The Athletic Crusade

D0107428

The Athletic Crusade

Sport and American Cultural Imperialism

Gerald R. Gems

UNIVERSITY OF NEBRASKA PRESS
LINCOLN AND LONDON

Abridged versions of chapter 4
appeared as
"The Athletic Crusade:
Sport and Colonialism in the Philippines"
in *International Journal of the History of Sport*
21, no. 1 (2004): 1–15,
and as
"Sport, Colonialism, and
the Reconstruction of Nature"
in *International Sports Studies*
24, no. 1 (2004): 32–41.
Chapter 7,
"Puerto Rico: Sport and the Restoration of National Pride,"
appeared in
International Journal of Regional and Local Studies
1, no. 1 (2005): 107–20.
© 2006
by the
Board of Regents
of the
University of Nebraska
All rights reserved
Manufactured
in the
United States of America
∞
Set in Quadraat by Kim Essman.
Designed by R. W. Boeche.

Library of Congress Cataloging-in-Publication Data
Gems, Gerald R.
The athletic crusade : sport and American cultural
imperialism / Gerald Gems.
p. cm.
Includes bibliographical references and index.
ISBN-13: 978-0-8032-2216-8 (cloth : alk. paper)
ISBN-10: 0-8032-2216-5 (cloth : alk. paper)
ISBN-13: 978-0-8032-4533-4 (paper : alk. paper)
1. Sports and state—United States. 2. United States—
Foreign relations—19th century. 3. United States—Foreign
relations—20th century. 4. United States—Territorial
expansion. 5. Sports—Social aspects—United States—
History. 6. Racism—United States. 7. Imperialism—
Psychological aspects. 8. Civilization—American influences.
I. Title.
GV706.35.G46 2006
796.0973–dc22
2005026035

OLSON LIBRARY
NORTHERN MICHIGAN UNIVERSITY
MARQUETTE, MI 49855

To the strong women in my life
—my mother, my sister, and my daughter—
with love

Contents

The Athletic Crusade

Race, Religion, and Manifest Destiny

Americans came late to the imperial game, or so historians have charged. Spain, France, and England had long since partitioned the New World and much of the old by the nineteenth century. At an 1884 conference Europeans carved up the African continent and staked claims to colonies. By 1914 European powers, led by Great Britain, controlled 85 percent of the earth's land surface. By that time the United States, itself a former colony, had become a major player in the imperial process.[1]

Only recently have American scholars questioned American imperialism. Previous studies glorified expansionism as a heroic struggle, a romantic adventure, a benevolent mission, and a Darwinian right or inevitability. Historians of the nineteenth and early twentieth centuries discarded the unheroic stories and those they deemed less worthy in constructing (some might say inventing) a national identity for a young country bereft of cultural roots.[2] Postcolonial scholars and revisionist historians have asserted a more critical lens. Viewed from the perspective of the conquered and colonized, the United States has been in a continual imperial mode since its colonial status, pushing ever westward. Once assured of continental dominance, it proceeded to international aspirations, and by the end of the twentieth century, to global expectations under the guise of a "manifest destiny."[3]

That term, coined in the 1840s, embedded racial, class, religious, and gender connotations that continue to affect and obscure the imperial process. Manifest destiny originally offered a racial and religious justification for the annexation of Texas, forcibly taken from the country of Mexico by WASP (white Anglo-Saxon Protestant) interlopers and their Tejano colleagues. The contributions of the latter, Catholic Mexican settlers unhappy with the policies emanating from Mexico City, have been, until recently, ignored or dismissed by American historians. People of color counted little in the construction of a national identity. The concept of whiteness adhered not only to skin color but to intellectual and physical capacities as well. British naturalist Charles Darwin published his seminal work, *On the Origin of the Species by Means of Natural Selection*, in 1859, pioneering evolutionary theory. British philosopher Herbert Spencer postulated that social evolution resulted from natural and uncontrollable forces, that is, a belief in the survival of the fittest. Lewis Henry Morgan, an early American anthropologist, categorized the evolutionary process into three stages with concomitant moral characteristics. He surmised that "primitive" societies exhibited communal and promiscuous habits, "barbarians" composed a middle stage of early agriculturalists, and "civilized" groups practiced monogamy and held private property.[4]

G. Stanley Hall, an educator and first president of the American Psychological Association, employed a similar classification in his theory of play. He determined that more savage societies played tag or chase games similar to hunters, while more civilized groups engaged in more sophisticated pastimes. Hall tied his notions of progress to morality, supporting Muscular Christianity and proper sport as a means to improve society. Ministers, too, championed the cause of manifest destiny by linking it to superior morality. Reverend Josiah Strong claimed that Americans possessed the "highest type of Anglo civilization" and that their brand of Christianity and civil liberty "contributed most to the elevation of the human race." By such logic Americans had not only a rationalization but a moral duty and an obligation to spread their culture abroad. William Graham Sumner, another minister and an influential professor of sociology and anthropology at Yale, argued for a natural aristocracy who gained their wealth and status via struggle and competition against weaker foes. His laissez-faire economics justified the seizure of natural resources for personal gain.[5]

The Darwinian scientific revolution of the mid-nineteenth century thus assumed racial, social, religious, and economic qualities and soon drifted into pseudoscience and biological theories of human evolutionary patterns that purported to rationalize racial and ethnic "differences." Phrenologists studied the structure and bumps of human skulls to determine levels of intelligence, and physiognomists analyzed facial features to ascertain one's character. Already-established stereotypes became rationalized, justified, and entrenched. By the twentieth century Social Darwinian reformers assumed the more benevolent aspects of the social gospel that accepted cultural pluralism. Israel Zangwill's 1908 play *The Melting Pot*, the subsequent pluralistic works of philosopher Horace Kallen, and the practical application of social science principles by Jane Addams and other settlement house workers shed new light on the acculturation process. Still, social scientists and physicians espoused euthanasia for those deemed to be feeble-minded or otherwise deficient. Such logic culminated in the horrors of Hitler's holocaust as he attempted to exterminate Jews, Gypsies, and "others" whom he perceived as lacking.[6]

Scientists who constructed such racial pyramids inevitably placed WASP males at the apex. The social construction of superiority, however, had been preceded by centuries of ethnic and religious strife that laid the foundation for such prognostications. Catholics, Jews, and Moslems had battled one another for nearly a millennium before Protestants entered the fray in the sixteenth century. The latter then contested with one another over myriad doctrinal differences. One such group, the Puritan founders of the Massachusetts Bay English colony in America, declared themselves a "chosen people." That self-identification of superiority initiated an ongoing westward expansion and expropriation of native lands based on racial and religious arrogance.[7]

Native Americans were portrayed as uncivilized heathens, or noble savages at best. The newly independent United States of America proclaimed the racial nature of its democratic republic in the Naturalization Act of 1790, which limited citizenship rights to free whites. By 1820 American Protestant missionaries began their proselytization of the Hawaiian Islands, long before the islands were usurped as American territory. White American settlers in the Texas region of Mexico soon revolted, declaring themselves independent from the Catholic Mexicans, whom they considered a mongrel race and less than white. The annexation of Texas by the United States prompted the Mexican War of 1846–1848, in which the United States gained California and the Southwest. Native Americans in the latter area forcefully resisted assimilation efforts for the remainder of the century.[8]

Blacks fared even worse. Conscripted as slaves, they served as a subjugated labor force, largely for the farms and plantations of the South. In an 1857 Supreme Court case involving a runaway slave, the chief justice asserted that "Negroes (were) beings of an inferior order with no rights which any white man was bound to respect."[9]

The American Civil War accorded blacks a technical level of freedom, but that legality never provided the privileges of whiteness. Despite the wholesale adoption of Protestant Christianity by African Americans, whites distanced themselves from nonwhites by disenfranchisement, miscegenation laws, and segregation practices. Bloodlines rather than skin color or appearance determined whiteness, and a drop of black blood might eliminate one from that exclusive fraternity. The U.S. Supreme Court affirmed exclusionary social practices in 1896 in the case of *Plessy v. Ferguson*, when Homer Plessy, who was seven-eighths white, unsuccessfully challenged the law that restricted him to a separate railroad car. The state of Louisiana contended, until 1974, that nonwhite status accrued if only one of a person's sixty-four ancestors qualified as black.[10]

The Chinese faced similar oppression and even greater exclusion. Californians in particular viewed the Chinese as a labor threat. In 1877 a congressman claimed that "there is not sufficient brain capacity in the Chinese to furnish motive power for self government. Upon the point of morals, there is no Aryan or European race which is not far superior to the

Chinese as a class."[11] Congress subsequently passed a series of Chinese exclusion laws, in effect from 1882 to 1943, that prohibited immigration. Japanese laborers faced a similar ban in 1907, as did Indian immigrants in 1917 and Filipinos in 1934.[12] Professor Daniel Brinton, president of the American Association for the Advancement of Science, declared that "the black, brown and the red races differ anatomically so much from the white . . . that even with equal cerebral capacity they never could rival its results by equal effects."[13] In addition to skin color, whiteness thus assumed intelligence, morality, and republican virtues.

General Leonard Wood, colonial warrior, governor, and presidential candidate, asserted that "no one . . . can question the inadvisability of the introduction of any other alien race, of a black, brown, or yellow strain into this country. We must make it a white nation."[14] In 1906 San Francisco schools began segregating Asian students from whites. In 1913 California passed the Alien Land Law, which even forbid property ownership by foreign immigrants. Such humiliation engendered hostility and anti-American riots in Japan and a long-simmering resentment that would hold repercussions and racial implications for World War II.[15]

Not only race but ethnicity and social class contributed to the measure of whiteness. By 1911 the Dillingham Commission on immigration had concluded that there were forty-five separate races and that Asians proved only one of many who failed to meet the standards of whiteness. Early Irish immigrants, for example, carried stigmas of class and Catholicism that had afflicted them under English rule. Irish laborers performed the most arduous tasks in the southern states, where slaves were considered more valuable as property. In the North, Irishmen were considered to be "a nigger turned inside out"; by 1850 Irish women constituted 75 percent of New York City's house servants, similar to the black slaves who served their southern masters.[16]

In 1874 William Wells Brown, an African American doctor who had apparently achieved a portion of whiteness, provided a generic description of the Irish: "These people are remarkable for open, projecting mouths, prominent teeth, and exposed gums, their advancing cheek bones and depressed noses carry barbarism on their very front. . . . Degradation and hardship exhibit themselves in the whole physical condition of the people . . . giving such an example of human degradation as to make it revolting. They are only five feet two inches, upon an average, bow-legged, bandy shanked, abortively featured, the apparitions of Irish ugliness and Irish want."[17] More than two decades later another writer advocated that "a Celt . . . lacks the solidity, the balance, the judgment, the moral staying power of the Anglo-Saxon."[18] Determinants of whiteness included perceptions of morality, discipline, work ethic, and social class as well as skin color by the late nineteenth century.

Skin color provided a primary determinant, however, and those of darker hue faced greater obstacles. Immigrants from southern and eastern Europe, particularly those of peasant stock, faced a longer road on their evolutionary journey to whiteness. Of the Slavs it was said that "only hunkies worked blast furnaces which were too damn dirty and too damn hot for a white man."[19] Another commentator on New York street life declared: "It is no uncommon thing to see at noon some swarthy Italian . . . resting and dining from his tin kettle, while his brown skinned wife is by his side."[20]

In 1891 eleven swarthy Italians won acquittal for the alleged murder of a New Orleans police chief. They were, nevertheless, lynched by a disbelieving mob. A *New York Times* editorial explained the belief in the inherent criminality of both Italians and blacks: "Those sneaking and cowardly Sicilians, who have transplanted to this country the lawless passions, the cutthroat practices, and the oathbound societies of their native country, are to us a pest without mitigation. Our own rattlesnakes are as good citizens as they."[21] Italians, often segregated with blacks, particularly in the South, became "dagos" or "white niggers." In 1922 Jim Rollins, a black man, won acquittal in an Alabama miscegenation case when the judge concluded that the Sicilian woman with whom he cohabited was inconclusively white.[22]

As Catholics, presumably ruled by the pope, both Irish and Italians seemed unfit or untrustworthy for full inclusion in the white republic. On that account Jews, too, failed to measure up. Although westernized, often-affluent German Jews won assimilation and a large degree of whiteness in the latter half of the nineteenth century, their Orthodox, eastern European brethren fared poorly as their communal Yiddish culture subjected all Jews to the WASP gaze of difference.

An 1893 *New York Times* piece on "East Side Street Vendors" stated: "This neighborhood, peopled almost entirely by the people who claim to have been driven from Poland and Russia, is the eyesore of New York, and perhaps the filthiest place on the western continent. It is impossible for a Christian to live there because he will be driven out, either by blows or the dirt and stench. Cleanliness is an unknown quantity to these people. They cannot be lifted up to a higher plane because they do not want to be."[23]

Xenophobes described Jews as lecherous perverts with high-bridged noses, bulging eyes, and thick lips. In 1916 Madison Grant, an influential eugenicist, declared that "the cross between any of the three European races and a Jew is a Jew."[24] The message to white supremacists was clear: Jews polluted the white gene pool.

Other ethnic groups confronted similar impediments in their quest for whiteness. Senator Henry Cabot Lodge called for restricted immigration and claimed that Slovaks "appear to have so many items in common with the Chinese."[25] Between 1878 and 1922 American courts deemed Chinese, Japanese, Hawaiians, and people of various combined racial origins as nonwhites and thus unworthy of citizenship, while Texas granted rights to some Mexicans based on skin color and Spanish heritage. Massachusetts determined that Armenians could be considered white because they were not black or Indian. In South Carolina, however, a Syrian proved insufficiently white, and an Oregon Hindu won temporary whiteness until a subsequent court reversed an earlier decision. In 1924 Congress finally heeded Lodge's call and passed a restrictive immigration law that assigned quotas to various ethnic groups, with northern Europeans being favored.[26]

The American obsession with race and racial characteristics required an evolutionary process for many ethnic groups in pursuit of whiteness and its accordant rights and privileges. Irish, Italians, Jews, Slavs, and other minorities eventually gained such status through their control of the labor movement, loyalty to machine politics, and the Americanization of the Catholic Church. Their gradual acceptance often came at the expense of African Americans, as whiteness became that which was not black and clearly set apart from it. As early as the 1830s whites had donned blackface to perform as minstrels who mocked black speech and expression.[27]

Minstrel shows provided only one means by which whites depicted the supposed inferiority of nonwhites to themselves and subject populations. By the latter nineteenth century "Buffalo Bill" Cody's Wild West Show enjoyed immense popularity as it traveled the country reenacting the whites' conquest of the Indians and displaying the Native Americans as primitives. Cody brought a simulated frontier experience to urban areas for those who had not experienced the process firsthand. By 1887 Cody had transplanted his vision of the Anglo triumph to European audiences when Indians assumed the status of exotic "others" caught in the throes of modernization.[28]

Cody's exhibition provided only a sideshow in the larger spectacle of the 1893 World's Fair, held in Chicago as the Columbian Exposition, a celebration marking the advent of European "civilization" in North America. Famed architect Daniel Burnham directed the construction of a stunning and eloquent "white city," illuminated by the daytime sunlight and by innovative electric lights at night. Classical architecture symbolized the order, discipline, harmony, grandeur, and idealism of modern bourgeois American civilization and its ability to transcend nature. The fairgrounds occupied former marshlands, which Burnham refashioned into a lagoon, a canal, and a magnificent basin. Moreover, the immense exposition buildings featured construction materials that rendered them temporary in nature, signifying Anglo abilities to fashion and refashion the environment, creating an artificial utopia by design.[29]

The program planners displayed a Social Darwinian perspective to human evolution as well by presenting three distinct levels of development—the savage, the semicivilized, and the civilized. White Europeans and Americans appropriated the latter role. Despite their protests African Americans failed to gain inclusion on any planning committees or exhibition space, except for inclusion in an Education Department display that espoused the value of schooling for nonwhite groups. Displays of African tribal life suggested a universal black experience, and in keeping with the organizers' moral and educational mission, the *Columbian Exposition Album* "hoped the Dahomans would take back the influence of civilization to West Africa."[30]

Protestant missionaries sought to convey both religious and cultural lessons. By the mid-nineteenth century they established residential boarding schools in Hawaii to inculcate the native children with their beliefs. Their efforts soon extended to Asia. Within U.S. borders, middle-class WASP reformers had already embarked on such a mission. The process of cultural assimilation began with the forced relocation of Native American tribes to allotted lands, or reservations, the imposition of agricultural or vocational lifestyles at the expense of nomadic or traditional ones, and institutionalized education under the guise of the more benevolent perspective of the social gospel. Mission schools, established by various Christian denominations close to the confined Indian populations, forced the English language and gospel hymns on indigenous children.[31]

The movement took on greater significance when the U.S. government established the Carlisle Industrial School for Indians in Pennsylvania in 1879. The institution housed Native Americans from seventy different tribes under government surveillance and tutelage. Grouped and classified homogeneously as "Indians," and bereft of their familiar environment, culture, and family support, individuals struggled to maintain their tribal identities. For many the collision of frontier cultures had produced mixed identities that intermingled race, religion, and ethnicity. Strict discipline required adherence to the English language and Anglo norms of dress and demeanor. The curriculum emphasized vocational preparation for an industrial workforce, but its most visible achievement occurred in the athletic program. Sport instilled discipline, teamwork, a strong work ethic, and perhaps most importantly, deference to authority in the form of a coach or game official that might ready one for a compliant workforce. Carlisle's famed football teams toured the country and drew enormous crowds. The school's most famous athlete, Jim Thorpe, earned further distinction as an Olympic champion. The perceived success of Carlisle's assimilation efforts fostered another twenty-five government schools for Native American children over the next two decades, and African Americans, too, followed a similar model of vocational training and deference to white culture at Booker T. Washington's Tuskegee Institute.[32]

Sport as a means to assimilate and acculturate such disparate groups assumed greater importance throughout the nineteenth and early twentieth centuries. After the Civil War even prominent preachers like Thomas Wentworth Higginson and Henry Ward Beecher espoused a "Muscular

Christianity" that promoted a strong mind in a strong body. The Young Men's Christian Association (YMCA) employed sport as a vehicle to attract and train bodies in the service of religion. G. Stanley Hall's play theory advocated the achievement of greater morality by training one's willpower. Under the leadership of Hall's disciple Luther Gulick, the YMCA ardently promoted sport as a mechanism for character development. Urban reformers, too, envisioned play as a practical and cultural end. By the 1880s playgrounds kept small children from the dangers of the street. Under the auspices of trained supervisors, coaches, and physical education teachers in the parks, playgrounds, and public schools, Progressive reformers believed that even the less cultured immigrant groups might be transformed into worthy Americans. For the vast majority who did not speak English, sport offered an effective means to teach civic virtues, democratic values, and respect for authority. The process of initiating child labor laws, compulsory education, and physical education requirements ensued throughout the states between 1880 and 1920. The Protestant missionaries, the YMCA, and the American government administrators employed similar strategies abroad.[33]

With indigenous tribes subdued and sovereignty over U.S. continental territory complete, the 1893 World's Fair marked the emergence of the United States as a world power. The showcase of American technology reflected a rapidly growing economic force, and despite the depression of 1893, the United States soon replaced Great Britain as the foremost industrial nation in the world. Historian Frederick Jackson Turner used the fair to announce not only that the American frontier was now closed but that it had forged a unique American character, which many deemed fit to assume international leadership. With the loss of the frontier, American producers needed new markets for their goods; imperial conquests offered the solution.[34]

American settlers in Hawaii had already overthrown the monarchy and usurped authority in 1893. The U.S. government annexed the islands as a territory five years later. The Spanish-American War of 1898 also brought Cuba, Puerto Rico, Guam, and the Philippines into the American realm. Samoa and Wake Island followed a year later, and the United States engineered a revolt in Panama in 1903, which won independence from Colombia and delivered the Canal Zone to the United States. Americans exported not only their commercial products to the new colonies but their racial attitudes as well.

Colonialism initially engendered much debate in American society, with anti-imperialists charging that the United States was forsaking its democratic and egalitarian ideals in such ventures. Henry Van Dyke, a Presbyterian minister, charged that the United States would be forsaking its ideals by colonizing other nations because the colonial subjects lacked representation in Congress. Others compared the United States to Great Britain and questioned why the Filipinos, who had already established their own provisional government, were not given liberation. David J. Hill, a former university president and assistant secretary of state, countered that the war with Spain was a just and moral one against Spanish oppression and that the United States had a duty to civilize its new colonies. Henry Adams, historian and great-grandson of President John Adams, wrote: "I think of the horror of a year's warfare in the Philippines. . . . We must slaughter a million or two of foolish Malays in order to give them the comforts of flannel petticoats and electric railways." Former Senator Carl Schurz, a German immigrant, complained that not all were fit for Americanization: "34,436 natives, 6,186 half-castes, 7,495 born in Hawaii of foreign parents, 5,301 Chinese, 12,360 Japanese, 8,602 Portuguese, 1,928 Americans, 1,344 British, 1,034 Germans, 227 Norwegians, 70 French, 588 Polynesians, 419 other foreigners. If there ever was a population unfit to constitute a State of the American Union, it is this [Hawaii] . . . a number of semi-civilized natives crowded upon a lot of adventurers."[35]

Still others rationalized imperialism on Social Darwinian terms. John Barrett, a U.S. minister to Siam, saw the Philippines as a resource, a market, and a naval port. He surmised that "the rule of the survival of the fittest applies to nations as well as the animal kingdom. It is a cruel, relentless principle being exercised in a cruel, relentless competition of might forces." John Procter, a U.S. Civil Service commissioner, agreed: "The tropics are peopled with millions of low social efficiency; and it seems to be the fate of the black and yellow races to have their countries parceled out and administered by efficient races from the Temperate Zone. . . . In the interests of civilization and humanity, this country should retain the Philippines." Ultimately, however, the government sided with Congressman Albert Beveridge, a staunch imperialist, who stated: "We will not repudiate our duty in the Orient. We will not renounce our part in the mission of our race, trustees under God, of the civilization of the world. And we will move forward to our work, not howling out regrets like slaves whipped to their burden, but with gratitude to a task worthy of our strength, and thanksgiving to Almighty God that has marked us as His chosen people, henceforth to lead in the regeneration of the world."[36]

The religious tone of Beveridge's speech matched the sentiments of many American church groups. Both they and the business interests opposed President William McKinley's original inclination to return the Philippines to Spain. Josiah Strong, a Congregationalist minister, had already sold 170,000 copies of his book *Our Country: Its Possible Future and Its Present Crisis*, which claimed that Anglo-Saxons professed the "purest Christianity and the highest civilization" and were therefore "divinely commissioned to be . . . [their] brother's keeper."[37] *The Advance* (May 18, 1898), a Congregationalist organ, asserted that "morally and religiously we should not shun an opportunity to lift up a barbarous people."[38] The *Eighty-Eighth Annual Report of the American Board of Commissioners of Foreign Missions* (1898) also stated that the Spanish-American War "opened the door wide for the prosecution of missionary effort in the Micronesian field. . . . Our missionaries may work unterrified by papal interference and Spanish treachery. . . . This is the Lord's doing and it is marvelous in our eyes."[39]

Episcopalians also considered the Catholics as "degenerates" in need of rescue, despite the fact that new territories were already Christianized.[40] They rationalized such renewed efforts as necessary to overcome papal influence, the lack of "civilization," and the notion that the colonial inhabitants were unfit to govern themselves—although Hawaii had a longstanding monarchy, and both Puerto Rico and the Philippines had revolutionary governments in place. Senator William Fulbright later warned that "throughout our history two strains have coexisted uneasily—a dominant strand of democratic humanism and a lesser but durable strain of intolerant Puritanism . . . leading us to look at the world through the distorting prism of a harsh and angry moralism."[41]

While religious leaders wanted the colonies for souls, and businessmen craved international markets for their goods, Captain Alfred Thayer Mahan, an influential naval strategist, had long argued for their strategic value. Caribbean outposts would be needed to guard the long-sought canal across Central America. Hawaii would protect the California coast from the "yellow peril" in China, while the Philippines gave access to the lucrative Asian markets and could buffer incursions by Japan. Such naval stations would allow the United States to challenge Great Britain and Germany for dominance on the seas.[42]

The earliest governors of the colonies came from the ranks of the military. Many hailed from the South, and a large percentage of those serving in the Philippines had fought against the Indians. They brought their racial sentiments with them. Soldiers wrote home, for example: "I am in my glory when I can sight some dark skin and pull the trigger." Another reckoned that the islands would not be pacified "until the niggers [Filipinos] are killed off like the Indians."[43] Senator John Tyler Morgan of Alabama proposed a plan to settle African Americans in Hawaii and the Philippines as a solution to "the Negro problem," until the Filipinos objected. John Galloway, a soldier in an African American unit, wrote that "whites have begun to establish their diabolical race hatred in all its home rancor in Manila, even endeavoring to propagate the phobia among the Spaniards and Filipinos so as to be sure of the foundation of their supremacy when the civil rule that must necessarily follow the present military regime, is established."[44]

Whites maintained segregation by selective membership in social clubs, such as Manila's Army-Navy Club, which required a personal reference from at least two directors. When enlisted African Americans fraternized too frequently with the native Filipinos, Governor-General William H. Taft sent the infantry back to the United States. Territorial laws forbade intermarriage between races, and Mrs. Campbell Dauncey, an Englishwoman in the Philippines, revealed that "while as to marrying a Filipino, no woman one could speak to would ever dream of such a horrible fate."[45]

In the Philippines and in the Spanish cultures of the Caribbean islands, mulattoes and mixed breeds proliferated and skin color was of little consequence. Racism had to be learned under the Americans, who had learned their colonial policies from long-established practices of the British Empire. WASPs denigrated subordinate groups in myriad forms of popular culture, such as newspapers, magazines, photography, art, and film, in order to portray their superiority to themselves and their subject peoples. The primary means of inculcation, however, proved to be education. In the war-torn territories the military established free public schools even before conquest and pacification were complete. William Howard Taft, the first governor-general of the Philippines, chose a school superintendent while still en route to Manila, stating: "We deem it of so much importance to have our superintendent of instruction on the ground as soon as possible."[46]

In the schools Taft indicated that the English language was to be a "common medium of communication . . . and will greatly assist in teaching them self-government on Anglo-Saxon lines."[47] Former U.S. vice president Charles Fairbanks opined that Filipino "boys and girls were learning the story of the majesty and beauty of the United States. They were learning the English language: they were learning the history of our country."[48] While the imposition of English had some practical validity for the polyglot and multilingual populations of the Philippines and Hawaii, it seemed oppressive to the thoroughly Spanish cultures of the Caribbean. As the official language in all of the American territories, English further limited access to democracy and government positions in particular for only the upper levels of the social strata, and an imbalance of power generated feelings of inferiority of subordinate groups throughout all imperial colonies.[49]

With English speakers at a premium, physical education became a primary means of instruction. Sports and games inculcated the characteristics valued by modern industrial society and the aggressiveness, competitive spirit, and leadership assumed to be the province of WASPs. Episcopalian bishop Charles Brent complained that "the constitutional fault of the Filipinos, a fault common to all Orientals, is sensuality . . . laziness, concubinage and gaming."[50] Cockfighting, in particular, enjoyed widespread popularity throughout all of the new American colonies, and educators hoped to instill more civilized, wholesome sport forms. They intended to build stronger physical bodies as well as moral character in their charges.

Nonwhite bodies were deemed inferior, easily measured by athletic competition. At the 1904 World's Fair, held in St. Louis, organizers held contests between Africans and Native American Indians under the guise of "Anthropology Days" to exhibit nonwhite debilities. The participants dressed in native garb to further emphasize their difference. When nonwhites, such as African American athletes in interscholastic athletics, excelled, scientists rationalized their success as a product of "natural, animal like" instincts, thus placing them lower on the evolutionary scale.[51]

Above all, sport served to assuage the crisis of masculinity that afflicted the WASP male bourgeoisie by the late nineteenth century. With the close of the frontier, strong, virile men no longer had wild lands or savage foes to conquer. By the 1890s a generation of young men lacked a war in which their male ancestors had proved themselves. Urbanization produced sedentary lifestyles, and industrialization relegated middle-class men to clerical roles or white-collar occupations that lacked physicality. The increasing feminization of culture threatened the traditional balance of social and domestic power. Boys spent too much time under maternal guidance, then went off to school, where female teachers directed their actions. Physicians and preachers derided the sallow, puny constitutions of weaklings, and too much stress resulted in neurasthenia, a psychosomatic condition that exhausted the nervous system. Effeminate men faced ridicule, and doctors judged homosexuality a grievous disease. Theodore Roosevelt believed that "the greatest danger that a long period of profound peace offers to a nation is that of effeminate tendencies in young men." Sport became a very visible antidote as a surrogate form of war, particularly in the brutal football games popularized on college campuses and in high school leagues.[52]

The Spanish-American War offered a brief interlude to test one's courage in more traditional ways. Teddy Roosevelt hastened to do so by forming the Rough Riders, a volunteer cavalry of cowboys and athletes who stormed the Spanish fortifications in Cuba, but relatively few others saw combat. Sport remained a more practical alternative, one that quickly produced a "jock culture" of hypermasculinity.

In fact, one of the sensationalized calls to arms against the Spanish involved the alleged necessity to protect Cuban women from lecherous assault. Honorable men felt obliged to defend the "weaker sex." Soon young boys engaged in character-building exercises and outdoor pursuits, such as the Boy Scout movement, designed to build strong men. As one general asserted: "Every soldier fears losing the one thing he is likely to value more highly than life—his reputation as a man among other men."[53]

Imperialists endeavored to teach such lessons to the multicultural populations of their empires. While British historians have thoroughly documented and analyzed such processes, American scholars have been more reluctant to do so until relatively recently. Most Americans are unaware of any imperial past. American studies programs have embarked on more interdisciplinary factors encompassing race, class, gender, and ethnicity, but they do so through an internal lens. The colonial voice has been largely silent. Only recently have Asian American and Latino scholars offered a critical perspective of colonial revisionism, yet none have examined sport. American sport historians, in particular, have greatly neglected imperial studies. This study attempts some rectification of that situation by examining U.S. incursions into other cultures on both a short- and long-term basis, with particular attention to the role of sporting practices in affecting power relationships and societal change. As late-nineteenth-century commercial expansion and the Spanish-American War prompted an immediate change in the United States' status as a global imperial power, I endeavor to examine American colonial practices beyond the North American continent, forsaking earlier conflicts with Canada and Mexico over matters of manifest destiny. I seek to find what values, if any, U.S. policies and sporting practices promoted in the already established cultures of Asia, the Pacific, and the Caribbean. In what ways did the United States use sport to increase its global hegemony? Did those cultures accept, reject, resist, adopt, or adapt such practices and their inherent value systems? How did those cultures change as a result? Did hybrid or alternative cultures evolve from such cultural interplay? Was the process volatile or relatively harmonious? Finally, what are the implications for the future?[54]

China and the Rejection of Christianity

China existed in relative isolation from European nations for millennia, but Mongol invasions in the thirteenth century resulted in temporary alien conquest. European interest in China escalated with Marco Polo's publication of his extended venture to the Asian land during the reign of Kublai Khan. Catholic missionaries began arriving in China in the sixteenth century, and British traders installed themselves at Canton in 1715. There they confronted an ancient culture steeped in Confucianism that differed greatly from their own WASP values. An authoritative, heirarchial social order valued obedience over individualism, and the clash of cultures resulted in the British wringing concessions from a weakened Chinese dynasty. British victory in the Opium War of 1839–1842 provided the United States with an entrèe into the Asian market, and it quickly secured the Treaty of Wanghia in 1844. Subsequent treaties in 1858 and 1860 extended American priviliges at the expense of the natives.[1]

An American Protestant missionary came in 1807 but took seven years to gain a convert. More American missionaries arrived in 1830. Three years later congregationalists established a school in Canton. In 1836 Baptists founded a school for girls in Macao. The establishment challenged the Chinese gender order, which placed no value on the education of females. Episcopalians arrived in 1842 and Methodist teachers five years later, but by 1853 the combined Protestant efforts had garnered only 350 souls.[2]

Commercial exchange provided a more symbiotic relationship as Chinese immigrants traveled to California in the gold rush of 1848. In 1852 more than twenty thousand disembarked in San Francisco. Although whites initially accepted the Chinese as a curiosity, they soon castigated their cultural difference and railed at their success as more efficient miners. Anglos questioned the masculinity of the Chinese who "scratched" at the ground to derive overlooked nuggets. One writer declared that they used their tools "like so many women, as if they were afraid of hurting themselves." Likewise, when battles between Chinese factions failed to produce fatalities, Anglos chided them as weak and inept. They imposed a foreign miners' tax in 1852 and drove others from the mines. Two years later the California Supreme Court refused any testimony by Chinese or any other nonwhites, effectively establishing white legal hegemony.[3]

In the 1860s Chinese laborers composed as much as 90 percent of the labor force that built the Central Pacific Railroad across the California mountains, braving conditions and accepting meager wages unacceptable to whites. A nativist backlash ensued, as white workers perceived the Chinese as a threat to jobs. In 1871 whites attacked the segregated urban ghetto known as Chinatown in Los Angeles, looting and killing. A similar riot followed in 1877 in San Francisco, as the Chinese became scapegoats for capitalist woes. American laborers viewed the Chinese as slaves and unfair competitors for jobs, rather than a class of workers even more exploited than themselves. Compounding the issue was the Chinese resistance to assimilation. Efforts to Christianize them met with futility. Newspapers and magazines characterized the Chinese as heathens, criminals, and degenerates in racialized cartoons. Consequently, Chinese in California failed to gain the privileges of whiteness, became disenfranchised, and, after 1882, legally excluded from immigrating to the United States until 1943.[4]

Chinese students in San Francisco had already been recalled to their homeland but not before the "Orientals" baseball club defeated an Oakland team by using a curve ball pitcher. After a defeat in the Arrow War of 1856–1860, Chinese leaders decided on a course of westernization, "adopting the barbarians' techniques to control the barbarians."[5]

Baseball and rowing clubs had formed in Shanghai as early as 1863. Other sporting enterprises soon followed, and Chinese scholars traveled to American schools in 1872, where they were perplexed by the game of baseball and the growing American emphasis that linked physicality to masculinity. Such notions transferred to China with the establishment of a YMCA in Shanghai during the 1870s. The Nanking Military Academy introduced physical education into its curriculum in 1875. Though the Chinese equated sport and physicality with menial peasant labor, baseball gained popularity, particularly among the students educated in America. Chinese teams appeared in at least four U.S. cities, and teams from San Francisco and Chicago barnstormed throughout the country. A Chicago sportswriter derisively remarked: "They play about as women would."[6] Another noted that "since the Chicago Chinese teams have been organized similar clubs have gotten up all over the country. If the game will serve to change the dress and habits of the Chinaman it will be of great benefit to him."[7] Such condescension regularly marked Anglo belief in its own superiority.

The Protestant American missionaries who flowed into China throughout the latter nineteenth century did little to alleviate the cultural clash. By 1877 the evangelists had founded more than two hundred Christian schools intent on undermining Confucianism and establishing a greater role for women in Chinese society. Traditional practices, such as footbinding, the taking of multiple wives, and arranging marriages, particularly troubled the Westerners who saw such customs as backward and barbaric. The introduction of Western technology and commerce, in which the missionaries freely engaged, further disrupted the Chinese economy. Railroads rendered unemployment for those affiliated with local transport occupations, and the manufactured goods of the Westerners displaced native craft industries.[8]

By the 1890s more than a thousand American missionaries resided in the country, and they preached both Christianity and sport as a way to save and modernize the ancient civilization. These Americans introduced calisthenics, games, and sports into their schools in the 1880s but met with resistance. The long gowns worn by upper-class men as a status symbol interfered with strenuous movement. The physical activity seemed too much like work, eschewed by the upper class, and the students tried to hire coolies to do the exercises for them. When such options failed they feigned illness or injury to avoid participation. Such Western practices seemed strange to the Chinese. A worker at one school remarked: "Every time Mrs. Smith conducted the drill people came flocking in to watch it, for they considered it more amusing than a theatre." Despite the native misgivings an 1890 conference among the various missionary groups resolved to continue physical training as a means to improve health and build character. By 1895 three Chinese colleges fielded baseball teams. St. John's University of Shanghai employed Chinese-Hawaiian coaches who had learned the game in the islands. Under the leadership of an Anglo headmaster, St. John's initiated physical education with archery and competition in track and field, conducting the first meet in 1890. The Tianjin YMCA introduced the game of basketball in 1896, and after 1900 the interscholastic competitions provided publicity for the schools and drew curious spectators.[9]

Such physicality proved too late for the Chinese, who lost the Sino-Japanese War of 1895, forcing them to cede Taiwan to the victors. Japan, already immersed in westernization and baseball, fostered the game on that island. Thereafter other European powers vied with Japan for territory on the Chinese mainland, as Germany, Russia, France, and Great Britain claimed portions of the country as commercial settlements. The economic depression of 1893 also renewed American interests in the vast Asian market, and in 1900 the United States declared an Open Door policy that safeguarded its own interests by calling for equal rights to trade and expansion.[10]

Such foreign invasions created a nativist retaliation by the proud Chinese. As early as 1891 a missionary reported: "The peoople are as hostile as ever and the anti-foreign feeling is as fierce as ever. During these eight years a perfect stream of the vilest pamphlets and placards have been pouring into this and other provinces from Hunan."[11] The so-called Boxer Rebellion erupted by the summer of 1900, resulting in the killing of missionaries and their Chinese converts. The Boxers besieged foreign compounds until they were vanquished by a multinational force, including U.S. soldiers and marines. A congregationalist publication professed that "a show of force is the only argument that appeals to an Oriental mind," and *Harper's Weekly* commemorated the Americans' heroic triumph by displaying Frederic Remington's painting "The Ninth U.S. Infantry Entering Peking."[12]

Undeterred, the U.S. emissaries renewed their commercial, religious, and athletic efforts. Both baseball and a seething nationalism continued. Schools conducted athletic meets in both Shanghai and Tientsin in 1902 and engaged in intercollegiate contests by 1907. Girls' schools engaged in baseball, basketball, volleyball, and track and field events, all pastimes requiring unbound feet for mobility. In 1908 Max J. Exner, an American physical educator, arrived to conduct classes and train teachers, and the YMCA organized basketball leagues. Still the cultural struggle continued. When the Chungking Methodist Boys' School introduced basketball in 1908, the American teacher reported that the students thought it "too much like work. . . . They tossed the ball like a lot of schoolgirls. . . . It took them a good while to get over being afraid of it." Edward Alsworth Ross, a sociology professor, traveled to China in 1911 and observed that "lissome young men with queues were skipping about the tennis courts, but they wore their hampering gowns and their strokes had the snap of a kitten playing with a ball of yarn." The American teachers thus questioned Chinese masculinity, especially the long, braided hair and long fingernails, the latter custom symbolic of elite status that denoted an absence of physical labor. The Americans considered such cultural symbols effeminate, and Chester Fuson, a teacher at the Canton Christian College, shamed his charges into participation in a 1908 track meet by accusing them of cowardice.[13]

By 1910 Nanking hosted the national athletic championships, organized by the YMCA and witnessed by forty thousand spectators over the five days of competition. Held in conjunction with the national industrial exposition, the affair represented a symbolic portrayal of Chinese advancement in Western eyes. The victor in the high jump competition reputedly won the contest by cutting off his queue, which had dislodged the bar on his first two attempts. Such an act signaled a definite breach with the traditional Chinese culture and a transition into the modern world.[14]

The Chinese government reformed the curriculum in its own schools to include physical education in 1905, but it favored the Japanese model, preferring an Asian cultural affinity rather than the Western impositions. China imported Japanese teachers and sent as many as eight thousand of its students to study in Japan in 1906–1907. The Chinese particularly disliked the threat posed by Christianity and had references to it, God, and Christ removed from textbooks. In addition, all government schools required rites to honor Confucius. The increasing secularization of the schools posed dilemmas for the Protestants, but the widespread use of English served the practical needs of commerce, and the adoption of sports and games signaled a more modern and healthier China. It proclaimed its greater inclusion in the outside world when China also agreed to join Japan and the Philippines in an international competition known as the Far East Olympics.[15]

The growing Chinese nationalism might thus be transferred to athletic rather than revolutionary outlets. Hawaii, however, proved a way station for both activities. Numerous groups, including Chinese, formed plantation labor forces where owners used baseball as a means of social control. Other Chinese students learned the game in Hawaiian schools. Sun Yat-sen journeyed to Hawaii in 1879 and learned baseball at the Iolani School and Oahu College before playing in China. His Chinese club masked its revolutionary purposes, and throwing baseballs had practical application for future grenade tossers. Sun Yat-sen later led the revolution that toppled the Manchu dynasty and made him the first president of the Chinese republic, in 1911.[16]

Eight clubs played baseball in the Shanghai league during 1912, and only a year later there were leagues in six provinces. The National Games, held in Beijing in 1914, also included baseball; yet despite the seeming emergence of the game, a Chinese team from Honolulu represented the country in international competition, purportedly defeating the New York Giants in a 1911 game in San Francisco and playing against West Coast college teams the next two years. A sportswriter admitted that the Chinese "were far better than the Japanese team from the University of Waseda last year."[17]

Both race and nationalism figured prominently in the adoption of Western sport forms. After the Japanese victory in the Russo-Japanese War of 1905, Japan assumed a preeminent role in Asian affairs. Given the racist sentiments in the United States, as many as thirty thousand Chinese students traveled to Japan for their education, where many learned the Japanese passion for baseball, and the role of sport as a means of retribution. The Honolulu team masqueraded as a nonexistent college club in order to procure games with American counterparts. They defeated both American and Japanese contingents and won a measure of respect from the foreign invaders. By 1915 the *San Jose Mercury* admitted that they were "gentlemen who would not corrupt white society with opium or take anybody's job away as cheap labor."[18]

The Far East Olympics offered the Chinese similar opportunities. The Far East Athletic Association, organized and administered by the American YMCA, drew the Chinese further into the Anglo sphere of sport. In 1913 President Woodrow Wilson even offered the Chinese ambassadorship to John Mott, head of the YMCA missions. Mott declined on the ground that he could do more good within the organization. Mott did not envision the opportunity that sport also provided the Chinese, who lacked the military might to repulse foreign subjugation. Sport became a viable means to reclaim national pride. The American organizers of the first Far East Games in Manila in 1913 typically assumed an ethnocentric satisfaction in effecting a modern Asia and rapprochement in international relations. Frank L. Crone, the acting director of education in the Philippines, wrote that "nothing previous to this meeting has shown so clearly the departure of the Oriental nations from the old conservative standards, for the interest of the East in organized athletic sports is only recent." Crone further applauded the harmony and understanding that would be generated, but Governor-General Cameron Forbes's opening remarks indicated little of either when he assumed an avuncular role by admonishing the participants: "I hope that all your contests will be carried on in the spirit of fair play, which in after years may govern your conduct in business and other vocations of grown-ups."[19]

An American missionary, Willard Nash, organized the East China Intercollegiate Athletic Association with six teams in 1914, just months after the Chicago White Sox and New York Giants passed through Shanghai and Hong Kong on a world baseball tour. A local Anglo tugboat captain explained the change in racial sentiments as he ferried the American ballplayers: "Times are not as they used to be. When I first came here it was the proper thing to kick a Chinaman if he got near enough to you, but now it is different. Why, you are likely to go to jail if you kill one."[20]

The sports boom in China proved largely a mirage, practiced mostly by Anglo expatriates and Christian converts. While whites might teach the Chinese how to play, they had little inclination to play alongside them. Thomas F. Cobbs, president of the Shanghai Baseball League, feebly explained the reason for excluding locals: "The same as in California. There are too many of them. The Chinese sometimes get excited just like occidentals, and were we to let them in our games there is no telling when a riot might break out and if it were to start, there would be no finish."[21] Nor was the Shanghai situation an anomaly. In the mission schools the Chinese teachers received a lower salary than their American counterparts, and the latter refused to live near their coworkers or even to play tennis with them. Intermarriage invited ostracism. The YMCA in Manila requested a separate building for the Chinese, to reduce gambling, prostitution, and the use of opium, as whites' condescending attitudes continued to permeate social relations.[22]

The YMCA and the Protestant missionaries still promoted the values of Christianity and sport, but world events channeled U.S. governmental interests toward Europe with the outbreak of World War I. China still hosted the Far East Games of 1915, and local athletes won the pentathlon, swimming, soccer, and volleyball competitions. They finished second to the Filipinos in baseball. Despite their adoption of Western sport forms, the war gave the Chinese greater cause to question cultural change, as the Christian nations mired in carnage and human suffering; missionaries in China betrayed their own remonstrances by arranging marriages to ensure Protestant unions for their students.[23]

After the war Shanghai hosted the Far East Games of 1921, including women's events. The Far East Games added volleyball and tennis for women in 1923, and swimming and track and field competition for females in 1930. The Chinese National Games of 1924 featured softball and women's basketball; in that respect the Westerners met one of their objectives in overcoming the tradition of bound feet, an impossibility for athletes. In 1922 Philip Beach Sullivan, a World War I veteran and Michigan grad, accepted a position at St. John's University as an economics teacher and coach. He directed the national basketball team in the 1923 Far East Games at Osaka and brought his baseball team to Japan for a contest with St. Paul's University in Tokyo. During that time another group of American Major League baseball players toured Asia, including China. The occasional infusion of American stars and coaches proved an inadequate means of sustaining American influence despite the ongoing efforts of the YMCA. At one mission school, boys refused to keep score in a basketball game lest the vanquished lose face. By 1923 a resurgent interest in traditional martial arts led to their inclusion in the National Games festival.[24]

Based largely in urban areas, the YMCA never reached the great mass of the peasant population in the countryside. The immigration quota law of 1924 fueled anti-American attitudes throughout Asia. Moreover, anti-Christianity sentiments persisted throughout the 1920s to hinder Protestant proselytism, as nationalists adopted the slogan "China for the Chinese." The government banned the teaching of religion in schools, and students agitated against foreigners. In 1925, in a protest over educational control of the schools, three Chinese universities refused to compete in an athletic meet with their Christian counterparts. The 1924 National Games, held in Wuchang, rejected organization by the YMCA. Under native administration the events drew forty to fifty thousand spectators on each of the three days of competition. The competition for cultural dominance worsened, and, reminiscent of the Boxers, nationalist soldiers attacked foreigners in Nanking on March 24, 1927, triggering a mass exodus. By 1928 only eight of the sixty-five evangelical missionaries remained in China, and their schools had closed. Despite a century of Protestantism less than 1 percent of the Chinese had accepted Christianity.[25]

Capitalism shared the blame for Anglos' inability to convert the Chinese to American ideals. Like the racism evident in nineteenth-century California, the exploitation of Chinese labor and resources continued by both

OLSON LIBRARY
NORTHERN MICHIGAN UNIVERSITY
MARQUETTE, MI 49855

the Americans and the British. A 1923 report, while generally laudatory of YMCA efforts, identified the impending causes of failure: "It is vitally necessary that a modern program of social betterment should be intensely developed in China . . . because the new industrialism now rapidly beginning will be even more cruel in its pressure upon the poverty-stricken working classes, and . . . the Christian church in China has not yet arrived at the era of social emphasis, but still inclines to a too exclusively individualistic program."[26]

The British, who had a longer history of interaction with China, had greater impact in inculcating a sporting ethos. The Chinese formed a national soccer association in 1924, and such Anglo sports as cricket, polo, tennis, and golf found patronage, along with equestrian events at the Shanghai racetrack. Intercollegiate athletic contests continued under the influence of American educators, particularly in baseball and track and field, and the YMCA initiated games of basketball and volleyball.[27]

Political events soon superseded sporting interests, however. In 1927 a civil war erupted between Communists and Nationalists, further disrupting religious efforts. The evangelicals' China Mission reported "serious disturbances," famine, banditry, and "all of Hunan in sympathy with the Soviets."[28] The atheistic Communist ideology proved a blow to both missionaries and capitalists. Over the remainder of the decade the Chinese Christian students assumed control of their own schools from their American masters, albeit in an unexpected and rebellious fashion.

Shortly thereafter Japan invaded Manchuria in 1931, precipitating the struggles that would engulf Europe within the decade. Both the Japanese and the Chinese Communists embraced baseball, however. Japan promoted baseball among its railroad workers in Manchuria, building twenty fields for that purpose. After 1932 Japan conducted a baseball tournament at Dalian that included the Philippines, Korea, and Taiwan, the latter two entities occupied by Japan at the time. The confrontation was also played out in the United States in a 1932 Pacific Coast League baseball game. Kenso Nushida, a Japanese American from Hawaii, pitched for the Sacramento Solons, while Lee Gum Hong faced him as the hurler for the Oakland Oaks in an exhibition game. Lee Gum Hong had previously pitched and coached the Wah Sungs, a Chinese American semipro team in Oakland. Yet he did not portray himself as American when he stated: "This is a battle of nations. I represent China. Nushida represents Japan. And China shall win."[29]

The Communist movement further eroded American sporting influence in the 1930s. The Red Army had instituted a comprehensive athletic program in the 1920s, and by 1933 it conducted a Communist sports festival at Ruijin, which included basketball, volleyball, soccer, tennis, table tennis, and track and field competitions. By the end of that year the Communists incorporated women into their offerings and established a women's basketball team at the Marx Communist University. American initiatives had largely concentrated on activities for males, thoroughly neglecting half of the population. Under native organization, the National Games included ten male sports and seven female sports by 1933.[30]

The egalitarian tenets of the Communist creed stood in stark contrast to American racial practices as well. The Chinese, considered white in Cuba, lacked the rights of whiteness in the United States. Two generations of Chinese Americans resided in the United States after the Exclusion Act of 1882, but they did so largely in segregated "Chinatowns," limiting their assimilation and acculturation. Despite their isolation in separate schools and recreation facilities, young men and women of the second generation adopted American sport forms that marked them as different from their parents. Some proved good enough, though not white enough, to reach the professional ranks. In 1915 the Portland Beavers of the Pacific Coast baseball league signed Chinese-Hawaiian Lang Akana to a contract, then reneged when white players refused to play with him. During the 1920s a select few gained a measure of acceptance on integrated teams or on Chinese teams in integrated tournaments. Most, however, continued their activities in seclusion. Thomas Chinn, a San Francisco tennis player, had to use the courts in the early morning "before the white boys and girls came out," at which time they had to be surrendered. Miscegenation laws remained in effect until 1948.[31]

After World War II the Communists solidified their hold on mainland China, and the Nationalists fled to Taiwan. The first National Games held under Communist rule in 1956 included American sport forms, such as baseball and softball, and a basketball tournament held three years later numbered more than thirty teams. The Cultural Revolution of 1966–1976 de-emphasized sport, yet, significantly, China reestablished diplomatic relations with the United States via table tennis players in a well-publicized international match in 1971. Chinese gymnasts, swimmers, and female runners achieved world-class status in the Olympic Games, and baseball reemerged in the 1980s. The Los Angeles Dodgers even built a field in Tianjin for the Chinese, but the Chinese opted for the Japanese model and the Confucian tenets of work ethic and discipline traditional to Chinese culture. Lawrence Lee, chair of the Hong Kong Baseball Association, asserted: "We cannot learn from the Americans because the Americans do not practice all the time. They just warm up about a half hour before the game. We cannot learn from them like we can learn from the Japanese."[32] Little had changed during the course of the century.

The Japanese had taught the Taiwanese well in their years of repressive occupation, but their former subjects exacted a measure of athletic revenge in 1968 when Taiwan's Little League team defeated the former world champs from Japan. The following year the Taiwanese vanquished the United States in winning its own world championship, engendering an eight-hour parade and a presidential audience upon the players' return to their home country. The team repeated its championship feat seventeen times over a twenty-seven-year period. Taiwan's dominance restored Chinese pride and dignity but led the U.S. administrators to impose a temporary ban on non-American teams in 1975. Continued Asian dominance in the 1990s resulted in further restrictions, and Taiwan's eventual withdrawal from the tournament. By that time Taiwan had formed its own professional league similar to that of the Japanese.[33]

Race, religion, and culture continue to be important factors in sport and power relationships. Sport served the Chinese as a significant political force. It was introduced by colonial powers with the intent of inculcating white Anglo-Saxon Protestant values and transforming the traditional culture, but the foreigners failed to subordinate the nationalistic impulses of the Chinese people. The Chinese adapted sport to their own needs and continue to use it to construct their own futures. Mainland China and

Taiwan now engage in sports exchanges and share basketball and baseball players in professional leagues. Both compete in international events that feature Anglo sport forms, yet they also adhere to traditional practices, such as dragon boat racing and Kuoshu (martial arts), that reinforce rather than diminish loyalties to established culture.[34]

Baseball and Bushido in Japan

Race and religion proved to be ongoing, contentious factors in Western relations with Japan. Christian missionaries arrived in search of souls in the sixteenth century but met with a ban against all, and martyrdom for some. Yet they persisted, returning in the 1850s, though the evangelicals did not record their "first heathen convert" until 1877. Commodore Matthew Perry, an American, arrived in Japan in 1853 and secured the so-called Treaty of Friendship, which opened Japan's markets to American goods the following year. During the Meiji period (1852–1912) the Japanese absorbed Western influences, including rapid modernization, industrialization, the adoption of Western governmental forms, educational models, arts, and sports. The formal abolition of the samurai class occurred in 1876, but sport proved a practical alternative as social tension accompanied the swift cultural changes.[1]

The discipline, teamwork, and self-sacrifice often required for athletic victories meshed with the warriors' bushido tenets of loyalty, courage, and honor. As Japanese schools inculcated Western ideologies, martial spirit and nationalism readily transferred to competitive ventures on the sports fields while also fueling patriotic, militaristic, and imperialistic aspirations. Teacher training for physical education began in 1878, based on European gymnastic models but also including drill, mimic fighting, fencing, and martial arts. Unlike China, Japan initiated a curriculum clearly designed to serve its own imperial ambitions. Each school maintained a medical officer, who was to keep boys healthy for conscription. Elementary school boys practiced storming forts and routing their enemies; on another occasion a fifteen-year-old boy and an eighty-year-old man swam the Sumida River despite a three-degree (Fahrenheit) temperature to demonstrate their endurance.[2]

American expatriates brought baseball to China as early as 1863, and teachers, missionaries, the military, and the YMCA promoted Western games throughout the region thereafter. In Japan the government imported American and European experts to bring Western science and technology to the island nation. One American teacher, Horace Wilson, brought a baseball and a bat when he embarked in 1871. He soon introduced the game to his students, and other American teachers spread baseball to Hokkaido, the northernmost island, by 1875. Japanese students sent to the United States for schooling also returned to their homeland with equipment and a love for the game. By 1878 adherents to the new sport had founded a private baseball club. Over the next decade other clubs formed and engaged in games with their rivals. The Americans and the Japanese shared a belief in the martial and masculine virtues of sport. Theodore Roosevelt stated that "the timid man who cannot fight, and the selfish, short-sighted, or foolish man who will not take the steps that will enable him to fight, stand on almost the same plane."[3] Sport proved a useful comparative tool that allowed the Japanese to measure their worthiness to assume Asian leadership and a place among the world's powers. China's sluggish pace in adopting the games relegated it to a less modern, less progressive status in Western eyes.[4]

A reactionary backlash to Meiji reforms marked the 1880s as America's democratic rhetoric failed to match its racist practices. U.S. immigration policy began excluding Asians in a series of legislative acts beginning in 1882, and American refusal to abrogate the unequal treaty arrangements that favored Western trade only exacerbated nationalistic sentiments over the next decade. By that time, baseball had already enjoyed widespread popularity and offered an opportunity for reprisal.[5]

The insult to Japanese pride continued, however, in 1891 when the Yokohama Athletic Club, which enrolled only Anglo members, dismissed a challenge by Ichiko, the elite national prep school, as inferior and unworthy. The Yokohama AC had barred Japanese spectators from its grounds over the previous decade in accordance with Western beliefs in Social Darwinian superiority and racial exclusion. Ichiko had to settle for a game against Meiji Gakuin, the Americanized Christian missionary school, in 1893. Ichiko's loss shamed the institution and engendered a Spartan training program of daylong drills as players endured pain stoically. Bunting and using relief pitchers became cowardly acts. Repeated challenges to the Yokohama AC were similarly disregarded until 1896, when an American English teacher at Ichiko brought the match to fruition. A recent victory in the Sino-Japanese War of 1894–1895 heightened nationalist fervor, and the students vowed in a written testament "to fight to the bitter end." The Ichiko team captain claimed that "the name of the country was at stake."[6] The team and its train of supporters met with taunts from the Yokohama AC fans, but Ichiko returned banzai chants as they prevailed 29–4 and celebrated with sake toasts as they sang the Japanese national anthem.

The student body president proclaimed: "This great victory is more than a victory for our school, it is a victory for the Japanese people."[7] Players were feted as national heroes, and the surprised Americans quickly called for a rematch, for which they recruited top players from the U.S. navy ships anchored in the Yokohama harbor. Despite the reinforcements the Americans succumbed 32–9 and suffered further indignities as the Japanese players spit three times on their sacred ground in ritual defiance of the racist ban and Japanese fans shouted obscenities. A Japanese newspaper trumpeted the result in front-page headlines, spawning baseball fever throughout the nation. English-language newspapers found excuses for the losses, and later that month, yet another team from a U.S. cruiser attempted to restore American honor. Accompanied by a naval band and U.S. government representatives, the sailors fell 22–6 before a standing-room-only crowd of ten thousand. Outside the field, Japanese employees of Anglo bosses who had shamed and dishonored them retaliated with acclamations for their warriors, who had redeemed their pride and self-esteem.[8]

The Ichiko Baseball Club's annual report of 1896 expressed the pain and redemption inherent in the political, cultural, and athletic confrontation. It stated: "The Americans are proud of baseball as their national game just as we have been proud of judo and kendo. Now, however, in a place far removed from their native land, they have fought against a 'little people' whom they ridicule as childish, only to find themselves swept away like falling leaves. No words can describe their disgraceful conduct. The aggressive character of our national spirit is a well-established fact, demonstrated first in the Sino-Japanese War and now by our great victories in baseball."[9]

The Americans requested yet another rematch on July 4. This time they garnered an all-star team that included a former pro who was then a sailor on the *Olympia* battleship, itself a symbol of U.S. might in the Pacific. The Westerners squeaked out a narrow 14–12 win, but over the next eight years Ichiko would prove superior in 9 of 11 contests against American teams.[10]

Despite the Japanese success, Caspar Whitney, the most prominent sportswriter in America at the time, minimized their prowess in an 1898 report. He described "little men" in "tiny houses," and rickshaws as "overgrown baby carriages" in "a country done over in miniature." Rather than recognize the discipline and determination that had garnered triumph, he remarked that "the Japanese temperament is uncertain and changeful . . . given to sudden flights and sudden flagging." He admitted the American losses in baseball, yet claimed that the Japanese had "that notable deficiency of all Orientals, the lack of steadfastness and perseverance." He further speculated that sumo wrestlers "would make but a short stand against a disciple of . . . Anglo-Saxon wrestling."[11] Nevertheless, such victories proved to the Japanese that they could not only compete in the modern world but succeed on the world stage. As American and European powers colonized the globe, Japan developed imperial visions of its own.

After the victory in the Sino-Japanese War, Japan perceived itself as the leading Asian power and eventual unifier of Asian peoples. By the turn of the century the United States considered Japan as a rival in the Pacific. The conquest of China in 1894–1895 established a Japanese presence on the Asian mainland and on the island of Taiwan, where boys were soon taught to play baseball. Moreover, the indemnities forced on China funded a major industrial and military buildup in Japan. General Leonard Wood argued that "Japan is going ahead in a perfectly methodical philosophical way to dominate the Far East and as much of the Pacific and its trade as we and the rest of the world will permit. When she has a good excuse she will absorb the Philippines unless we are strong enough to prevent it."[12]

As early as 1897 white settlers feared a Japanese takeover of the Hawaiian Islands and called for annexation by the United States. The Hawaiian government imposed a restriction on Japanese immigration, which spurred a protest by Japan. Yet Japanese settlers maintained ties with the homeland when the Asahi baseball team of Hawaii traveled to Japan in 1905, and Japanese teams barnstormed to the island and the U.S. mainland thereafter. When Waseda University sent its team to the United States in 1905, the players enjoyed fervent fan support in San Francisco, Los Angeles, and Seattle. The *Los Angeles Times* described the "short legged, black haired . . . brown batter(s)" and "a short, fat, greasy-faced Mongolian," who expressed "the firm conviction of the Japs that the 'white boys' could not play ball with the men from Tokio [*sic*]" in a Waseda victory. Such ties and racial difference would raise suspicions of collusion by the start of World War II.[13]

When Russia breached the boundary of Korea and threatened Japanese control of the region, the Japanese retaliated in the Russo-Japanese War of 1904–1905. Their dominance led to formal annexation in 1910, three years after the so-called Gentleman's Agreement, which excluded Japanese workers from the United States. Such racial policies led to anti-American demonstrations in Japan that carried over to the baseball field. In the 1905 game between Waseda and Keio universities, fans disputed a call by C. T. Mayes, an expatriate American who served as the umpire. Normally polite and respectful, they chased Mayes over the left-field wall and forced him into hiding. Baseball games between schools in Japan assumed rivalries similar to college football confrontations in the United States. Japanese players gained the status of "Senshu," or warriors, who served as the new samurai.[14]

Japanese athletic prowess matched the country's growing political stature. A Chicago alumnus living in Japan wrote to his former coach that his rickshaw driver was much faster than the American university runners and that another ran 12½ miles nonstop. He asserted: "When the exposition comes off here in 1917 I am going to have a Jap set a mark for the marathon race that no white man can touch."[15]

Baseball continued as the primary test of racial comparisons as teams from both countries traveled across the Pacific after the turn of the century. In 1908 Keio University defeated the U.S. Atlantic Fleet team, then finished second in a Hawaiian tournament. The Great White Fleet, symbolic of American military might, arrived in Japan in October 1908 while on its global tour. Uncowed by the formidable armada, Japanese students played a series of baseball games against the visitors, defeating or tying the fleet's all-star contingents. The A. J. Reach Sporting Goods Company ensured dominance by sending a group of barnstorming professional players throughout Asia in the 1908–1909 off-season. The Reach team won all 17 games in Japan, to the chagrin of the Japanese. The Japanese government funded another trip by Waseda University to the United States. Trips to Japan by baseball teams from the universities of Washington, Wisconsin, and Chicago soon followed. The excursions were inevitably characterized as "invasions," and Waseda played accordingly, defeating Washington four times in 1908. The American schools endeavored to educate the Japanese in the amateur ideology and sportsmanship perceived to be absent among navy and professional teams—"to show that rowdyism has no place in Base Ball [*sic*], that kicking against decisions and browbeating the umpire is not a necessary adjunct of the game."[16]

The emphasis on sportsmanship masked cultural differences and the outcome of the racial confrontation. The infield chatter of the Wisconsin players offended the Japanese fans' sense of decorum as Wisconsin lost 3 of 4 games with Keio University in Tokyo in 1909. American publicists admitted that the Japanese were "imbued with bushida [*sic*] spirit" and that they played with an indomitable fighting spirit which is lacking in most American college teams."[17]

The following year, 1910, the University of Chicago stipulated particular conditions and took extensive precautions to ensure a better performance. Concerned that the Washington and Wisconsin players had compromised their morality and ability by frolicking with geishas, Coach Stagg informed the Japanese hosts that his players were in "strict training" and would be unable to accept Japanese "hospitality."[18] Players were instructed to stay "away from such places in Japan . . . which are commonly visited from impure motives or morbid curiosity" and "without exception [to] add to the warfare each and every man has to fight for his own self control. . . . Do not go where you would not be willing to take your mother and sister and sweetheart."[19] An accompanying faculty member ensured adherence to the prohibitions. Stagg refused to play the best teams on successive days and received extensive scouting reports from Americans in Japan, some of whom coached Japanese teams.[20] One report stated:

> *They are proud and usually count themselves superior to all foreigners. . . . They root like mad, arouse themselves, and fight like the soldiers they really are. . . . The little fellows are sometimes tricky. . . . They are tempted sorely by the rough American tactics sometimes used against them. They bear such things in silence usually, but feel it deep inside. . . . Don't call the little brown players "Japs" for they are sensitive. . . . Never show anger under any provocation. . . . A few "banzais" (cheers) for the opposing team will add spirit . . . and create good feeling.*[21]

Further correspondence referred to both sides as "warriors" for the fall "invasion" and feared meeting one's "Waterloo."[22] Stagg's team practiced with the Chicago professionals, while the Waseda University squad prepped in the Oahu Baseball League in Hawaii throughout the summer. Stagg's diligence paid off, however, as Chicago swept the Japanese in 10 straight games before enormous crowds, then declared itself "champions of the Orient."[23]

Eager to learn from their conquerors, the Japanese sent students to America to observe their sporting practices and techniques, in particular those of the master coach, Amos Alonzo Stagg, at Chicago. They also organized a national baseball tournament for high schools in 1911, followed four years later by a national middle school championship. Keio University imported an American coach before its 1912 trip to the United States, and Japanese political confidence grew with athletic prowess. Japan sent three athletes to the 1912 Olympics in Stockholm as it increased the size of its navy. It further asserted its prominence in the Far Eastern Olympics, initiated by the YMCA in the Philippines that same year. Elwood Brown, the YMCA director in Manila, envisioned a pan-Asian alliance via sport based on Coubertin's Olympic ideology, and he counted on Japanese pride as a catalyst for inclusion in his already well established Filipino games. The Japanese eagerly agreed to the athletic competition, which could demonstrate their physical superiority, but they harbored opposing views on the role of political leadership in Asia.[24]

Political relations between Japan and the United States deteriorated precipitously in 1913 when legislation in California forbade alien land ownership. Aimed at, and humiliating to, the Japanese, the measure brought a formal protest; yet the athletic wars continued. In 1913 the Chicago White Sox and the New York Giants played each other in Tokyo during a worldwide tour, and in 1915 the University of Chicago baseball team returned to Japan, narrowly winning all 10 games against Japanese schools, although the victory over Keio University in Tokyo was a disputed one.[25]

The Japanese continued to learn from the Americans, incorporating that which proved beneficial or practical while denying cultural incongruities. By 1909 the Mizuno Company began producing its own baseball equipment, rather than importing the sporting goods of the American Spalding Company. The proselytizing YMCA had long been a factor in Japan, even providing hygienic and recreational services to its army during the Russo-Japanese War. In 1916 the Japanese government used the YMCA as its model when it organized thirty thousand youth clubs throughout the country. The clubs served imperial and nationalistic purposes but denied the Christianity inherent in YMCA programs.[26]

Japanese nationalism made a prominent appearance at the Third Far Eastern Olympics in 1917, held in Tokyo. Twenty thousand fans per day witnessed the Japanese victories, and the YMCA foresaw a burgeoning Olympic spirit that promoted peaceful competition as World War I raged in

Europe. "The dust clouds of strife and hatred are uprising on the battlefield of Europe; the dust of furious but friendly conflict is ascending on the athletic field of Japan . . . without inspiring the lust of killing. . . . The armaments are vaulting poles, discus plates, baseball clubs. The rifle-shot on the battlefield echoes in Japan; it is the report from a starter's revolver."[27]

Elwood Brown, the YMCA director in the Philippines and founder of the games, even allowed for a measure of modernity in Asia achieved through sport, though he tempered his remarks with continuing racial connotations repugnant to Asians. Brown stated:

> *When, fifty years ago, Japan came out of her seclusion and selected from the civilization of the world her special brand, she overlooked sports. . . . But now . . . she welcomes the opportunity to play. One who did not know Japan might think that her meet would include an archery tournament, or a mock duel with samurai swords, or at least an exhibition of jiujitsu. But the archery contests occur on estates hidden from the general public, the two swords of the samurai are rusting in the family storehouses, the jiujitsu combatants toss each other behind closed doors. Instead there is volley ball, football, baseball. There are high jumps, shot-puts, tennis games. There are foot races, hurdle races, bicycle races. And Pentathlon, Decathlon and Marathon. . . . The Imperial Princes, small, serious lads, flanked by responsible looking personages in Prince Alberts and high hats, walked decorously to specially prepared seats, while the military band played the National Anthem of Japan.*[28]

Brown further remarked that it was strange to see the Chinese, "a dispassionate race," cheering, and he gave faint praise to the "better ordered college yell" of the Filipinos then under American tutelage. But, he wrote, "from the baseball field comes a wild confused cannibalistic cry led by an apparently frantic dancing Dervish; the star pitcher of Japan has put over one of his famous plays."[29] Brown surmised:

> *Today Japan is exultant. She has won the Third Far Eastern Championships, and for two years may wear on her proud brow the golden wreath which was presented . . . by the World Olympics. But beneath*

> *these surface bubbles of self-glorification one cannot help feeling that there is flowing a quiet national courtesy. The Western world may be grinding its best youth into mincemeat, but the Eastern world is making its lads into fine, strong citizens. On the battlefield Western civilization may be scattering its good-will and brotherhood to the four winds, but on the athletic field the East is welding a great amulet which will encircle the Far East in a band of international fellowship.*[30]

Brown's analysis, however, misinterpreted Japanese intentions. Wholesale acceptance of the Western athletic ideology proved problematic for the Japanese. They adopted Western sport forms but retained their interest in martial arts and the bushido spirit. Athletic contests served to test Japan's might against other Asian nations and the United States. The latter factor assumed even greater importance after World War I when President Woodrow Wilson refused to approve a racial equality clause in the Treaty of Versailles so dearly desired by the Japanese. Sport became a primary means to demonstrate their parity. Under Coach Suisha Tobita, Waseda engaged in "death training." The stern taskmaster claimed: "If the players do not try so hard as to vomit blood in practice, they cannot hope to win games. One must suffer to be good." He further stated that "players who lose and don't cry, don't care enough."[31] His players learned their lessons well, going undefeated in 1925.

Heita Okabe, sent to the United States to study sport at American colleges, became a disciple of Amos Alonzo Stagg at Chicago. The organic intellectual in Gramsci's hegemony theory, Okabe served to bridge the cultural gap between the two nations. He absorbed Stagg's lessons thoroughly, even playing on the freshman football team. Their correspondence continued for at least a dozen years (1918–1930), and Okabe became a prominent sports figure in Japan and coach of its track and field team. His adherence to Western ideas, however, caused social and political tension in his homeland.[32]

As a teacher in Tokyo, Okabe tried to introduce American football into the school system, though soccer remained more popular. He caused an international stir when he resigned his position as a martial arts instructor at the Kodokan (association of Japanese wrestlers) over a match with American professional wrestlers in 1921. More than twenty years after Caspar Whitney's prediction that Japanese wrestlers stood little chance against Anglo-Saxons, the long-awaited contest offered to test such allegations. Okabe, however, considered such an event a clear violation of Stagg's interpretation of amateurism.[33]

Sport continued to provide Japan with international exposure when it hosted the Far Eastern Games at Osaka in 1923. Just two years later, however, Okabe created a nationalistic furor when, as coach of the national track team, he withdrew his squad from the Asian games at Manila after filing nearly thirty protests over three days of competition, charging incompetence by the Filipino judges and collaboration by the YMCA organizers when Japan's lead in the point totals drastically diminished. Okabe wrote: "I was thinking of Mr. Stagg when I thought of withdrawing, and finally I decided to follow the spirit of Stagg and announced the withdrawal of Japan's team."[34]

In doing so Okabe also violated the bushido sense of honor. As a quitter he and his team were ostracized by the other Japanese athletes, who refused to travel home on the same ship until the Japanese government intervened and offered support for Okabe's position. He returned to Japan, where he made four public speeches in explanation, and Japanese media portrayed the affair as a war against the Filipino lackeys. The United States had recently passed the Immigration Act, which excluded the Japanese from American citizenship.[35]

Baseball provided yet another opportunity for retaliation. Both U.S. president Warren Harding and Major League Baseball commissioner Kenesaw Mountain Landis had sanctioned a 1922 postseason tour by Major Leaguers to Japan as a means to increase international interest and provide instruction. Yet the American pros lost decisively, 9–3, to the Mita Club of Shibawa, a signal victory for Japan. The Japanese further applied their lessons against the University of Chicago during the latter's 1925 trip to the country. Tobita Suishu, famed authoritarian coach of the Waseda team, had spent years instilling *konjo*, the Japanese fighting spirit, in his players, who engaged the Chicagoans in four of the battles. Whereas the Chicago players had been undefeated in two previous expeditions, this time they won only 2 of 8 games and were held scoreless in six of the contests.[36]

Baseball fueled nationalistic sentiments and reaffirmed Japanese masculinity. When an American women's team arrived in 1925, the Japanese showed little interest, leaving the players stranded. The high school championships of 1927 drew eighty-five thousand fans, and the winner, Wakayama High School, earned a trip to the United States. Upon the team's triumphant return, so many fans crowded the railway station that it took the team two hours to disembark. Another two thousand showed up just to watch a practice session. An American reporter detailed the samurai spirit, martial music, banzai cheers, and bushido code of honor. He noted that Japanese sporting goods manufacturers offered equipment autographed by native rather than American stars.[37]

Such nationalism did not bode well for the YMCA or Protestant missionaries. The evangelical mission recorded only 343 attendees at its Tokyo Bible School in 1927, less than one per day on average. They further reported that converts were disowned by their own families and that Christian shopkeepers were boycotted. By 1940 Christians accounted for only 0.1 percent of the population.[38]

Despite such religious differences, sport offered opportunities for some conciliation. Okabe, at least, maintained his Olympian beliefs. Now stationed in Manchuria, he wrote Stagg that he hoped "to reconcile Japan and China via sport with the spirit of fair play and good sportsmanship. . . . I am glad that that great spirit of Stagg is pl[a]ying the fundamental role in this also."[39] Stagg responded: "You will accomplish more than the diplomats and politicians can ever bring about. It pleases me very much that you are thinking such noble thoughts and planning in such noble ways."[40] Stagg collaborated with Okabe, even writing the introduction to one of his protègè's books that promoted Stagg's philosophy in Japan.[41]

Japanese nationalism, however, superseded such idealistic notions. In the Far East Games of 1930 the Japanese overwhelmed the Philippines, China, and India to demonstrate their mastery of Asia. The nearest competitor in the track and field events lagged nearly 100 points behind. Japan sent a team of female swimmers and men from Meiji University to compete against U.S. athletes in Hawaii, and the University of Chicago baseball "invasion" of Japan only swelled Japanese pride, as the Maroons went 5-9-1, winning only 2 of 10 games against the Japanese colleges.[42] Militarism kept pace with the Japanese victories. By 1931 compulsory martial arts training became part of the school curriculum. Bushido emphasized patriotism, conformity, obedience, and toughness of mind and body. In the schools, sports also became a means of inculcating a fascist ideology that opposed a growing Communist movement in Japan. Organized athletics henceforth served the state.[43]

Another tour by Major League stars in 1931 included Lou Gehrig and other future Hall of Famers to ensure American superiority, but even that team almost lost to Keio University. Buoyed with confidence Japan flexed its military muscles as well, seizing Manchuria. The following year yet another troupe of Americans came to Japan for instructional purposes—this time accompanied by catcher Moe Berg, who purportedly spied for the U.S. government.[44]

In 1932 Japan demonstrated its athletic prowess on the world stage as its male swimmers won five of the six Olympic events and another captured the triple jump in track and field. Still, American journalists persisted in referring to the Japanese athletes as "little brown men" who were "diminutive but doughty."[45] Two years later Harvard's baseball team belatedly made the pilgrimage to Japan, but America's most prestigious educational institution lost the majority of its games, falling to six different opponents. That same year a group of American League All-Stars, including Charlie Gehringer, Babe Ruth, Lou Gehrig, and Jimmy Foxx, barnstormed Japan, going undefeated. They gained only a one-run victory over their Japanese counterparts in Osaka, however, as eighteen-year-old Eiji Sawamura became an instant national hero by successively striking out the American power hitters. Still, recognizing them as warriors, Japanese fans gave "banzai" cheers for the sluggers, while Earl Averill earned a sword as a badge of honor after a particular home run. The following year Japanese players toured the United States, winning 93 of 102 games played. The Japanese soon began their own professional league with the intent of beating the Americans in a true world series. President Franklin Roosevelt supported the initiative as a surrogate to war, but the Japanese military campaigns in China soon precipitated a greater competition for control of Asia.[46]

Japan had already withdrawn from the League of Nations in 1933 when the latter condemned its seizure of Manchukuo. A year later Japan abrogated the naval treaties on disarmament and allied itself with Germany and Italy in 1937. That same year Japan embarked on a full-scale war with China. The National Mobilization Law followed in 1938, and slogans such as "East Asia for East Asiatics" denoted the racial character of the ensuing conflict.[47]

Japanese nationalism thus superseded the progressive promise of sport and led to the use of sport as a resistive force. The adaptation of Western sport forms served both racial and nationalistic ends, allowing the Japanese to combat Anglo perceptions of superiority, Western colonialism, and notions of Asian leadership. Sport allowed for the reemergence of traditional cultural values, particularly the warrior ethic of bushido.[48] That determination had been evident as early as 1905 in the Ichiko baseball song that extolled victories over the American teams and ended as follows:

Ah, for the glory of our Baseball Club!
Ah, for the glitter it has cast!
Pray that our martial valor never turns submissive
And that our honor will always shine far across the Pacific.[49]

The final verse held an ominous portent of World War II. Sport thus served not as a surrogate to war but as a preparation for hostilities. Japanese dissatisfaction with Western culture grew with American rejection of racial equality and cultural parity, and in reaction to Christian proselytism. Competing visions of regional leadership undermined any idealistic notions of a sporting camaraderie. While the Japanese adopted whiteness in the form of Western technologies, industrialization, sporting practices, goods, and even modes of dress, they did not perceive any greater benefits in the Christian religions. American missionaries, including the YMCA, labored in futility despite the attractions of sport to the Japanese.

Perhaps even more abhorrent to the Japanese were Americans' racial attitudes. The messages of democracy, freedom, and liberty espoused by American missionaries and statesmen rang hollow when the Japanese were not taken seriously on the athletic fields or at the conference tables. While American politicians and emissaries proclaimed equality and fraternity, they hardly practiced it. The U.S. government's policies safeguarded American trade in the form of protective tariffs, protected American evangelists abroad despite (or in the cause of) public advocacy of religious freedom, prohibited Asia immigration, and assumed that the New World had much to teach the older civilizations of Asia and even those of Europe, as evidenced by President Woodrow Wilson's diplomatic efforts to structure the Treaty of Versailles, which ended World War I, and by the initiation of the League of Nations. The Americans failed on all counts. They achieved only a temporary peace; they assumed an isolationist stance that precluded membership in the League of Nations, dooming it to failure; and Japanese designs on Pacific leadership remained unchanged. Americans' belief in their country as a world model to be emulated held steadfast, even as Japan and the American-occupied Philippines began to question such self-righteous presumptions and the hypocrisy of U.S. practices in its racial relations.

Sport and Colonialism in the Philippines

Under Spanish control for nearly three centuries, the Philippines opened the port of Cebu for world trade in 1860. An American firm quickly established an office in the city, signaling the start of American intervention in the islands. By the end of the century the United States possessed the entire archipelago as a colony. Paul Kramer has stated that the ensuing occupation served as a "a laboratory for reform" that merged imperialism with progressivism. Such reforms attempted wholesale changes in governance, administration, education, cultural beliefs and values, and even recreational practices.[1]

In 1989 Jan Beran published a seminal and insightful article on the introduction of American sports to the Philippines. She analyzed the role of the schools, teachers, and the YMCA in the transition from traditional folk games to organized and competitive athletics that taught American ideals. Beran concluded that the process proved to be one of relatively beneficent assimilation. More recent studies of imperialism, colonialism, and acculturation suggest that the process is more complex.[2] Sports are not value-free entities; nor are their producers. Though more subtle than government impositions, sports and their administrators play a key role in the evolutionary process of cultural change. In the case of the Philippines, that change brought racial, gender, and religious relationships into question and ultimately fostered a new product unforeseen by either side.

Having acquired the Philippines through the brief Spanish-American War of 1898, the U.S. government faced considerable opposition to procuring the archipelago both within the United States and in the islands. Some anti-imperialists argued that the new territory would prove a drain on national resources, while Carl Schurz, formerly a senator and secretary of the interior, argued that Filipinos were "a large mass of more or less barbarous Asiatics . . . far less good-natured, tractable, and orderly than the negro [*sic*] is."[3] Even coreligionists warned that "the inhabitants of the Philippines include . . . Kanakas and Malays who are half-civilized and in rebellion; canny Chinese and shrewd Japanese and—in the interior—thousands of naked negritos [*sic*], wild and untamed as the red aborigines."[4] As racial concerns affected some, others thought the concept of colonies a betrayal of the American heritage and its democratic promise of independence.[5] Many Filipinos agreed with the latter stance as their rebel army had already declared a war against their Spanish overlords and had them surrounded in Manila when the American army arrived, then surreptitiously claimed the victory. Nevertheless, the rebels maintained their own governmental headquarters, produced a constitution, and chose a national assembly.[6]

Given such circumstances the U.S. government needed a way to rationalize further deployment and occupation of its "liberated" domain. Colonial proponents proved ready with economic, religious, and ideological reasons. The overheated American economy had surpassed the industrial output of Great Britain and the European powers by the 1890s but had stalled in the depression of 1893. Producers needed new markets for their goods, and the Philippines offered a gateway to the rest of Asia. Protestant missionaries saw a chance to win souls and perceived it as their duty to provide a "Christian education," neglecting to consider that the largely Catholic Filipinos were already Christians. As early as July 1898 an interdenominational conference met in New York to divide up the spoils among Baptists, Methodists, and Presbyterians; congregationalists had already determined that "morally and religiously, we should not shun an opportunity to lift up a barbarous people."[7] This and similar statements assumed it to be the "white man's burden" and a moral imperative to bring civilization, technology, and a particular brand of the Christian religion to those deemed to be lower on the Social Darwinian ladder.

Supreme Court justice David Brewer declared the United States to be the "purest form of Christianity." In his 1904 address to the YMCA, an organization destined to be among the chief proselytizers in the Philippines, he stated: "Here in the Republic, in the Providence of God, should be worked out the unity of the [human] race—a unity made possible by the influences of education and the power of Christianity."[8] Such global intentions carried distinct economic, racial, and religious manifestations. The United States, however, arrived late to the geopolitical banquet of the "survival of the fittest." Great Britain and the European powers had already carved up much of the world as their dominions, and little remained. If the United States was to achieve its manifest destiny and vie for world leadership, expansionists argued, then the government had not only a right but a duty to claim the Philippines.

The U.S. government had already established, at least to its own satisfaction, the uncivilized, primitive condition of the Filipino peoples and their need for benevolent guidance, despite the protestations of the Philippines' revolutionary government. As early as 1887 Dean Worcester, a zoology professor at the University of Michigan, had traveled to the Philippines in search of specimens. His second expedition, from 1890 to 1893, and his subsequent forays into physical anthropology established Worcester as an "authority" on Filipino tribes when he opportunistically published his speculations with the outbreak of the war. President McKinley appointed Worcester to the First Philippines Commission in 1899, and Worcester supervised its final report, recommending U.S. rule. He returned to the islands as part of the second commission in 1900 and served as its secretary of the interior until his resignation under scandalous circumstances in 1913, after which he engaged in private business until his death in Manila in 1924. Throughout Worcester's life, his books, articles, photographs, and lecture tours earned him substantial sums by characterizing Filipinos as half-naked savages, headhunters, and primitive barbarians. Though Worcester was a zoologist by training, Americans considered him an expert in the nascent field of anthropology, giving his opinions as an autocratic colonial administrator added weight. Among educated Filipinos he was, perhaps, the most reviled and resented of American officials.[9]

Combined with the publications of Robert Bennett Bean, a University of Michigan anatomist who emphasized racial differences, Worcester's work established the Filipinos as genetically inferior and unable to govern themselves without proper American guidance. As late as 1913, fifteen years after the American invasion, Worcester stated of the Negrito tribe: "These people are probably the lowest type of human beings known and have been described as not far above the anthropoid apes." He labeled the Ilongots "a tribe so primitive that they are unable to count beyond ten," and described the Moros as "unexcelled pirates and slave traders, treacherous and unreliable to the last degree."[10]

The cameras and phonographs used to capture the images and sounds of the natives further established the scientific and technological precedence of the Anglos, enhancing their own views as superior. In the United States Thomas Edison produced "newsreels" from his New Jersey studio, in which he staged or reenacted battles and skirmishes of the Filipino-American War. African American actors played the parts of vanquished Filipinos, who inevitably lost or ran from heroic whites. Various forms of media thus inscribed racial superiority for audiences at home and abroad.[11] Despite his own studies to the contrary, Worcester claimed in a 1914 book that "before the American occupation of the Philippines the Filipinos had not learned to play. There were no athletics worthy of the name."[12] He recommended baseball to "strengthen muscles and wits."[13]

The baseball campaign had already been long under way. American soldiers had introduced the Filipinos to baseball and boxing as early as 1898, shortly after they arrived in the country. Baseball soon became part of the Americans' educational initiative as soldiers were pressed into service as teachers even before colonial administrators established a civil government.[14] Baseball, the American national game, linked participants and spectators to particular cultural values that they intended to transmit to the Filipinos. An American expatriate explained his fellow citizens' emphasis on the game: "For many of that day's American officials, playing baseball was as cleansing and creative as total immersion to a Baptist." The American-owned *Manila Times* declared, "Baseball is more than a game, a regenerating influence, or power for good."[15]

The U.S. Army had just begun to notice the value of sport in the 1890s, not only for maintaining the morale of its troops but for inculcating particular value systems. Sports served as a more pleasurable form of exercise, distracted participants and spectators from the less wholesome forms of entertainment, and established esprit de corps and a martial spirit. General Franklin Bell, commander of U.S. forces in Manila, stated that "baseball had done more to 'civilize' Filipinos than anything else."[16]

The Filipinos had cause to question the civilization and morality that the Americans brought. Gambling ran rampant; American brothel owners institutionalized prostitution, which the government rationalized as a necessary evil; and adventurers amassed fortunes by exploiting Filipino resources and labor. Governor General Taft admitted that "here Oriental corruption, through gambling, prostitution, and other vices, flourishes in its most exuberant form, and it is so easy for an American in authority to acquire a great deal of money. . . . The real danger in the administration is the inability to secure, not honest Americans, but honest Americans who will not become dishonest under the temptations."[17] Four years later the situation had not improved, as Bishop Brent, the Episcopalian leader, charged that "the Orient is no fit place for persons, especially young men, who have not moral stamina. The Philippines are almost the sure undoing of the weak."[18] Even the seemingly inviolate American women strayed into scandalous romances and illicit affairs. One local commentator remarked: "It is a curious thing about the Tropics. It certainly does something to one's moral standards."[19] Such logic thus rationalized immorality not as an Anglo fault but as a condition of a corrupt environment. The perception of sport as wholesome, disciplined, virtuous, and healthy seemed a godsend.

The practice of schooling Filipino children in baseball continued after the arrival of American teachers in 1901. Mary Fee, one of the new American schoolteachers, stated that games between town teams and including girls were under way by 1903. Manila showcased a baseball park by 1902, and an interscholastic tournament and baseball leagues appeared by 1905. Fee offered the opinion that "those children got more real Americanism out of that corrupted ball game than they did from singing 'My Country 'tis of Thee' every morning."[20]

Americans, in fact, tried to re-create the United States in the Philippines. Protestant missionaries began arriving in March 1899 to distribute Bibles and convert the Filipinos to their version of Christianity. American officials soon imposed their particular morality as well by banning cockfighting, lotteries, and gambling houses. They initiated English language instruction in the schools in 1898 as a common parlance with the intention of replacing the multitude of dialects and tribal languages. School administrators adopted public education models from the Massachusetts public schools and the Tuskegee Institute, which emphasized vocational training, and the racial segregation practices of the American army and stateside society found ready adherents in the Philippines.[21]

Despite the promises of education and sports, Americans continued to racialize and emasculate Filipinos. More than 75 percent of house servants in the colony were males, whom their employers referred to as *muchachos*, or boys. One such employer, an American woman, wrote: "Your first impression will be that we keep trained baboons to do the housework, for the probability is that a half-naked, dark-skinned creature is rushing up and down the hall on all fours, with big burlap sacks under his hands and feet. He is only the monkey-like coolie who polishes the narra floors."[22] General Leonard Wood re-created the frontier in the Philippines and justified his use of force against those he considered "savages" and "religious and moral degenerates." When a soldier who served as a deputy governor under Wood took a Muslim woman for his wife and assumed a Muslim title, he was expelled from his post. Lt. Benjamin Foulois, Woods's tennis partner, declared the Moros to be "a race of children [who] . . . have to be treated accordingly." Similarly, white Americans taught their racial attitudes to the Filipinos, urging nonfraternization with the black U.S. Army units stationed in the islands.[23]

White Americans secluded themselves in the Manila YMCA, in social clubs, and in the designated summer capital of Baguio, two hundred miles north of Manila. The U.S. government called on Daniel Burnham to transform the historical capital, Manila, and to design a summer capital at Baguio, where the cool mountain breezes better suited Americans. Burnham traveled to the Philippines in the fall of 1904 for the purpose of "adapting the city of Manila to the changed conditions brought about by the influx of Americans, who are used to better conditions of living than had prevailed in those islands. . . . The two capitals of the Philippines, even in their physical characteristics, will represent the power and dignity of this [U.S.] nation."[24]

Burnham indeed aimed at achieving an imperial facade, incorporating ideas from his American city plans. Parks, play fields, and natural preserves served the people, but a complex of government buildings was situated near the bay and elevated, with the Hall of Justice at the highest point. Diagonal streets radiated from the civic center "because every section of the Capital City should look with deference toward the symbol of the Nation's power."[25] A grand boulevard, later named for American war hero Admiral George Dewey, skirted the bay, and a magnificent park, the Luneta, arose from landfill dredged from the harbor. Yet the best and potentially most prosperous land remained reserved for Americans. A military reservation occupied the harbor front, the private Army-Navy Club was situated on the south side of the Luneta adjoining the oceanfront, and the private and opulent Manila Hotel rested on prime property to be leased to Americans for the next ninety-nine years. Burnham described the location as "magnificent. . . . This site will be finer than anything in any capital in the world . . . [the] most prominent spot in Manila."[26] The elegant hotel served as both a repository and an attraction for expected tourists.

The public buildings copied those designed by Burnham for Washington DC, and Manila's streets soon assumed the names of American heroes and politicians. Its wealthiest suburb, Forbes Park, honored the governor general who tried most earnestly to Americanize the Filipinos.[27]

Burnham drew from his European travels in further planning for Manila, suggesting the " 'canals' be developed, as in Venice. Possessing the bay of Naples, the winding river of Paris, and the canals of Venice,

Manila has before it an opportunity unique in the history of modern times, the opportunity to create a unified city equal to the greatest of the Western World with the unparalleled and priceless addition of a tropical setting."[28] Manila thus expressed the epitome of the City Beautiful movement, but one reliant on Western, and particularly American, ideals of aesthetics and social order, where site and monumental structure established and objectified dominance.[29]

Burnham's plan for the summer capital at Baguio expressed similar intent. The mountains and climate of northern Luzon Island reminded Burnham of the Adirondack region of his native New York, and he drew inspiration from both the British summer capital at Simla in colonial India and his own previous city plans for Washington DC. In Baguio, Burnham set the business district on a level meadow, between the municipal building, which he located on a ridgetop, and the government buildings placed "on the natural Acropolis formed by Governor's Mountain and its flanking hilltops."[30] Burnham Park, with an artificial lake, offered romance, solace, and reflection, while an open plaza fronted the government complex, whose setting gave it "preeminence over all other buildings of the city."[31] The *Inland Architect*, a trade journal, praised the designs to "develop civilizing influences side by side with commercial advancement."[32] In the smaller villages Americans restructured streets and housing in accordance with their own norms, and the native populace was taught to observe American holidays.[33]

The Filipinos did not suffer American impositions gladly. Shortly after the American takeover of Manila, a skirmish between U.S. soldiers and Filipino revolutionary troops on February 4, 1899, erupted into a full-scale and brutal guerrilla war of resistance. By 1900, 75 percent of the entire U.S. Army was engaged in the suppression. The United States claimed victory in three years, and President Teddy Roosevelt declared the remaining resistance fighters "bandits." Still, fighting continued on the main island of Luzon until 1911, and on the southern island of Mindanao until 1916, with two hundred thousand Filipinos, mostly civilians, losing their lives. Filipino revolutionary leaders were hung, deported, or co-opted, yet a strong underground movement persisted. The American colonial government banned the revolutionary flag and required an oath of allegiance for governmental positions. It established the Federalist political party, composed of Filipino collaborators or accommodationists, who were subsequently chosen for office by Governor General William Howard Taft. Despite the Americans' pronounced intentions of universal education and suffrage, only about 3 percent of Filipinos qualified to vote, allowing the wealthy to retain positions of power, as they had under the Spanish.[34]

Although Americans banned oppositional parties during the hostilities, even the Federalists sought independence or statehood by 1904. Secretary of State Elihu Root stated "Statehood for Filipinos would add another serious problem to the one we have already. The Negroes are a cancer in our body politic, a source of constant difficulty, and we wish to avoid developing another such problem."[35] The local, American-owned *Manila Cablenews* commented: "All of us who have lived in the Far East know that in practice these yellow and brown peoples must be guided and often driven in a forward direction so that they do not obstruct the progress of the world nor infringe on the rights of other nations."[36]

Filipinos vehemently protested such racist characterizations, particularly the American practice of exhibiting the primitive Igorot tribe in a series of world's fairs and expositions. At the St. Louis World's Fair of 1904, a Filipino "village" presented nearly naked, barefoot "natives" in loin cloths. Under the guise of educational "Anthropology Days," ethnic groups competed in athletic and pseudo-athletic events. The latter included a greased pole climb and a mud fight that clearly implied the physical and cultural superiority of Anglos. Educated Filipinos asserted that "the Igorottes [*sic*] were no more representative of the Philippines than the most savage Indians are representative of Americans."[37]

To the charges of Filipino laziness, the Filipinos countered that "the charge is that the Filipino will not work! The sentence is not complete; it should read: 'The Filipinos will not work for foreigners.' That is to say, they will not work for the vampire, and the wolf whose sole intent is to amass wealth by the labor of others."[38] Such tensions fueled the nationalist movement, which resulted in three new political parties in 1906. They merged the following year as the Nacionalista Party, calling for immediate independence and a democratic government. In the 1907 elections they won sixteen of thirty-one governmental positions and a majority in the Philippine Assembly, and Filipinos marched on American buildings, tore down and trampled the U.S. flag, and replaced it with revolutionary symbols. The Nacionalistas soon tried to overturn the imposition of the English language, only to be vetoed by the governor general. The colonial Supreme Court had already banned the very popular nationalist plays in the Tagalog language as seditious.[39]

The Americans enjoyed a larger measure of success with the younger generation in the schools, though education, too, remained a contested terrain. In August 1900 the Filipinos in two cities of Batangas Province boycotted the schools. From a population of 80,000, fewer than 400 students enrolled, and in the rural areas American soldiers and police had to drag the children to classes. Filipinos perceived the secular public schools established by the Americans as Protestant institutions, and attendance quickly dropped from 200,000 in 1902 to 150,000 the next year. Colonial administrators reached a compromise by seeking the help of the American Catholic hierarchy in formulating a plan that allowed for religious instruction. Welcoming the chance to bring additional Catholics within their domain, American cardinals dispensed the evangelical Jesuits and other priests to combat the proselytizing Protestant schoolteachers. Between 1903 and 1912 Catholics established 903 private schools as a counter to secular education.[40]

Still, sports, games, and poverty drew children to the free public schools, and physical education became a primary means of acculturation. Even Filipino intellectuals had called for greater physical education in the schools as early as 1898, suggesting Jose Rizal, a multisport athlete and patriot considered to be the father of his country, as a role model for youth. W. Cameron Forbes, who served as governor general from 1909 to 1913, gladly obliged.[41]

Forbes, the grandson of Ralph Waldo Emerson and scion of one of the founders of the Bell Telephone company, held great faith in the powers of sport as a means to health and character building. Forbes had played football and baseball as a youth and favored golf and polo as an adult. In 1894 he coached the freshman football team at Harvard and served as the varsity coach in the 1897–1898 seasons, remaining undefeated against archrival Yale. Appointed as a Philippine commissioner from 1904 to 1908,

Forbes served as secretary of commerce and police before assuming the role of vice governor from 1908 to 1909 and of governor general from 1909 to 1913. During that time Forbes used part of his own considerable fortune to construct a polo field and golf course at Baguio. He became closely involved in soliciting memberships for the country club and in its accompanying real estate ventures, but ownership of the *Manila Times* by his brother generally shielded him from controversy.[42]

In the summer capital of Baguio and in Manila, where Americans constructed the public spaces as a way to demonstrate the racial and social hierarchy, large streets, avenues, or boulevards received American names while lesser thoroughfares got Filipino designations. The wealthy lived apart from the poorer classes, and Bishop Brent constructed a private school in Baguio for American boys, where students participated in riding, swimming, golf, and tennis. Brent stated that "the aim of the school is to promote Christian character, intellectual vigor, and respect for the body. . . . Every boy will be required to bring a Bible." Sport and social clubs served as segregated refuges for the Americans, some remaining so into the 1950s.[43]

The public schools purported to be more egalitarian, serving the uneducated poor by teaching them vocational skills, the English language, and American cultural values. The schools accomplished the latter largely through sports. The Bureau of Education began organization of interprovincial competition between schools on the main island of Luzon in 1904. By 1905 both boys and girls engaged in required physical education. A principal reported that "each boys' class has a team in baseball, indoor baseball, volley ball and basket ball. Each girls' class has a team in indoor baseball and volleyball."[44] Within five years tennis courts and tracks were added to school facilities to instill competitive spirit, discipline, work ethic, and community pride. Formal interscholastic competition began by 1905 and included district leagues and interprovincial championships, with teams traveling hundreds of miles for the big events.[45]

Sport also enabled the Americans to channel the Filipinos' nationalism into athletic rivalries. When the Waseda University baseball team arrived from Japan for a series of games in 1905, the contests approximated a surrogate war. Having just defeated the Russians in actual combat, the

Japanese brimmed with confidence. One thousand fans turned out for the match with Cebu. An American reported that "the rivalry was spirited. Once or twice, it bordered on bitterness. In short, the game was for blood. Having defeated a white foe in war, no doubt the Japs could not brook defeat by their neighboring islanders." When Cebu triumphed 3–1, "bedlam broke loose, Japan was whipped, and the Cebu men became heroes." More than five thousand spectators attended the game in Manila, including Bishop Brent, then president of the Philippines Amateur Athletic Federation, and the Chinese minister to Washington. The Filipinos prevailed 3–2 and ultimately earned a one-game edge in the series. Such encounters served as cultural tests. Baseball offered a common denominator for comparative supremacy as Japanese aspirants challenged the Filipino protègès of the United States.[46]

Such tours allowed Americans to reassert notions of their own superiority as well. When the Reach All-Stars traveled to the Philippines in 1908, they won 10 of 12 games, losing only to U.S. military teams composed of outstanding athletes. Likewise, when the University of Chicago made its Asian tour in 1910, it lost only to the U.S. Marines in 4 games and shut out its Filipino opponents. The university also got a $1,000 guarantee for its efforts from local white organizers. When an all-Filipino team toured the United States three years later, it returned with a 16-38 record, signifying, to Americans at least, that Filipinos still failed to qualify on the athletic and cultural measuring stick.[47]

By 1910 boxing matches allowed Filipinos to reclaim a sense of masculinity when an African American promoter, Frank Churchill, began conducting weekly bouts in a Manila gym. Filipino tribes had engaged in combative games and even deadlier rites, such as headhunting, as symbols of virility and readiness for marriage, but regulated bouts organized by weight divisions provided for more equal competition between opponents. Early Filipino boxers demonstrated their toughness by refusing to wear cups that protected their genitalia, considering that American practice to be effeminate. American military personnel were particularly attracted to boxing and cockfighting, much to the dismay of the religious missionaries. One missionary reported to his bishop that the soldiers engaged in "much drinking and gambling" and that church services averaged an attendance of fewer than eight.[48]

While class differences hindered religious efforts among Americans, race undoubtedly hampered endeavors among the Filipinos. The works of Michel Foucault have demonstrated the relationship of power and knowledge relative to the social construction of the body. In the Philippines the characterization of nonwhite bodies remained contested terrain throughout the American occupation. Soldiers commonly referred to Filipinos as "goo-goos," "monkeys," or "niggers." One of the first soldiers to arrive in the islands described the natives as "dirty" and said, "It is nothing to see a niger [*sic*] (we call them nigers [*sic*]) woman pretty near naked."[49]

Upon arriving in the islands in 1912, more than a decade after the initiation of widely publicized educational and assimilation programs, George Dorsey, a doctor of divinity, wrote: "Most of these pirates . . . look . . . like undersized, underfed mulattoes. On closer investigation you decide that they are a new breed of men. They look a little like the Japanese, a little like the Malays . . . a little Like negroes [*sic*]. These are the Filipinos, our Little Brown Brothers. But, when a white man addresses them they degenerate instantly."[50] Unsurprisingly, another American reported two years later that the Filipinos hated whites and wanted their independence immediately.[51]

As whites continued to characterize Filipinos as boys, diminutive Little Brown Brothers, animals, pirates, barbarians, and additional racial slurs, they accentuated physical and intellectual differences that they felt rationalized their own sense of superiority. While Filipino men served as lackeys or house servants, the native women were relegated to sexual objects. Another soldier admitted that "the Americans were inclined to treat the natives as a whole with contempt, but with no other feminine association these soldiers made exceptions with any woman who appealed to their sexual instinct." By 1912 the venereal disease rate for soldiers in the Philippines was the highest in the whole U.S. Army. Rather than question the soldiers' immorality, the surgeon general blamed the lack of hygiene among the Filipino prostitutes and the cheap cost of procurement (25 cents).[52]

The whites' prurient interest extended to the increasing numbers of American tourists who traveled to the islands in search of primitive and exotic images. Uninterested in the Christian Filipinos, the whites went to Baguio to photograph naked Igorot girls with large breasts and men in G-strings with their "genitals nearly exposed." Like the tricksters of subaltern groups in the United States, such as Native Americans and African Americans, some educated Filipinos manipulated such racial stereotypes for their own advantage. One Igorot who had lived in the United States as a house servant for several years and who spoke excellent English returned to Baguio, where he posed with a hatchet in warrior's garb to attract paying photographers. Carlos Bulosan, a writer who later migrated to the United States, spent part of his youth posing naked in the Baguio marketplace for "American tourists who seemed to enjoy the shameless nudity of the natives."[53] Such tricksters turned the tables on whites by creating false, inauthentic images and taking the Americans' money in the process, enriching themselves on the moral foibles of the supposedly more intelligent Caucasians.

Other Filipinos resisted racialization, adhering instead to their own cultural standards. The Igorot caddies at the Baguio Golf Club, for example, declined offers of Western clothing and worked in their traditional loincloths. The waiters in the club dining room donned the required white jackets but refused Western pants.[54]

The racialization of nonwhite bodies extended to the African American troops in the Philippines, some of whom sided with the Filipinos. Deserters rallied to the Filipino cause; one such sympathizer, David Fagen, became an officer in the insurrectionists' guerrilla army. Black athletes took their revenge on the athletic fields, relishing their victories over condescending white soldiers. The 25th Infantry Regiment, composed of African Americans, retained the baseball championship of the Philippines from 1899 to 1902. Ongoing black fraternization with the natives contributed to the recall of the African American units to Hawaii, and from 1906 to 1916 U.S. congressmen made annual proposals to eliminate blacks from the military.[55]

The schools, however, endeavored to ameliorate any liberation sentiments, and sport provided an important means of integration and social interaction. Physical education accounted for more class time than all other subjects except reading and phonics. The Bureau of Education stressed competitive athletics so much that by 1916 formal policy awarded bonus points based on grade point averages or to make up deficiencies for those students who participated in provincial meets. Competitors in the Manila Carnival gained even more favor.[56]

Organized in 1908, the Manila Carnival served as a commercial fair to promote business and as occasion for the national athletic championships. The athletic spectacle spurred town and tribal rivalries while fulfilling the Filipino love of festivals and pageantry. By 1912 the carnival hosted national championships in men's and boys' baseball, basketball, volleyball, and track and field, as well as girls' basketball and open competition in swimming, tennis, running, golf, polo, soccer, football, and bowling. The carnival also featured a baseball tournament, which included Waseda from Japan, and the first Far Eastern Olympics.[57]

Governor General Forbes took a personal interest in promoting the competition. He awarded complete uniforms to the top divisional teams in baseball and basketball, trophies for track and field competition, and prizes at the provincial level. By the end of his tenure more than 1,500 uniformed baseball teams competed for the awards and 95 percent of the schools' enrollment participated in sports and games. When Patnongon won the provincial volleyball championship in 1913, the team received a police escort and a parade through their town, where banners festooned the streets lined by a thousand people as a band paid musical tribute. To win such honors and acclaim, even Filipino teachers and administrators fostered sport. Luis Santiago, principal of the San Mateo intermediate school, organized intramural baseball teams at the lowest grades to serve as a farm system for his varsity. He sent his pitcher and catcher to Fort McKinley during vacation breaks to learn from American military teams, and he even pitched himself in an interprovincial game. By 1911 his school team had beaten the American soldiers in 3 of their 5 games, and he and his charges had clearly inculcated the American competitive spirit and a need to win.[58]

The comprehensive athletic plan included the schools, playgrounds, settlement houses, and YMCAs in the Philippines in a closely knit network that surpassed even the civic and regional associations in the United States. The director of education boasted that "it is believed that no country in the world, certainly no State in the American Union, has such a carefully worked out plan to make athletics national in scope and to determine who are the athletic champions."[59]

Despite the claims of the education department, that plan rested largely with the YMCA. The Young Men's Christian Association arrived with the California contingent of the U.S. Army and by 1907 had requested tax exemption as a religious organization. By 1909 it had erected a building in Manila complete with athletic facilities to deter young American males from the saloons and brothels.[60] The Y quickly established ties to the colonial government. Elwood Brown arrived to direct the Y in 1910, and he founded the Philippines Amateur Athletic Federation in 1911 to instill a particular concept of fair play. Governor General Forbes served as the first president of the organization and Brown as secretary-treasurer. Brown reported to his superiors in the United States that "a great many of the evils that grew up in athletics in the States before definite control was established will never find a foothold in the Philippines or in the Far East."[61] As early as 1911 school officials allowed Brown to prepare the official recreation manual, and a Y staff member served as acting director of public education. Brown soon trained the playground directors. By 1913 Brown served on the Playground Committee under the secretary of public instruction, and within two years the Board of Education gave support to the YMCA. The integration of an evangelical missionary organization with the secular government clearly surpassed the U.S. constitutional prohibitions on the separation of church and state as colonial administrators favored a particular brand of Christianity.[62]

Brown's organization of the Far Eastern Athletic Association initially included China and Japan and soon extended membership to other Asian countries. Brown won the approval of Pierre de Coubertin as soon as he dropped the "Olympiad" designation from his Far Eastern Games. The organization of sport on a regional basis had two aims: to bring Asia into the modern world (as defined by Anglos), and to assimilate Filipino tribes in a focused nationalism against foreign opponents. The YMCA annual report of 1913 stated: "Nothing previous to this meeting has shown so clearly the departure of the Oriental nations from the old conservative standards, for the interest of the East in organizing athletic sports is only recent."[63] Once again, the New World, led by the United States, firmly believed in its desire and mission to teach the Old World.

Through his involvement in the schools, Brown had helped to spread both basketball and volleyball, sports developed by the YMCA in the 1890s. The Far Eastern Athletic Association enabled him to introduce such sports beyond the Philippines, including them in the Manila Carnival and banking on Japanese pride and belief in their own superiority leading them to adopt the games as a competitive challenge.[64]

Despite the Y's intentions of regional integration through sport, it retained a policy of segregation in Manila, deemed hypocritical by Filipinos. It allowed for open competition between the races but maintained separate buildings for whites, Filipinos, and Chinese. Interracial competition, however, allowed the Filipinos to challenge notions of Social Darwinian superiority. In the Philippines Amateur Athletic Federation (PAAF) volleyball tournament of 1915, Filipino clerks defeated their American bosses in the semifinal round. Filipinos employed a playful strategy deemed "deceptive" and unsportsmanlike by the less creative Americans. When the Filipinos allegedly employed 52 hits before returning the ball to their white opponents, who promptly sent it back with a single blow, the Americans changed the rules. Henceforth, the Anglos got unlimited bumps and sets, while Filipinos were limited to three.[65]

In addition to Filipino victories in baseball and volleyball, boxing, with its opportunities for retaliation, soon became favored by Filipinos. Poor natives found some pride in their toughness and found greater largesse in winning. Eventually the government prohibited bouts between women and required that boys in the featured fights at the stadium be at least age sixteen. Such restrictions did little to diminish the sport's popularity. By the 1920s the Philippines produced their own champions, including a world titleist in flyweight Pancho Villa. Despite a zealous following at home, American sportswriters accorded Villa a muted respect that racialized his abilities. Damon Runyon classified him as a "demon" and less than human, while another claimed that "his brown sweating body flashing back and forth like a caged monkey. . . . It was impossible for anything human to get around so fast."[66] Like Jack Johnson, the black heavyweight champion who had preceded him, Villa offended contemporary racial attitudes by consorting with white women, lavishing his money on a Ziegfield dancer and "Broadway dolls" during his two-year sojourn to the United States. He flamboyantly carried a $1,000 bill in his watch pocket and shopped for jewelry at Cartier. His lifestyle hardly fit the abstemious middle-class WASP aspirations of the American reformers, but when he died of blood poisoning from infected teeth in 1925, Filipinos considered it a national tragedy. Stores closed and streets were draped in black as one hundred thousand mourners attended his Manila funeral.[67]

Numerous other Filipino fighters also challenged the notions of white privilege and prowess. Welterweight Ceferino Garcia later developed the "bolo punch," a weapon symbolic of his Filipino identity, and he attracted a large following among Filipino workers in the United States as he pummeled his way to the championship. In such a context the racially superior attitudes espoused by whites held no validity, as even the poorest and uneducated of the masses could make sense of the results of a boxing match. Sport provided the great equalizer.[68]

Both the Y and the school authorities took credit for the improved health and performances of the Filipinos. As early as 1911 the director of education claimed that baseball had replaced the cockpit and that "this new spirit of athletic interest . . . is actually revolutionary, and with it came new standards, new ideals of character."[69] By 1917 the health service claimed that athletics had decreased cases of tuberculosis, a year after the Philippine Constabulary asserted that its recruits were physically larger than those of a decade earlier, "due no doubt to athletic training the younger generation has been and is receiving in the primary, intermediate, and high schools of the Islands."[70] Despite such improvement Filipino bodies were deemed inferior to those of whites, as native soldiers received only one-third the salary of their white counterparts. At the American Physical Education Association convention of 1919, president William Burdick admitted that the schools of the Philippines "show a progress and a conception of physical training that do not seem to exist here in America."[71] In the Philippines, students who failed physical education were not promoted to the next grade level. The Bureau of Education maintained that exercise was necessary to make Filipinos taller and bigger and "that the stock of the race can be improved considerably."[72]

Despite such grandiose assertions, the American crusade in the Philippines elicited mixed results that more clearly demonstrate the interrelationships of cultural adaptation rather than wholesale assimilation. Geographical features, such as jungles, mountain ranges, and the more than seven thousand islands that compose the archipelago, and its resultant polyglot population thwarted American efforts to enculturate the Philippines' inhabitants. American cultivation of the elite, more educated Filipinos and the increasing appointment of these privileged Filipinos to governmental positions only further entrenched the caste system of the Spanish, rather than bring true democracy to the islands. While more Filipinos gained suffrage, they voted only for wealthy landowners, a situation still unchanged.[73] Filipino nationalism only increased as the American government delayed an independence date until "the colonized met the expectations of the colonizer."[74] American control of the economy by the U.S. government and the expatriate community only exacerbated tensions and led to the formation of a still-extant Communist movement in the Philippines.[75]

Protestants gained few inroads in their high hopes for conversion. By 1918 only 1.3 percent of the Filipinos had converted, and those who did faced ostracism, harassment, and even murder. Catholic priests even threatened YMCA members with excommunication.[76] Despite the Y's widespread sports programs and government influence, the organization's executive secretary admitted in 1922 that "as for the work that we came out here to do, there seems little likelihood of its immediate accomplishment."[77] The Y faced even greater opposition from the Catholic church in the 1930s, and the Far Eastern Games initiated by the YMCA dissolved in discord in 1934 over the Japanese incursions into China. The consequent governing body assumed Japanese rather than American leadership.[78]

The American educational system produced limited gains. As early as 1913 a special investigator informed President Woodrow Wilson that English was rarely spoken outside of the schools and Manila. Americans, in fact, had affected a patois hardly intelligible to newly arrived English speakers. By the late 1920s the quality of spoken English had declined, forcing American army officers to learn Tagalog. After forty years of U.S. rule only 26 percent of Filipinos could or would speak the colonial language. Less than half of the population reached fourth grade; 38 percent never reached third grade. By 1940 the schools were considered a failure, and illiteracy remained at 40 percent in 1948.[79]

Athletics fared somewhat better in the idealistic quest to promote democracy. Boxing became a major sport in the Philippines, and basketball superseded baseball as the national sport. In 1924 the University of the Philippines, founded by the Americans in 1908, initiated a local version of the American National Collegiate Athletic Association (NCAA). Yet some Filipinos still resisted the commercial aspects of modern sport. Only two years later the YMCA reported that a considerable number of mediocre players had entered only one event in the tennis tournament simply to gain a competitor's pass and avoid the admission charge.[80]

Interscholastic athletic programs fostered greater activity by young girls and necessitated dress reform. Outside of the required physical education endeavors, however, few women chose to participate. Only three teams entered the PAAF's 1926 tournament for women's indoor baseball, and the girls' volleyball championship enrolled only two teams. Lack of patronage in recreational sports led to the closing of Manila's skating rinks as well.[81]

Basketball proved more popular, and educators claimed that the players achieved better health and higher grades than nonathletes. The first national basketball tournament occurred in 1924, and the sport became a popular obsession. Filipino female physical educators at the University of the Philippines resurrected the residual Spanish sport of fencing in 1925, along with gymnastics and swimming. Girls had their own interscholastic provincial track and field championship the following year. National tennis and swimming championships began in 1923 and 1927 respectively, as the liberation of Filipino women kept pace with the nationalist movement, in contrast to the restriction of interscholastic sport for females in the United States, where educators favored noncompetitive "play days."[82]

American moralists failed to eliminate cockfighting or gambling, and the introduction of boxing only channeled betting to human competitors. Nor did Filipinos accept PAAF dictates regarding amateurism and eligibility. By the 1920s nonclub members were "invited" to play for championship games. Three volleyball teams showcased such "ringers" during the 1926 championship, including ten of the sixteen players on one team. The Filipinos emulated the Americans' competitive nature and their emphasis on winning, a fact soon substantiated by the 1929 Savage Report, which found similar improprieties on U.S. college teams.[83]

Filipinos took more readily to American popular culture, affecting Western dress and names and consuming Western movies, songs, cars, media, and products. Perhaps they sensed the hypocrisy in Social Darwinism or in American impositions of morality, particularly when fifteen colonial provincial treasurers were convicted of embezzlement between 1898 and 1914.[84] Race and religion impeded the lessons of the Americans, and Filipinos adopted or adapted only those cultural forms that they deemed most important or applicable, combining them with their existing native practices to form a negotiated hybrid culture with its own ideas, beliefs, and practices.

Filipinos gained their treasured independence after World War II, but the Filipino economy remained tethered to American interests. The Bell Trade Act of 1946, part of the Philippines Rehabilitation Act, provided the United States with free trade rights, access to the country's resources, public utilities, and land for military bases. The latter provided some sense of security for Filipinos at the cost of sovereignty. The Americans thus kept the Communist threat at a distance at the peril of their former colonists. The Military Bases Agreement, despite protests, gave the United States a rent-free lease for ninety-nine years. Filipinos got jobs, but at wages well below those of their American coworkers. The towns of Angeles and Olongapo became dens of vice and iniquity catering to the lusts of young American service personnel, hardly the noble civic establishments envisioned by zealous missionaries and middle-class progressive reformers. Clark Air Force Base consumed 132,000 acres, with more than fifty thousand squatters mired in poverty amid the plenty of American materialism. One analyst remarked on the "mutual suspicion, distrust, contempt, and hostility. After six decades, the American still fears that if he goes into the Filipino community he will be gypped, clipped, stripped; and the Filipino is still a stranger in the American community." Indeed, Americans continued to act with seeming impunity. Between 1952 and 1964 thirty-one Filipinos lost their lives at the hands of Americans, yet none of the instances went to trial. When two more killings of Filipino scavengers went unheeded, thousands of Filipinos marched on the U.S. embassy in January 1965.

Their efforts provided compensation to victim's families, but one got only $787.[85]

Like their parents and grandparents, the Filipinos adapted to the American presence. In 1964 they pilfered 564 bombs as well as food from the American military warehouses. The dynamite from the bombs served nutritional and recreational needs as fishermen garnered even bigger catches with a new technique produced by underwater explosions. The government, too, had taken steps to establish greater independence. In 1961 the legislature passed the Sports Federation Law, finally disbanding the half century of centralized governance created by the PAAF and granting each of its sport associations the autonomy that it had long sought as a nation. Thereafter it renegotiated the leases on the military bases (which finally ended in 1991) and sought greater trade with other countries. Boxing and basketball, however, remained key components of an evolving national culture, one no longer imposed by the United States but searching for an identity that might unify the multitude of island peoples.[86]

Hawaii as a Cultural Crossroads of Sport

Hawaii served as an early stop in Anglo globalization efforts and the concurrent cultural imperialism. Captain James Cook's landing at Kauai in 1778 soon introduced alcohol, tobacco, diseases, and guns to the native culture; Kamehameha conquered the neighboring islands with the support of the new weapons by 1810. The first American missionaries arrived in 1820, and Hawaii became a multicultural frontier, a liminal place where whiteness was not the norm, long before the term *Manifest Destiny* echoed throughout the American West.[1]

The transition in Hawaiian sporting culture commenced shortly thereafter. Charles Stewart, one of the early missionaries, remarked in 1823 that surfing was "a daily amusement at all times. . . . Hundreds at a time have been occupied in this way for hours together."[2] Both men and women excelled at the activity, and their prowess brought prominence and prestige, particularly for chiefs, whose physicality reinforced their social status. Contests of strength, skill, and chance dominated Hawaiian culture, and challenge matches in boxing sometimes ended in death. Widespread gambling on such events, as well as in canoe racing and bowling, offended missionaries, who were further outraged by the hula dances they deemed as lewd and by the communal lifestyles of Hawaiians, which included the sharing of wives and children.[3]

Such sharing perplexed one Anglo, who remarked that "the ease with which the Hawaiians . . . can secure their own food has undoubtably [sic] interfered with their social and industrial advancement. . . . [It] relieves the native from any struggle and unfits him for sustained competition with men from other lands. The fact that food is supplied by nature takes from the native all desire for the acquisition of more land. . . . Instead of grasping all he can get, he divides with his neighbor, and confidently expects his neighbor to divide with him."[4] Although correctly analyzing the natives' disadvantages in the capitalistic economic struggle that transpired over the next two centuries, the writer underestimated the hardiness of the Hawaiian people and their culture.

The cultural transition ensued as the clergy moved to ban the native games and install their own version of "civilized" society, but Hawaiians resisted such impositions. Equally perplexed by the British, French, and American strangers who contested for power and the myriad Protestant sects who opposed Catholic proselytizing and vice versa, Hawaiians turned away from such bickering. One native Hawaiian reacted to the fire and brimstone approach by stating: "The preacher is mocking us and calling us by hard names. He would have us, too, shut up in raging fire if we do not believe in his God. What a railing, cruel and revengeful man."[5]

Within a generation the missionaries enjoyed a great measure of success, however. They did so by introducing residential boarding schools to inculcate youth, gaining advisor positions with the monarchy, and instituting judicial, commercial, and capitalist systems unfamiliar to the natives. The religious school system, initiated in the 1820s, long before similar ventures took Native Americans from their parents in the United States, won converts and protègès to fill governmental appointments. One early missionary rationalized the process as follows: "It was thought that by taking scholars who were quite young into a boarding school, they could be preserved in a measure from the pollutions of a heathen society, be trained to habits of regularity, neatness and civilization, and receive a mental and moral culture more thorough than it was possible to bestow upon adults."[6]

Missionaries wrote the first constitution in 1840, and by 1848 American advisors had convinced the monarchy to undertake the Great Mahele, the division of the land into private plots for sale, despite a petition of protest to King Kamehameha III. In 1850 the land became available to non-Hawaiians. Missionaries each got 560 acres at minimal cost. Native Hawaiians, who had existed in a barter and subsistence economy for hundreds of years, could not pay the new land taxes; by 1890 foreigners owned 75 percent of the acreage.[7]

The Vagrancy Acts of 1852 required those without property to work, and many sought meager wages on foreign sugar plantations that had existed since 1835. Laborers toiled fourteen-hour days for 12¼ cents per day (women got only 6 cents), which they spent at the company store. It is little wonder that one overseer noticed that "the native laborers do but little when my back is turned."[8]

Sport offered one means of instilling the Anglo work ethic. The wealthy enjoyed a racetrack at Lahaina on Maui as early as the 1850s, but baseball proved more suitable for the workers and for the intermingling of cultures. Alexander Cartwright, considered the "father of baseball," arrived in the islands in 1849, but the game had already been introduced by the missionaries at the Punahou School, founded for their own children in 1841. Cartwright prospered in several commercial ventures, served as advisor to five monarchs, and built a number of community organizations, but Punahou fostered greater influence in baseball by promoting interscholastic games and town leagues. As plantation owners imported Chinese, Portuguese, Japanese, Filipino, and Korean workers to replace the Hawaiians dying from diseases introduced by Westerners, the game spread to the multicultural labor force, but not always with the perceived benefits of teamwork, time discipline, and deference to authority. However, the use of English, taught in the schools, displaced the native and ethnic languages to become the common parlance.[9]

Entrepreneurs introduced commercialized leisure to the islands with the opening of a roller skating rink in 1871 that charged both skaters and onlookers. By 1875 the opening game of the four team baseball league in Honolulu drew two thousand spectators. Albert Spalding and his traveling tour of professional players arrived in Hawaii in 1888 on their world tour to publicize the game. Unfortunately, they arrived on a Sunday and the blue laws enacted by the missionaries as early as the 1820s forbade play on that day. Despite King Kalakaua's support, Spalding honored the Protestants' religious ban but donated a silver trophy for Hawaiian league play. Sport sometimes brought cohesion to divergent groups. The first polo match, in 1880, featured British naval officers against a local contingent. Hawaiian *paniolos* (cowboys) on Maui adopted the game within the decade. A few years later, in 1894, an American and a Hawaiian teamed up as doubles partners to defeat two Englishmen at tennis. The Hawaiian Lawn Tennis Association offered their first championships the next year.[10]

The British had introduced tennis to the islands at tea parties during the 1880s. The Japanese organized a fencing tournament for King Kalakaua in 1885. As early as 1887 Punahou (then called Oahu College) commenced track and field competition, and integrated football games followed by the 1890s. The Honolulu YMCA initiated basketball play in 1896, the same year a golf club was founded, and volleyball began in 1900.[11]

The proliferation of sports, instituted largely by a white minority, constituted a cultural imposition and generated a Hawaiian backlash. Natives resurrected canoe racing in 1875, and hula dancers entertained King Kalakaua at his 50th Birthday Jubilee in 1886. The king opposed the cession of Pearl Harbor to the United States, and both he and his successor, Queen Liliuokalani, restored Hawaiian pride and a sense of nationalism by reviving the Hawaiian language and native dances. Hawaiian music became a form of resistance as lyrics became politicized and chants backed Hawaiian sovereignty. Sensing the loss of their privileges and established hegemony, the all-white Hawaiian League imposed the so-called Bayonet Constitution on King Kalakaua in 1887, stripping him of his power, yet the anti-American National Reform Party won all seats in the Oahu elections of 1890. The king died in 1891, but Queen Liliuokalani proved to be as strident in her nationalism. Her intransigence resulted in an 1893 coup led by American businessmen supported by a U.S. government diplomat and a contingent of marines. The new "provisional government" soon effected a new constitution that rescinded voting rights, disenfranchising fourteen thousand while establishing an electorate of only 2,800, most of them white employees of the Dole Company. Not surprisingly, Sanford Dole, the son of missionaries, assumed the presidency, despite the fact that whites represented only 22 percent of the polyglot population. When a coup failed to restore the queen to her throne, she endured imprisonment. Despite objections from U.S. president Grover Cleveland, the whites declared Hawaii an independent republic.[12]

The U.S. government debated the annexation of Hawaii on commercial and racial grounds. Senator Henry Cabot Lodge admitted that "we have a record of conquest, colonization, and territorial expansion unequaled by any people in the nineteenth century."[13] He advocated annexation as a boon to commerce. Senator Richard Pettigrew of South Dakota disagreed for racial reasons, stating that the United States could "not afford to add more dark-skinned races to (its) population . . . with the negroes [*sic*] of the South, the Chinese of the Pacific Coast, the Indians of the West, and the dagoes of the East."[14] The advent of the Spanish-American War in 1898 spurred renewed interest in the islands as a way station to the Philippines, and the new administration of President William McKinley supported the annexation.

Restrictions on Asian immigrants followed, and the Japanese government protested. Fearing a Japanese takeover, the *Honolulu Star* newspaper asserted that "it is the white race against the yellow. . . . Nothing but annexation can save the islands."[15] The U.S. government complied with the request despite Hawaiian protests, limiting citizenship and political offices to literate whites and ensuring a white, commercial oligarchy in the islands that controlled virtually all trade, but not culture. January 17, 1898, served as a legal holiday to commemorate the overthrow of the monarchy. The YMCA celebrated with its first field day, but sport became a means of resistance, adaptation, and retaliation for subordinate groups. Nationalists, led by Queen Liliuokalani, boycotted the American flag raising ceremony in August 1898.[16]

With annexation came a greater political voice, particularly at the local level, where the Home Rule Party in Maui enjoyed success and elected the first native to Congress on the refrain of "Hawaii for Hawaiians."[17]

The plantations, where baseball had served as social control and a means to unite a disparate labor force in a common bond, became contested terrain. Workers attacked overseers and managers and perpetrated acts of arson. Insubordination, work slowdowns, and a multitude of strikes limited production and profits. Many workers clung to such traditional sports as Japanese sumo or Filipino sipe, but integrated play allowed others to express racial pride and retaliation.[18]

In 1903 girls from the Hawaiian Kamehameha School defeated Anglos from the YMCA in basketball, a game the Y had invented. Despite strained political relations between Japan and the United States, Hawaiian baseball provided a buffer between the two nations. More than thirty thousand Japanese migrant workers came to Hawaii as contract laborers for sugar cane plantations between 1885 and 1894. A Japanese Christian missionary, Takie Okumura, followed in 1894 to minister to his countrymen. Okumura organized baseball games as a more wholesome means of recreation to divert the workers from alcohol and prostitutes. Steere Gikaku Noda, a Japanese Hawaiian, founded the Asahi Nisei team in 1905, serving as treasurer, manager, captain, and star pitcher. The Asahis made their first trip to Japan in their inaugural season and also traveled to the Philippines and Taiwan thereafter. Two years later the St. Louis College, a Hawaiian high school, made the trek to Japan, where it won 2 of 5 games against Keio University. The next year Santa Clara College of California met Keio and the multicultural teams of Hawaii in the Honolulu summer league.[19]

In the wake of exclusionary practices aimed at the Chinese, a Chinese Hawaiian baseball team began touring the United States in 1910, winning the majority of its games. The team went 105-38-1 in 1913 (54-5 against college teams.) They taunted the University of Chicago pitcher as they pounded his offerings, and they beat Stanford, St. Mary's, and Occidental on their 1914 California tour. They ridiculed both the umpire and their opponents in the win over Occidental, for which the Los Angeles Chinatown community feted them with a banquet.[20]

Sporting practices also helped stem the cultural flow. Surfing and canoe racing, banned by the missionaries because of their associated gambling and scanty attire, continued clandestinely. By the turn of the century, haole (white) boys had become attracted to the Hawaiian pastimes. By

1908 American businessmen had formed the Outrigger Canoe Club with an eye toward commercial opportunities at Waikiki Beach. They entertained Theodore Roosevelt's Great White Fleet in its Hawaiian stop with match races against a Hawaiian club, won by the natives. Other white clubs centered around the Honolulu Harbor included a women's organization. Competing surfing clubs enjoyed similar facilities at Waikiki by 1911. George Freeth, a product of a mixed Hawaiian-American marriage, taught Californians surfing and water polo as a swimming instructor at the Los Angeles Athletic Club and Redondo Beach, and the Californians soon co-opted surfing as their own.[21]

Duke Kahanamoku promoted surfing in Australia in 1916, but he became more famous as an Olympic swimming champion, garnering six medals (four gold) from 1912 to 1932. Pervasive racism characterized American society at that time, and some questioned Hawaiians' right to represent the United States; but the victories of Kahanamoku and other Hawaiian swimmers as "bronze skinned men," neither white nor black, won a measure of acceptance in the dominant culture. Kahanamoku, in fact, had effected both an integrated environment and American Olympic swimming prospects as one of the founders of the coed and interracial Waikiki Hui Nalu Canoe Club. The club resulted from a racial affront when the Healanis Club solicited Kahanamoku's paddling prowess for a canoe race but later denied his application for club membership. The integrated Hui Nalu Club sponsored a swim team, and the Hawaiians supplied a multicultural corps of Olympians over the next two decades, including such stars as Warren Kealoha, Pua Kealoha, Harold Kruger, Clarence "Buster" Crabbe, Ethelda Bleibtrey (who won gold medals at the 1920 Olympics), and Mariechen Wehselau Jackson (who won gold and silver medals for the women in 1924).[22]

The Hawaiian environment allowed for competitive events for women, and female swimmers became the mainstay of U.S. Olympic teams in the 1920s. Americans took pride in Hawaiian accomplishments, and in their own liberalism regarding the inclusion of Hawaiians in the Olympics. The YMCA provided complimentary memberships, and Kahanamoku parlayed his recognition into a movie career and political office. Colorful, cheerful, and charming, yet gentle and caring, Kahanamoku represented a transcendent figure. His fame brought the friendship of dignitaries, his marriage to a white woman portrayed new racial attitudes, and his adherence to Hawaiian foods, language, and issues merged cultures harmoniously. Still, Chinese and Filipino baseball players often faced exclusion or restriction to the Negro League.[23]

The diversity of Hawaiian society and its sporting relationships offered experiments in integration long before most mainland communities. Close ties between the Japanese residents of Hawaii and their homeland brought Japan's Waseda University to Oahu in 1905. In 1910 it played in the Hawaiian league throughout the summer. Chinese, Japanese, Filipinos, and Portuguese athletes all competed in the Honolulu Baseball League, while the Chinese and Japanese also maintained separate associations. Baseball fostered interisland competition and industrial leagues that featured integrated rosters. By 1919 baseball offered some hope of conciliation; as one plantation manager explained: "Every Sunday we have baseball games between the Filipino laborers and our young Japanese and Portuguese boys in which our timekeepers and some of our overseers join. . . . In looking around at the universal unrest amongst labor and thinking of the absence of it upon these Islands, we feel that an unremitting endeavor should be made to keep our laborers contented and happy."[24]

The plantation workers had registered their discontent in 1907 when thousands struck over unequal wages. Three thousand Japanese and Filipino laborers marched through downtown Honolulu carrying portraits of Abraham Lincoln to symbolize their struggle for freedom and equality. Baseball served as a means of social control on plantations; nevertheless, Oahu workers struck again in 1920 for equal pay, a nonracial wage scale (lighter-skinned Portuguese workers were favored over Asians), maternity leaves, and better recreational facilities. Employers often segregated activities to inhibit racial cooperation in the multicultural labor force. Hawaiian authorities even restricted integration by legal means in two court cases in 1916. In both trials a Japanese and a Filipino were denied citizenship as nonwhite aliens, and an appeal to the U.S. Supreme Court upheld the verdict.[25]

The assignment of the African American Twenty-Fifth Regiment to Hawaii in 1913 brought some opportunities for racial interaction. The soldiers proceeded to win the Hawaiian baseball championship from 1914 to 1918 and played against barnstorming professionals from the mainland. The black infantry unit added the island track and field title to its athletic laurels as well. Endeavoring to capitalize on the more liberal relationships and the varied population, J. Ashman Beaven embarked on a career as a sports promoter in Hawaii, establishing athletic leagues and a Catholic Youth Organization. He built the Honolulu Stadium in 1925, to which he brought teams from Japan and Korea as well as Major League stars from the mainland.[26]

While sport nurtured integration in the islands, bureaucratic structures still maintained stratified class divisions on the plantations and in the educational system. Punahou High School, established by the white missionaries, maintained its elite haole status, while McKinley High School served the working class and a multicultural populace. Students from the former school still assumed a proprietary right to leadership and affluence; as one stated in 1928: "It's all settled; we, the Punahou boys, will be the lunas [supervisors] and McKinley fellows will carry the cane."[27]

McKinley and other schools continued to challenge such notions of superiority and gender through their sporting endeavors and successes. The local working-class adaptation of football, played barefoot on both Oahu and Maui throughout the 1940s, enjoyed substantial support, drawing five thousand fans to a championship game played in a stadium. Barefoot football emphasized speed and rugged play, which was perceived as more masculine than white styles of play. Plant stuffings served as simulated shoulder pads, as poor practitioners adapted equipment to fit their budgets. One player, Shoichi Igarashi, declined recruitment to the high school team, telling the coach, "I want to play against men, not boys."[28] By the 1920s teams abounded in working class neighborhoods, featuring Japanese, Chinese, Portuguese, and native Hawaiian players. For the Asians in particular, barefoot football allowed them to retain cultural values. Paul Taniguchi claimed that playing barefoot football was "more natural." Some spectators provided Japanese players with *musubi* (rice balls), while others bet on chop suey dinners for the victors. The Recreation Commission counted more than two thousand players in barefoot leagues in 1922. By 1930 football overshadowed baseball in popularity, and the university team reflected the growing heterogeneity of Hawaiian culture. The University of Hawaii first traveled to the West Coast in 1923. Two years later it enjoyed an undefeated season, with three of its ten victories coming against Occidental, Colorado Agricultural (Colorado State), and Washington State. The 1938 team featured fifteen different ethnic groups on its twenty-four-man traveling squad.[29]

In the more liberal racial environment of Hawaii, girls also challenged Anglo societal norms and assigned roles by playing on baseball and softball teams in their working-class neighborhoods. Hawaiians had adapted the Anglo sports to their own conditions by that time. Beach volleyball eschewed six-man teams in favor of four or two players to test speed, agility, and stamina. The Hawaiian version eventually gained mainland interest and a lucrative television contract. Barefoot football, also played on the beach, found less interest when exported to the mainland after 1920. Contrary to most economic exports, however, the sporting trade extended to both sides of the Pacific. The Asahis baseball team, winners of fifteen championships in the Hawaiian league, traveled throughout the Pacific to Japan, the Philippines, and Taiwan for games.[30]

As a cultural crossroads Hawaii became exoticized by mainlanders. Hawaiian music gained popularity, and sporting fashions transformed the beach to a site of sexual attraction when Ruth Stecker, a Hawaiian swimming champion, unveiled a one-piece suit that was rapidly copied. The resultant bathing suit law of 1920 intended to prohibit such lasciviousness but to no avail. Stecker's innovation prompted an immediate and ongoing cultural change with great ramifications for the realms of fashion, sport, and gender relations.[31]

Tourists began flocking to exotic locales, such as Hawaii and Cuba, where they might escape, at least temporarily, the repressed inhibitions of Protestant America. Golf courses and beachfront resorts soon transformed Hawaiian real estate and further commercialized the idyllic culture, much to the chagrin of the dwindling native population. By the 1930s the Maui County Fair included a Wild West show and an Ice Follies, along with horse racing and a Soap Box Derby. Despite such cultural incursions, the polyglot residents managed to retain a number of traditional ethnic sports, such as sumo among the Japanese and *sipa* and cockfighting among the Filipinos. Among the latter, boxing won particular favor.[32]

The Philippines had already produced a world champion in Pancho Villa, king of the flyweights from 1923 to 1925. Filipinos in Hawaii practiced a form of slap boxing known as *kamaro*, and plantation boxing bouts drew crowds of five thousand by the 1930s. As American nativism and racial prejudice subjected Filipinos to the same indignities as other nonwhites, boxing offered a means of retaliation. Like the Chinese and Japanese before them, Filipinos faced an immigration prohibition with the Tydings-McDuffie Act of 1934. The California Athletic Commission had already tried, but failed, to bar Filipino boxers from that state in 1930. Both California and Hawaii had large Filipino communities, and their athletes carried the aspirations and pride of the residents, who provided great support to their efforts. At least a dozen Filipino fighters operated in California, and Hawaiian promoters relied on Filipinos to turn a profit when the state legalized the sport in 1930. The boxers symbolized retribution for all Filipinos when they sought reprisal with their fists. Speedy Dado took the California state bantamweight title in 1932, while Dado Marino, a Hawaiian, gained the world flyweight crown in 1950.[33]

Aquatic sports also retained their attraction and continued to foster Hawaiian pride. Hawaii hosted the 1927 national Amateur Athletic Union swimming championships at the Waikiki War Memorial Natatorium, and Hawaiian swimming teams captured U.S. national championships in 1930 and from 1939 to 1941. Surfing and canoe racing also reveled in a 1930s resurgence, the latter resurrected by multiethnic clubs who had adopted the native sport in a reversal of the dominant cultural flow. Despite a century of white impositions, the vibrant Hawaiian culture continually reasserted itself rather than remain a receptacle of passive subordination.[34]

Sporting culture and more hospitable relations continued to flow across the Pacific and through Hawaii. Japan's Meiji University sent its baseball team to compete with the Asahis in Honolulu in 1924. Its men's and women's swim teams competed in Hawaii thereafter, and its basketball team returned in 1933 for a game against the University of Hawaii as the Japanese occupation of Manchuria threatened Western powers.[35]

World War II interrupted that ongoing cultural negotiation, bringing large numbers of mainland military personnel to the islands' many combat bases, forever changing the geographic, social, and cultural landscapes. As Japanese Americans faced incarceration on the mainland, the Asahis baseball team changed its name to the Athletics, although the Japanese totaled 37 percent of the Hawaiian population. The Hawaiian Baseball League purposely transferred Japanese players to different teams to promote rapprochement. Despite stellar credentials as an intercollegiate athletic star, Jackie Robinson played with the Honolulu Bears in the Hawaiian football league in 1941 because no stateside professional teams hired black players. Only in Hawaii did race matter less than ability, and it would be another six years before Robinson changed the racial landscape of the U.S. mainland as a Brooklyn Dodger.[36]

Henry Tadashi "Bozo" Wakabayashi elected to attend college in Japan, where he pitched his team to two championships before a Hall of Fame career with the Hanshin Tigers. Wally Yonamine played pro football for the San Francisco 49ers before choosing a pro baseball career in Japan. Other Hawaiian athletes opted for American colleges; some, like Herman Wedemeyer, a former barefoot player, found stardom and professional contracts, as sports provided an entrèe to the Anglo world and greater socioeconomic status. Another Hawaiian athlete, Kenso Nushida, a Nisei who played for the Sacramento team in the Pacific Coast League, brought his Hawaiian culture to the mainland, entertaining his teammates with island music.[37]

Barefoot football continued on the Hawaiian plantations and under the sponsorship of canneries as a form of social control. Employers provided wholesome forms of recreation, including boxing, baseball, and basketball, to keep workers from pursuing activities that might render them less productive. Companies supplied equipment and facilities and even provided medical care for injuries without cost to the players. Such paternalism, however, failed to produce docile employees. In 1946 all but one of the thirty-four sugar plantations faced strikes, and the pineapple workers followed suit in 1947. Owners gradually withdrew their support for the activity thereafter.[38]

Despite the agrarian conflicts, tourism further increased after the war, spurred on by a commercialized, artificial portrayal of island culture as featured in the Kodak Hula Show. The Korean and Vietnam wars brought new martial legions to the sunshine, beaches, warm breezes, and palm trees. After the wars many soldiers returned as tourists, fueling the construction of high-rises, shopping malls, and golf courses until Hawaii resembled mainland communities, losing its uniqueness and much of its exoticism.

Culture, however, remained a battleground as elements of the polyglot Hawaiian population, including middle-class whites, reacted to developers' intrusions in the 1970s. Native rights groups formed, some seeking complete independence, others wanting separate nation status within the U.S. governmental structure, and still others demanding reparations payments. Led by Japanese-Hawaiians after World War II, native politicians had already succeeded in overthrowing the Republican Party, which had dominated public affairs since annexation. Among those who parlayed sporting fame into political office, Steere Gikaku Noda, founder of the Asahis, and Sam Ichinose, a boxing promoter, served in the legislature. Tourism accounted for a third of Hawaii's jobs, but protesters railed against the loss of native traditions and the commodification of culture. Producers released more than one hundred albums of Hawaiian music in 1978 alone, but much of it trivialized natives as "lazy but happy."[39]

A consolidation of the disparate protest groups, known as the Native Hawaiian Renaissance, resulted in concerted success. Four of the five major companies that had prevailed over the Hawaiian economy were dismantled or sold by the 1980s. Nonnative members of the governing board of the Kamehameha Schools, reserved for native Hawaiian children, came under fire. Lobbying efforts and boycotts of the public schools led to the reinstatement of Hawaiian language in the classrooms, banned since 1896. Opposition to the use of Kahoolawe as a bombing site for military training engendered a lawsuit that returned the island in 1994 to be held in trust for native Hawaiians "until the formation of a sovereign Hawaiian nation."[40] Schoolchildren paddled their canoes to Kahoolawe for lessons in their ancestral culture.

Hawaiians won rights to traditional fishing grounds and had commercial trawlers banned. Beaches used for native swimming and surfing gained state park designation, thus thwarting the plans of hotel developers. On Maui, natives regained control of nearly thirty thousand acres, most of it for a return to the communal lifestyle of their ancestors. Environmental organizations, whose membership spanned the pluralistic population, resisted developers' efforts, oceanfront homebuilders, and government projects. On Molokai, islanders first marched to protest a tourist ranch that catered to adventure sports tourists, then committed acts of sabotage and arson to ensure its demise. The protesters had no opposition to sports, for they continued to play baseball and volleyball as they hunted and fished, but they took exception to the resort's profligate use of the scarce water supply. In 1993 President Clinton offered a formal apology for the 1893 overthrow of the Hawaiian monarchy, yet the independence movement continued to gain strength. In a 1996 poll 73 percent of native Hawaiian voters chose sovereign status.[41]

The cultural renaissance continues. Hawaiian language and cultural studies are included in the required elementary curriculum. In Hilo, on the isle of Hawaii, residents conduct the annual Merrie Monarch Festival to honor the nationalistic King Kalakaua. The 30th Annual Ukulele Festival drew more than nine hundred participants in 2000, and the Waimanalo Canoe Club, one of many such clubs, boasts more than one hundred members engaged in outrigger racing.[42]

Sport has held a prominent place in the long history of colonialism and the nationalists' ongoing concerns over cultural hegemony. Hawaii's natives and pluralistic ethnic groups had American sports imposed on them as a means of instilling social control, "civilizing" influences, and democratic ideology. They resisted, adapted, and adopted such cultural dictates in recurring cycles for nearly two hundred years. In the process the cultural crossroads of Hawaii witnessed and hosted migrants from not only the U.S. mainland but also British, Japanese, Chinese, Portuguese, Filipino, and Korean populations. When a small minority of whites proved unable to sustain cultural dominance, the racial and ethnic mix forced integration and cooperation, noticeable in sporting ventures, long before statehood and the contested legalization of civil rights in the continental United States. In the case of Hawaii, cultural imperialism proved to be less than a unilateral process, as surfing migrated to the mainland and then gained an international following and as Hawaiians traveled to Japan to become sumo wrestlers. Outrigger canoe racing, declared the state's official team sport by the legislature in 1987, and native Hawaiian culture have enjoyed a recent resurgence of interest and continue to prosper. Hawaii's varied residents now coalesce around political issues rather than racial ones, indications that the continually evolving, negotiated culture of Hawaii holds valuable lessons for us all.[43]

Cuba and the Rehabilitative Qualities of Sport

The Taino and Siboney Indians who settled Cuba enjoyed a free and playful existence until enslaved by the Spanish in the sixteenth century. Their pastimes included a ball-and-bat game that is a significant symbol of modern Cuban sporting culture, representative of a more successful resistance to domination. Given Cuba's location as a gateway to the Caribbean and to Central America, other nations, most notably the United States, began to intrude on the Spanish colony by the nineteenth century. American companies engaged in banking, shipping, mining, and sugar and coffee production by the 1830s. American engineers built the first railroad in Latin America during that decade, and five thousand annual tourists from the United States soon followed. By the 1850s American entrepreneurs had established ranches and tobacco plantations. The sugar, coffee, and tobacco plantations brought longing glances from American slaveholders looking to expand their dominion, but three annexation attempts by the U.S. government at midcentury proved unsuccessful. American workers and settlers continued to take up residence nevertheless, bringing their language and their Protestant religion with them, factors that distressed the Spanish authorities.[1]

Cuban boys sent to the United States for schooling in 1858 returned to their homeland six years later with bats and balls. Baseball spread rapidly thereafter. Within two years Cuban stevedores played a game with an American ship's crew. In 1868 the Havana Baseball Club defeated an American team in Matanzas. The Spanish government banned the game the following year to no avail. Esteban Bellan, a Cuban player who temporarily moved to the United States, found employment as a professional with the Troy Haymakers and the New York Mutuals over the next three years. By 1873 Cuba had its own professional league, and Bellan appeared in an 1874 game for Havana against Matanzas. The latter team built Cuba's first baseball stadium that year. The aristocratic Almendares club took the field in 1878, and an American company team traveled to the island that same year. Havana featured at least thirteen teams in the following decade. Hundreds of clubs proliferated throughout the island, spurred on by a burgeoning jumble of baseball periodicals. The zest for the game was matched by passion. When Santa Clara lost the first provincial championship to Sagua la Grande in 1890, its fans set the grandstand ablaze.[2]

Baseball fans included young women, who presumably were more decorous than their male counterparts. As early as 1882 *El Base-Ball*, one of the early periodicals, stated that "women are at least as attentive or more so than young men to the North American game; and they are always enthusiastic for the victory of the club or the players that they support." The article claimed that almost all baseball clubs had an honorary board of directors "consisting entirely of women."[3]

For young, middle-class Cubans the game symbolized modernity and removal from the staid colonial world of the Spanish, who favored the blood sports of bullfighting and cockfighting, deemed barbarous by more "civilized" nations such as the United States. American technology quickly spread to the island, bringing gas lighting, an ice factory, telephones, electricity, and phonographs in conjunction with baseball. With the new technology came new ideas and a new religion. Baptists founded their first church in Havana in 1883, and seven others followed within the decade. One commentator claimed that "the country has been overrun by Americans, who have introduced every form of Protestantism, from Episcopalianism, to Quakerism, and even Shakerism." Protestants preached an individualism contrary to the Spanish Catholic communalism but attractive to the ambitious middle class. Despite government bans on the new religion and the consequent jailing of its pastors, new ideologies took hold. Baseball, too, fostered revolutionary practices as players defied repeated bans on the game. Cuban players even became avid missionaries for the sport, transporting it throughout the Caribbean to the Dominican Republic, Puerto Rico, Nicaragua, Venezuela, the Yucatan, and Mexico.[4]

Sport held great economic and social promise, particularly for the downtrodden. American and Spanish endurance walkers competed in pedestrian races by the 1880s. The Philadelphia Athletics, an American professional team, traveled to Cuba for competition against island counterparts in 1886, the same year that slavery was banned in the colony. The New York Giants began winter play in Cuba four years later, to be followed by a long succession of American barnstormers. Professional baseball fueled the aspirations of many who lacked the wealth and socioeconomic status to attain an education, a learned profession, and consequent respect. Professional athletes earned their salaries through physical prowess, independent of class affiliation or access to higher education. Widespread gambling on ball games required the most highly skilled athletes, regardless of class or color. Cuba offered such opportunities in its own professional and company teams, while possible ties in America suggested even greater riches for some.[5]

Nevertheless, many of Cuba's social athletic clubs enforced strict membership policies. The Havana Yacht Club, founded in 1886, and the Jockey Club clearly required lofty standards. Other skating, hunting, and cycling clubs necessitated the expendable incomes found among their middle-class members. Race figured perhaps more than income, as many of the athletic clubs denied membership to blacks well into the twentieth century.[6]

Baseball provided the means to overcome such class and racial divisions, as Cuban nationalism and civic pride emerged in athletic contests even before the nationalist revolution of 1895. In order to defeat neighborhood, civic, regional, and American rivals, teams sought the best players. By 1893 El *Base-Ball* affirmed that "one can hardly find any Cuban town that does not already claim as its own a club, perfectly uniformed and prepared to play."[7]

Nationalism spurred periodic revolts aimed at independence from the Spanish masters throughout the nineteenth century, only to end in dismal failure. The revolt of 1895 proved more successful, however, partly due to baseball. Aurelio Miranda, a founder of the Havana Baseball Club, claimed that the game served as a classroom, teaching patience, tactics, and strategy. Teams adopted revolutionary names or those of nationalistic heroes. Team meetings or practices fomented revolutionary fervor; the colonial government disbanded the Cardenas club in 1881 over such issues. By 1895 baseball teams in Cuba and Cuban teams in Tampa and Key West in Florida were diverting funds to Jose Marti's liberation movement, causing the Spanish once again to ban the game on the island. When the war for independence erupted in 1895, many of the game's top players joined the revolutionary army as officers. Emilio Sabourin, a founder of the Havana Club team and the first professional league, faced imprisonment and eventual death in Spanish Morocco.[8]

The war continued for three years, drawing great attention from the American media and from the banks and business interests with holdings on the island. The rebels intended to address class divisions in the society by redistributing the land, a fear of the Cuban bourgeoisie as well as of the Americans. Americans were equally disturbed by the alleged atrocities of the Spanish Army in Cuba, as blatantly charged by America's yellow press, led by Joseph Pulitzer's *New York World* and the New York *Journal* of William Randolph Hearst. Protestant organizations lent their voice to calls for intervention on religious or humanitarian grounds, and President William McKinley sent a battleship, the USS *Maine* to Havana, which arrived in the harbor on January 25, 1898. Three weeks later, on the night of February 15, a mysterious explosion rocked the ship, tearing it to shreds as the vessel sank. Among the 266 sailors and marines killed in the blast was William Lambert, an African American and the star pitcher of the ship's baseball team, which had been the champions of the navy. Americans suspected

Spanish treachery, and the yellow press called for revenge. "Remember the *Maine*" became a shrill war cry, and Congress acquiesced in April, precipitating the Spanish-American War.[9]

Similar to events in the Philippines, the arriving American forces dismissed the successes of the insurgent, largely black Cuban army, and American generals relegated the nationalist patriots to inconsequential duties. A brief four-month campaign resulted in the conquest of Cuba by a disorganized American army over an even more ragged but courageous Spanish opponent. In the midst of the military struggle, buoyed by the spirit of territorial gain, the U.S. Congress annexed Hawaii. The resultant peace negotiations with the Spanish brought an instant empire in the form of the Philippines and Puerto Rico and the temporary governance of Cuba.[10]

The declaration of war had included the Teller Resolution, which promised an independent Cuba, but the new Cuban constitution required approval by the United States, and the resultant Platt Amendment gutted that pledge by establishing an American protectorate with undue influence on the Cuban government, economy, and military. The United States got a permanent naval base at Guantanamo Bay, and Cuban officials were educated in America. Cuba's handpicked first president, Tomas Estrada Palma, spoke English, converted to the Quaker faith, and held U.S. citizenship. Despite the anti-American demonstrations fostered by the Platt Amendment, U.S. intervention proceeded after the war. Secretary of War Elihu Root had already congratulated Governor-General Leonard Wood for the "establishment of popular self-government, based on a limited suffrage, excluding so great a proportion of the elements which have brought ruin to Haiti and San Domingo." The "elements" to which Root referred were black Cubans, many of whom composed the liberation army. By 1905 an American visitor observed that "Negroes . . . are deprived of positions, ostracized and made political outcasts. The Negro has done much for Cuba. Cuba has done nothing for the Negro."[11] The early promise of baseball seemed negated by American impositions and racial attitudes.

American middle-class, WASP standards of morality influenced further edicts by the occupational government. The Woman's Christian Temperance Union (WCTU) appeared in Cuba in 1899, shortly after the end of hostilities, and the American Society for the Prevention of Cruelty to Animals lobbied for a ban on bullfights and cockfighting. The government duly obliged and prohibited gambling as well. There proved one exception to the latter, however, as Governor-General Wood, a jai alai player, approved the building of a fronton in 1901, thus earning its managers a handsome sum of more than 11 million pesos per year. Cubans viewed such actions as hypocritical and promptly reinstated cockfights with the termination of the American occupation in 1902.[12]

The fact that Wood engaged in the sport of jai alai indicates an early crosscurrent of cultural flow, yet Americans intended a wholesale adoption of their democratic ideology by the Cubans. Schools became one of the first priorities of the U.S. Army, and the military retained control by maintaining three of the four positions on the Board of Education. The school system followed the model of those in Ohio and Philadelphia, and English-language instruction began as early as kindergarten and continued through all grades. Cuban teachers were sent to Harvard and other American colleges for educational training each summer. Elite Cubans maintained private schools, however, to avoid the racially mixed classrooms of the public educational system.[13]

The Americans had a particular interest in teaching morality to the Cubans, whom they deemed lacking in Anglo virtue. In 1905 the secretary of war installed Wilson L. Gill with the title of general supervisor of moral and civic training in Cuban schools. Gill organized the schools into miniature governing bodies with elected officials and their own police courts. James Wilson, governor of Matanzas province, ordered English books for the school library because, he wrote, "unquestionably our literature will promote their knowledge, improve their morals and give their people a new and better trend of thought."[14]

American notions of morality aligned closely with Protestant precepts. Rather than contend with one another for Catholic souls, the Protestant missionaries carved the island into separate jurisdictions, with cities in excess of six thousand inhabitants remaining fair game for all. Aided by American corporate sponsors, the Protestant sects established at least a hundred schools that emphasized vocational training as well as religious instruction. Episcopalian bishop Albion Knight wrote to the acting governor Charles Magoon in 1907: "Because of the prevalence of blacks in this locality I have selected this point as the place to locate an industrial school for the negroes modelled on the plan of Hampton, Tuskegee, and Lawrenceville."[15] Despite the Americans' best intentions, such practices only doomed blacks to an unequal share in Cuban society.

The Cubans did not accept the American initiatives readily. In the election of 1900 the National Party, which sought independence, won most of the positions on town and provincial councils, and Cuban lawyers successfully opposed American attempts to introduce the jury system and an act of habeas corpus. When the Cubans elected black countrymen, rather than the whites favored by General Leonard Wood, Wood deemed them to be "irresponsible, unreliable, . . . and proof of their incapacity for independence."[16]

Sport provided yet other lessons in race and nationalism. The Cuban X Giants, an African American baseball team, traveled to Havana for games with several Cuban teams in 1900. By 1904 Cuban teams began touring the northeastern United States. Major League teams soon began winter play in Cuba, and the triangular competition among white, African American, and Cuban teams, combined with resentment of the American occupation, which had resumed in 1906 after a brief sojourn, only escalated the surrogate wars and the popularity of the game. Cuban League teams drew as many as twelve thousand spectators for Sunday games, with victories over the Americans "consolidating feelings of nationhood and general solidarity that went beyond race, class, or politics."[17] In 1909 two Cuban teams beat the Detroit Tigers, defending champions of the American League, in a series of games, including one in which a Cuban pitcher threw a no-hitter for eleven innings. Such performances led to enhanced opportunities for the Cuban players, with the best white Cubans signed by the American Major League teams and black Cubans relegated to Negro League play. Baseball thus provided an opportunity for skilled players but, ironically, also reinforced the racial divide.

The gains offered by baseball and education were offset by racial segregation as well as by class and religious differences. The Protestant clergy failed to impose sabbatarian restrictions as the lure of baseball superseded religious services and Sunday school. The various yacht clubs, the Jockey

Club, and the auto racing circuit founded by the Americans and the Cuban gentry catered to the upper class, while patronage of a bowling alley, roller skating rinks, and tennis clubs required a middle-class income. Wealthy Cubans who had attended schools in the United States returned to their homeland to establish the Havana Sports Club and the Vedado Tennis Club in 1902. Both eventually competed in baseball, basketball, and American football. The latter played against American colleges and the University of Havana, which eventually installed an American coach and an American athletic director.[18]

The YMCA sent its first organizer to Cuba in 1904 and opened its gym the following year. Its promotion of basketball and volleyball proved popular, but the Y had less success with its program of moral uplift. To many Cubans the Y's message smacked of hypocrisy, and even its representative admitted that "while drinking is very common, drunkenness is very rare, except among the Americans. Gambling is very common, especially in the form of betting." In addition to the betting on baseball games, the jai alai matches allowed by Governor-General Wood had undermined the Y's moral campaign.[19]

The YMCA received considerable help from the American administrators, including a $1,000 contribution in 1905 from H. G. Squires, an American minister. The YMCA building boasted the only swimming pool in Havana at that time. The new game of basketball brought new faces to the gym but also resulted in the muttering of unsavory language, which the Y's representative described as "vile" and "fearful." He admitted that his limited knowledge of Spanish precluded his knowledge of even more unseemly utterances. Moreover, the Cubans wanted to start a basketball league on Sundays, despite the Y's ban on sabbatarian games. The difference between the Catholic and the Protestant perception of Sunday became clear upon questioning. The Cubans insisted that it should be a day for frolic and amusement.[20] Wrote the director about one encounter with a native Cuban: "I asked him if he ever took time to think of God, and he said that he did every day except Sunday. . . . It is slow work."[21] The YMCA continued to expand its offerings to include bowling, track, and billiards, yet it attracted mostly American sailors.

A burgeoning black rights movement combined with the Liberal Party's campaign against the abolishment of the Platt Amendment resulted in another revolt in 1906. By that time thirteen thousand North Americans owned land in Cuba, and the rebels declared that "the properties which we will commence to destroy by fire . . . in case we do not reach an accord with the Government, will be those of American citizens." The U.S. government quickly sent the navy and the marines to safeguard American interests. They remained until January 1909.[22]

Anti-American sentiments lingered, and by 1908 government officials reported a general hostility. Cubans believed that they had "exchanged the Spanish yoke for an American yoke."[23] Black Cubans began organizing an "independent negro party," which the Americans characterized as "the beginning of the race problem in Cuba."[24] The independent party was outlawed in 1910, and even nonblack Cubans felt cheated. The U.S. acting governor, Charles Magoon, entered office with a treasury surplus of $26 million in 1906, but government patronage and collusion with New York bankers had reduced that surplus to only $3 million by 1907.[25]

Sport provided an inadequate and uneven means of retribution. Cuban teams battled Americans on the baseball diamonds, and the University of Havana defeated the YMCA's basketball squad in 1906. The university had even beaten U.S. military teams on the football field, but Louisiana State University avenged those losses with an overwhelming 56–0 victory on Christmas Day 1907. Competition carried over to the track; as one administrator remembered: "It was the desire of the National University to meet us on the track and administer a good dose to us. I must say that they hardly gave us a fair chance and that their method seemed to be intended to give them the victory at all costs. They thus yielded to us in the choice of some other day than Sunday. . . . Our victory placed us among the front ranks in the athletic circles in Cuba, and put us in a position to make suggestions as to better management of amateur contests."[26]

The YMCA followed its victory by organizing a track and field meet during the Havana carnival, similar to its later ventures in the Philippines. The event drew four thousand spectators, and J. E. Hubbard of the YMCA gloated: "We shall soon be the guiding light in amateur sport. . . . You will see how we will thus shape the policies of all athletic organizations in the

Island." Hubbard felt that the Y attracted young Cubans away from their nationalistic sport clubs and that American victories demonstrated Anglo superiority.[27] The YMCA even deviated from its usual policies to engage in the most masculine of sports to prove its point the following year. Although the Y's team tied with the university football team earlier during the season, the two met in the championship, a culminating athletic feature of the 1909 carnival. In a game played in the rain, the Y used deceptive passes and a reverse to gain a 12–5 win, then held a party in celebration. Hubbard reported: "We are now arranging a trophy room to keep our spoils of war, banners, and photographs."[28] Such images provided reminders of dominant and subordinate status in colonial societies.

Sport still provided hope and promise, however. Cuban baseball teams barnstormed throughout the United States during the second occupation, and no less than nine Major League squads traveled to Cuba during that time. On their home soil the Cubans scored notable triumphs, winning 7 of 11 games against Cincinnati in 1908, splitting 8 games with the Philadelphia A's the next year, and taking 8 of 12 from Detroit in 1909. Early in 1910 a Havana team even defeated the Tulane University football team.[29]

Cuban nationalism mounted simultaneously. In 1908 voters ousted the Protestant Tomas Estrada Palma, who had been handpicked by the United States for the presidency, in favor of a rebel hero, Miguel Gomez. Nevertheless, U.S. economic control and property holdings continued apace as American railroads, mines, and sugar plantations spread throughout Cuba. The loss of land by poor, mostly black peasants precipitated yet another revolt in 1912 that approximated racial and class warfare versus wealthy whites. The U.S. government denied an appeal by the rebels, and the Cuban army killed more than six thousand, some by lynching.[30]

American popular culture continued to intrude on the traditional lifestyles of Cuba. In Havana the social athletic clubs, fraternal associations, American Legion, YMCA, WCTU, English-language newspapers and periodicals, Protestant churches, and country club Anglicized and Americanized the city. Big bands and burlesque shows catered to musical interests, and thousands of prostitutes offered carnal pleasures. In the countryside large American corporations, including the Hershey, American Fruit, and United Fruit companies, transformed rural areas into company towns with athletic facilities, theaters, amusement parks, and dance halls. Americans owned more than a third of the country's sugar mills and nearly a hundred of these fielded baseball teams. Baseball provided the local population with a form of entertainment and served the owners as a means of social control, providing otherwise unruly workers with a more wholesome use of their time.[31]

The Catholic Church in Cuba fought cultural impositions vigorously, particularly those of a Protestant religious nature. It succeeded in limiting the gains of the YMCA, but Cuba soon began losing its human as well as its natural resources. In 1911 American League president Ban Johnson prohibited teams from traveling to Cuba after several defeats questioned the Social Darwinian presumption of whites' superiority. Thereafter, American professional teams began hiring the best of the light-skinned Cubans for their own ranks. Both Rafael Almeida and Armando Marsans appeared with the Cincinnati Reds in 1912, and Mike Gonzalez enjoyed a long career with the Boston Braves (1912–1929) before his rise as a coach and manager. Perhaps the most distinguished Cuban player, pitcher Adolfo Luque, started his long Major League stint (1914–1935) with the Boston Braves but reached the World Series with Cincinnati in 1918 and 1919. To engage Luque's services Cincinnati had to prove his whiteness with an affidavit. Luque won 27 games for the Reds in 1923, and thirty thousand Cubans honored him with a parade through Havana upon his return. Such players faced racial taunts, stereotypes, and "bean balls" thrown at their heads, but their success initiated a transition in the perceptions of race and whiteness that eventually paved the way for Jackie Robinson and the globalization of professional rosters.[32]

Professional boxing raised similar issues in Cuba and culminated in a bout of international significance. A professional match had taken place in 1909 and a boxing academy had opened soon thereafter, but interracial bouts often disrupted the social order and any triumphs by black fighters challenged the accepted racial hierarchy. The government banned the sport in 1912; nevertheless, Havana served as the site in 1915 for one of the most controversial of all fights. For nearly a quarter century white heavyweights had refused to fight blacks in championship bouts. White fighter Tommy Burns, an undersized claimant, assumed the crown after the retirement of the undefeated Jim Jeffries. Burns proceeded on a world tour, hounded by Jack Johnson, king of the black heavyweights. An Australian promoter secured a championship match in 1908, in which Johnson toyed with and pummeled Burns. Johnson's flamboyant and profligate lifestyle challenged whites, and his sexual escapades and marriages to white women antagonized all but the most radical of observers.[33]

Johnson's general offensiveness to the principle of white superiority engendered a search for the "Great White Hope" who would reclaim the crown. Jeffries came out of retirement for a celebrated 1910 contest to restore white supremacy, only to suffer his first loss in a knockout. Johnson remained the champion until 1915 when, forced to flee the United States due to charges on immorality laws, he eventually agreed to a championship contest in Cuba. His opponent, the raw but white giant Jess Willard, won a controversial title by knockout in the twenty-sixth round and immediately reinstated the color ban at the heavyweight level, the symbol of ultimate masculine prowess. Cuba proved a ready site for interracial combat.[34]

Whites in Cuba reinforced such attitudes. For example, the Loyal Order of the Moose admitted: "The Havana lodge is open to all Cubans, Spanish and other nationalities who can read, write, and speak the English language. We want only good men of the white race, who are in good standing in the community and engaged in lawful occupation."[35] Ethnocentrism still prevailed in the YMCA as well. The Y had expanded its program to offer baseball, swimming, and water polo, explaining that "to the Cuban youth physical development is his idol. There is nothing he will not do to attain a strong big-muscled body." The Y's physical education director further railed against "characteristically Latin" traits of sexuality that contributed to one's machismo.[36]

Cubans tried to reassert some control over their own destinies as they founded another professional baseball league in 1917. The political and economic situation necessitated more drastic action, however. The growing bureaucracy required formal titles to land, forcing surveys that poor peasants could not afford. The resultant loss of their land compelled many peasants to accept seasonal work in the sugar cane fields. When a right wing faction seized the election, another revolt ensued. Baldomero Acosta, a former pitcher for the Washington Senators, led the rebel forces in western Cuba as workers raided the estates of the wealthy, stole cattle, and generally destroyed property. Inevitably, U.S. ships and marines arrived in 1917 to provide security for American business interests and to support the conservative government.[37]

By 1918 the United States dominated the Cuban economy, accounting for 76 percent of its imports and 72 percent of its exports. American companies controlled nearly half of the sugar and tobacco production. Cuban workers retaliated with two general strikes in 1919. Despite such resistance their efforts seemed feeble in the face of American economic and cultural power. Havana became an exotic American playground that fulfilled illicit pleasures no longer available as Prohibition encompassed the puritanical states. Gambling casinos, a multitude of brothels, and risquè theatrical performances provided much more than physical escape from the mainland. The cultural amalgamation that had occurred over the previous two generations denigrated Cubans and affected their self-worth. One Cuban remarked: "Indolence is natural for us. . . . White Cubans descend from Spaniard [*sic*] and Cubans of color from Africa, two races equally lazy."[38] Fortunately, sport still allowed Cubans to test such beliefs.

While the American corporations and elite social clubs still maintained their segregation practices, baseball and boxing provided opportunities for racial comparison and for renewal of Cuban pride. Light-skinned Cubans appeared in growing numbers on Major League rosters, and one New York sportswriter claimed that "St. Louis and Cincinnati would be out of the league altogether if it were not for their Cuban allies."[39] Black Cuban stars found employment on teams in the Negro National League in the United States, which began play in 1920. During the 1920–1921 winter league season, the African American Bacharach Giants joined the Cuban League but left for home only halfway through the schedule in last place. When Babe Ruth arrived for a ten-day exhibition in 1920, Jose Acosta, a Cuban knuckleballer, struck him out three times. Cuban ballplayers gained even more glory when they spurred nationalistic sentiments by winning the first Central American Games baseball championship in Mexico City in 1926. They repeated as champions in 1930, 1935, and 1938, and Cubans added the soccer title in front of their own fans in Havana in 1930.[40]

Cuban women, too, assumed a more active role in athletic endeavors. More than fifty clubs fielded women's teams by 1930, some on the tennis courts but most as school or industrial basketball squads. Among the men, the YMCA complained that it had trained the Cuban basketball players only to have them desert to the Cuban national clubs. After losing the 1921 championship trophy, the Y invoked Amateur Athletic Union guidelines that required players to remain on one team throughout the season. At the university, students objected to the ban on black athletes and organized their own club as an alternative.[41]

Boxing allowed even more direct challenges and produced national heroes. Authorities lifted the ban as bouts began attracting tourist dollars, especially with the Johnson-Willard spectacle. In 1921 the government established a national commission to regulate matches, and Golden Gloves amateur competition reached Cuba by the next decade. Cuban fighters had already begun seeking contests in the states; Eligio Sardinas, boxing under the belittling appellation of Kid Chocolate, won the junior lightweight crown in 1931 and followed that with the world featherweight championship a year later. Sardinas moved to Harlem, where he continued to break racial barriers. Restaurants recognized his celebrity by disregarding their segregation policies for his visits. He dated Cotton Club dancers and heaped candy on Harlem youngsters. African Americans gave him a standing ovation at the Apollo Theater. Like Jack Johnson, he squandered his money on a lavish lifestyle that included six cars, but the Cuban government, then under the nationalistic dictator Fulgencio Batista, provided him with a house and a lifetime pension for bringing honor to Cuba.[42]

By the 1930s Cuban nationalism boiled over as factions fought over the country's direction. Five political assassinations in 1932 paved the way for the rise of Batista in a 1933 military coup. The rebels had even used the Havana YMCA building to secretly store guns and ammunition. A year later the YMCA surrendered in its religious crusade to bring a Protestant morality to Cuba.[43]

Despite the political upheaval, baseball still buoyed Cuban spirits. The national team won the 1935 Central American Games title despite having to compete against professionals from Mexico, Nicaragua, and Panama. Political factions united in support of a Havana team in a 1936 series with the St. Louis Cardinals. A Cuban team followed that victory with the world amateur championship in 1939 and 1940, and a Cuban team beat the Boston Red Sox during spring training the following year. Cubans resumed their dominance of amateur baseball with successive world titles from 1946 to 1953, and Cuban boxers won prominence in American venues; but the cultural convergence fostered by sport weakened traditional Cuban culture. American movies, foods, clothing styles, music, and other forms of material and popular culture continually eroded Spanish influences. In return, Cuban dances, such as the rhumba, cha cha, mambo, and conga, won temporary popularity in the United States. African American Negro League stars helped Cuba obtain the Caribbean Series championship in 1948, and a Cuban woman, Isora del Castillo, played third base for the Chicago Colleens, a professional team in the All American Girls Baseball League during 1949–1950. Cuba added the inaugural Pan American Games baseball crown to its laurels in 1951.[44]

The Cuban Sugar Kings, whose name reflected nationalistic pride, joined the Triple A International League as a Cincinnati farm team from 1954 to 1959 with the intention of eventually securing a Major League franchise for Cuba. Whereas the Havana Cubans were restricted to using only white players because of Florida's segregation laws, the Sugar Kings faced no such prohibitions. The *Montreal Star* reported that they "started five Cuban Negroes," who were "showy and flashy," and that they were "accompanied by a conga band of eleven musicians who supplied a rhythmic beat when the Sugar Kings came to bat."[45] The next year, the Kings made the playoffs, and a Cuban reporter framed the win over Syracuse in heroic terms. He described "patriotic spirit—yells, songs, explosions of delirious support for the players who defended . . . the national flag as if we were in full war and that was actual combat between two armies, and not a passing sports event."[46] American Major League teams managed to thwart Cubans' nationalistic hopes, however, by signing the best players, white and black, to big league contracts after Jackie Robinson's breakthrough.

Cuban boxers, including Kid Gavilan (Gerardo Gonzalez) and Benny "Kid" Paret, battled for the welterweight championship and became television stars in the United States. Gavilan showcased his indigenous "bolo punch" and danced a rhumba in the ring as he held the title belt from 1951 to 1954. In a 1953 bout he mocked the undefeated, college-educated Chuck Davey while exposing the contender's weaknesses. Despite $2 million in earnings, Gavilan had little to show for his rule of the welterweight division and retired to a life of destitution. Paret fared worse, losing his life in the ring in a televised bout with Emile Griffith.[47]

Like the boxers, professional baseball players felt exploited. They suffered humiliation and racial animosity in the United States and labored for less compensation than their white counterparts. By the 1950s even middle-class workers in Cuba were experiencing similar degradations as employees of American companies. For the working classes and the peasants, poverty only increased. Cuba was ripe for revolution, and as in 1895, baseball assisted the rebellion. A United Fruit Company player explained: "You know we couldn't meet in public, so we had to meet during our baseball games. We'd hold a big game and during it hold our planning meetings." A pitcher and ardent baseball fan, Fidel Castro, led the revolutionary army. After that army's success, a Communist sports model unfolded. Sport became a right rather than a privilege, and private clubs were abolished. Commercialized sports, such as pro baseball and boxing, also faced extinction, and athletes channeled their energies into securing nationalistic glory for the homeland and the revolution. After repelling the 1961 Bay of Pigs invasion, Cubans celebrated with an amateur boxing tournament, which became an annual festival of patriotism. Cuban boxers won fame as Olympic champions, and fifteen thousand practiced the sport under the tutelage of coaches in state schools. The Cuban system proved so successful that nine foreign Olympic teams employed Cuban coaches in 1992.[48]

The formation of the Instituto Nacional de Deportes, Educacion Fisica y Recreacion (INDER) in 1961 fostered mass sport as a means not only to identify and train elite athletes but to improve the health of all. By 1989 Cuba enlisted twenty-eight thousand physical education teachers in schools and clubs to promote national fitness. Castro claimed that "imperialism has tried to humiliate Latin American countries, has tried to instil [sic] an inferiority complex in them; part of the imperialists' ideology is to present themselves as superior. And they have used sport for that purpose." Unable to compete with the United States economically or militarily, Cuba intended to use sport as a political tool; its athletes and coaches became representatives, diplomats, and ambassadors. By the 1990s the Cuban government was investing $80 million annually in its sports program. Given the U.S. economic boycott of the nation, exchanges in baseball, basketball, and volleyball remained one of the few links between the once-close neighbors.[49]

Olympic boxing and track champions won glory and respect for the small island nation throughout the latter half of the twentieth century, but baseball remained at the core of Cuban culture. Cuba won the first Olympic baseball championship in 1992, and its athletes garnered twenty-five medals in 1996 and improved even further on that total in 2000 (with twenty-nine medals). But perhaps the most satisfying athletic event of the recent past occurred in the baseball series with the Baltimore Orioles in 1999. The Americans took a narrow 3–2 win in Cuba, but the Cuban team won decisively, 12–6, in Baltimore. More importantly, Fidel Castro and the capitalists Bud Selig, the baseball commissioner, and Peter Angelos, the Orioles' owner, shared a communal moment in a mutual love of baseball.[50]

Despite foreign influences, multiple U.S. occupations, and internal political upheavals, sport, and particularly baseball, has remained the one constant in Cuban life. It has served as a ritual, a spectacle, and a carnival conducive to Cuban society and has nurtured a nationalistic spirit, reconstructed a fragmented culture, exhibited machismo in times of oppression, and restored dignity and national pride to the Cuban people.

Sport and the Restoration of Pride in Puerto Rico

Race, religion, and revolt dominated the history of Puerto Rico. After Christopher Columbus discovered the island in 1493, colonization by the Spanish occurred in earnest in 1506. With the Spanish came Catholicism and disease. The latter decimated the ranks of the native Indians, and African slaves replaced them beginning in 1508. The island sustained attacks by the English and the Dutch over the next two centuries, and island residents revolted against their Spanish masters by 1848. Spain abolished slavery in 1873 and granted Puerto Ricans their independence in 1897. Unfortunately for the islanders the USS *Maine* exploded in Havana, Cuba, only five days after the establishment of the provisional cabinet.[1]

With the declaration of war, U.S. troops invaded Puerto Rico in July and controlled the island in three weeks' time. Spain granted Puerto Rico to the United States in the peace treaty that ended the war, thus resulting in the American annexation of an independent country. Despite local opposition the United States initially installed a military government and a local police force, and recruited a native garrison, although the latter's membership was restricted to whites only. Stereotyping the Puerto Ricans as "lazy," the Americans instituted vagrancy laws, established an eight-hour workday, and banned cockfights. Secretary of war Elihu Root, in his 1899 annual report, rationalized that "before the people of Porto Rico [sic] can be fully intrusted [sic] with self-government, they must first learn the lesson of self-control and respect for the principles of constitutional government, which requires acceptance of its peaceful decisions. This lesson will necessarily be slowly learned. . . . They would inevitably fail without a course of tuition under a strong and guiding hand."[2] Root referred, in part, to Creoles' attacks on large landowners both during and after the war, events that allied the wealthy with the new government and placed class interests above nationalism.[3]

Such alliances also centered around race. As in the Philippines, American WASP anthropologists studied the native peoples, extolling the redemptive values of their Spanish past and denigrating their African aspects. Jesse Fewkes studied the Puerto Ricans for three years and determined them to be "primitive, illiterate, idolatrous, destitute, superstitious, and dark-skinned." As Spanish influences, gambling, dueling, and cockfighting assumed Catholic qualities of association.[4]

Americans determined that such barbarities and immoral ties had to be eliminated and new ways learned. They installed boards of education in 1899, required the teaching of English as well as Spanish in the schools, and designated moral training "as distinct from secular or religious teaching"—to distinguish the program from the Catholic curriculum in private schools. All teachers had to be familiar with "American" methodology, and a teacher training institute was established for that purpose.[5]

The imposition of the English language continued throughout all grades despite opposition. American administrators and editors arbitrarily changed the Spanish spelling of Puerto Rico, Anglicizing it to "Porto Rico," which became a journalistic tradition over the next generation.[6]

Suffrage pertained only to literate adult males, who voted for a representative in the U.S. Congress who had no electoral vote of his own. The

U.S. president appointed a governor and the executive council, while the U.S. Supreme Court adjudicated all final appeals. The Foraker Act of 1900, which established a civil government, also prohibited ownership of more than five hundred acres of land but lacked strong enforcement. In 1898 93 percent of Puerto Rican farmers owned their own land, but a United States–imposed land tax soon drove them from their property, similar to the situation in Cuba. American periodicals, particularly *National Geographic*, lauded the rich natural resources of the island. Large corporations and wealthy individuals soon controlled the best land, much of it under plantation cultivation. In 1904 nationalists founded the Union de Puerto Rico, an oppositional party that clamored for independence.[7]

As in Cuba, baseball preceded the Americans to the island. Cultural and personnel flow between the Spanish islands brought the game from Cuba to Puerto Rico. By 1896 the Almendares and Borinquen clubs battled each other in San Juan. Within four years, company and school teams engaged in tournament play. The entry of the Americans brought a more varied and comprehensive sporting culture to the island. Included among the first requests to the adjutant general were "a modern athletic club for recreation with billiard rooms, bowling alleys, a library, outdoor field sports, running and wheel [cycling] tracks, ball grounds and beer sales to allow for proper recreation."[8] Soldiers apparently introduced boxing to the island with a match at a local boat club in 1900. The YMCA, too, inserted itself in San Juan and began raising money for its programs. By 1910 it had won a building site from the Puerto Rican legislature; it dedicated the structure built there in 1913. Proselytism through sport quickly ensued, as the Y introduced basketball, volleyball, fencing, tennis, handball, and track and field meets. The Y offered medals, trophies, banners, ribbons, and pennants to attract the boys and young men. The first track meet, held in 1916, drew 110 participants, 101 of whom were natives. The Y felt that "through this Athletic Meet we gained access to many young men and boys who had not been in touch with the Association."[9]

The YMCA failed to connect with many Puerto Rican baseball players, however, because it refused to let its team play on Sundays, the primary date for island games. Another factor that hindered YMCA efforts involved its adherence to racist segregation policies. W. G. Coxhead, the physical director of the San Juan YMCA, related that he had to turn away a Puerto Rican who was "too dark and of Negro blood, though the young man seemed to be a gentleman." Blacks had contributed money to the construction of the YMCA building under the assumption that all were welcome. The Y returned their membership application fees, and a perplexed Coxhead stated that they "don't see themselves as colored; but claim they are Porto Ricans." Coxhead further intimated that "the color question with which we have to deal here is new to me and I find it causes me some embarrassment but is a thing to which I will have to learn to adapt myself."[10] Such cases illustrated the different perspectives on social status. For Puerto Ricans, class carried more weight than the color of one's skin. For Americans, skin color determined class. Racism thus became part of the American educational agenda.

The YMCA began women's teams in both basketball and volleyball, and the popularity of female opportunities resulted in the hiring of twelve female teachers. The women's success, however, proved short-lived, as the men commandeered the gym for their own purposes. The government instituted physical education classes in the schools, and the playground movement took hold in San Juan during the World War I era. Women participated in physical education classes at the local university and engaged in tennis play by the 1930s, but the Latin macho culture generally relegated their sporting endeavors to the background. Like the children of immigrant parents in the United States, sport and physical education under the guidance of trained teachers and specialized coaches meant to impart the lessons of teamwork, self-sacrifice, work discipline, and democracy in practical ways for those who spoke little or no English. Yet Joseph Cannon, U.S. speaker of the house, asserted in 1916 that "the people of Porto Rico have not the slightest conception of self-government."[11]

The Puerto Ricans had apparently learned their lessons well enough at the YMCA, where a native team won the basketball league championship. Other Hispanic members, in a reverse cultural flow, used the facilities as a fronton. Such adaptations gave early evidence that the imposition of culture would be a long and difficult task.[12]

The U.S. government decided to grant citizenship to Puerto Ricans in 1917, but without fanfare on the island. Nationalist leaders opposed the move, and nearly three hundred Puerto Ricans went to court to renounce their new status. World War I produced a temporary allegiance when a German submarine torpedoed a Puerto Rican ship. More than one hundred thousand islanders registered for the military draft, and a Puerto Rican regiment embarked to protect the Panama Canal Zone. The island returned to its liminal status after the war. U.S. authorities directed English-only classes at the secondary level (above grade six), but few outside of urban areas chose to practice the foreign tongue. By 1920 only one-third of Puerto Rican children even attended school.[13]

The native population clung to its language and lifestyle despite the efforts to Americanize the culture. Cockfights continued throughout the island, government prohibition notwithstanding. The indigenous residents saw little value in adopting the materialist ambitions of capitalism when the plantation workers earned no more than $4 a day for ten to twelve hours of toil. Some made as little as 50 cents per day, with $2 being the top wage for women. Plantation managers routinely ignored the eight-hour workday prescription during the 1920s. L. W. James, the American trade commissioner in Puerto Rico, claimed that a *jibaro* (rural worker) worked only enough hours to meet his physical needs: "The idea of saving something for a rainy day was beyond his comprehension. . . . He combines the care-free ideals of the redskin and the impetuous temperament of the Spaniard." Such comparisons established WASP, middle-class values as the norm. Consequently, employers reduced the hourly wage in order to get additional labor from their employees. Sugar workers struck for a minimum wage in 1920, but the exploitative conditions hardly improved their lives. By the end of the decade nearly three quarters of rural adults remained illiterate and 80 percent of rural peasants were landless; by 1930 U.S. corporations owned 60 percent of the sugar industry, 60 percent of the banks and public utilities, and 80 percent of the tobacco business.[14]

Some Puerto Ricans sought refuge in the United States, many settling in New York City. There they founded the Alianza Abrera Puertorriquena (Puerto Rican Workers Alliance), a socialist organization, in 1923. Others found solace in baseball. That same year the immigrant community formed the Porto Rican League in New Jersey. The following season a team from New York's East Side, known as the San Juan Baseball Club, entertained the Puerto Rico Stars from the island. Such personal, social, and cultural flow would persist throughout the century, becoming known as the Nuyorican movement, which contributed to the fragmentation of a the Puerto Rican culture. In the United States the Nuyoricans became stereotyped as youthful gang members in the popular theatrical play *West Side Story*. Official government documents, such as the 1965 Moynihan Report, described a culture of poverty that transcended generations. Such racialized characterizations branded poor females as "welfare queens" by blaming the ghetto residents rather than the social conditions that created their circumstances. The gradual and limited assimilation of the Nuyoricans, their increasing use of the English language, and their ties to Democratic Party politics would eventually create a hybrid culture that borrowed from both venues and that remains an issue with nationalists.[15]

Baseball teams traveled to Puerto Rico in increasing numbers for winter league play after World War I. The governor advocated American ball games, as well as gymnastics, tennis, and track as alternative activities to the enduring cockfights. While baseball continued to prosper and find advocates, other American efforts languished. Salaries proved insufficient to attract Anglo teachers and coaches, and the use of locals undermined the government's emphasis on English usage.[16]

The YMCA, proponent of a Protestant Muscular Christianity, faced even greater hurdles. Despite constant promotion of its programs and principles, the director wrote that "Catholic influence is strong here and undoubtedly greatly hinders the progress of the work of the Association."[17] The Y included boxing, offered prizes for recruitment, and even brought the Brooklyn Central YMCA basketball team to Puerto Rico to compete with local teams, but the new director, Everett Symonds, reported in 1927 that "our second goal of greatly increasing our membership did not become a reality . . . and . . . the hope of building another wing on the building has not been realized."[18] He complained that athletes joined only to play sports and then quit after their season. The fact that U.S. companies contested paying taxes on the island also raised anti-American sentiments, and the Y's membership dropped even further the next year. By 1931 membership turnover reached as high as 75 percent, and the Y admitted that very few visited the building except for sports and exercise. Their religious message went unheeded.[19]

During the 1930s Puerto Rican athletes began to establish reputations beyond the island, enhancing a greater national identity and self-esteem. In 1930 Puerto Rico entered the competition in the Central American and Caribbean Games as a separate nation, distinct though not completely separate from the United States. Boxing, legalized in 1927, provided Puerto Ricans with their first athletic hero when Sixto Escobar won the bantamweight championship of the world. The sixth child of a plantation labor boss, Jacinto Escobar, and his wife, Adela, Sixto Escobar won the National Boxing Association title in 1934 and solidified the undisputed world championship with a knockout victory over Tony Marino in 1936. Escobar began boxing at age sixteen and was never knocked out throughout his career, inspiring a generation of Puerto Rican youths. His February 21, 1937, win over Lou Salica in San Juan delivered the first title match to be held on the island. One writer claimed that Escobar "brought the game of boxing at [*sic*] Puerto Rico from nothing more than club-fighting to international spotlight, and spawned a whole new generation of fight fans and boxers." One of this "new generation," Jose Torres, who later became an Olympic and world light heavyweight champion as well as president of the World Boxing Organization, stated that Escobar helped Puerto Ricans overcome their colonial inferiority complex during an era "when the island suffered an identity problem; when it had a confused culture; when we saw any non-Puerto Rican individual as superior to us." Puerto Rico beamed at Escobar's accomplishments and their restoration of national pride. It showed its appreciation by naming a San Juan arena after him. His obituary in 1979 named him "the father of modern Puerto Rican boxing" and "a national shrine."[20]

The Nationalist Party expressed its newfound pride in a peaceful independence march in 1936. Brutally suppressed by the government, the march resulted in seventeen dead and more than two hundred wounded marchers, and it became known as the Ponce Massacre. Despite repression, poverty, and exploitation, sport enabled Puerto Ricans to reclaim their national self-esteem. Physicality mattered to workers, and sport provided the most visible means of direct comparison with supposed superiors.

Victories spawned confidence. Their nationalism erupted in 1936 with the assassination of Francis Riggs, the American chief of police, and similar but unsuccessful attempts on the governor, a judge, and a labor leader. Puerto Ricans found some solace in other athletic heroes. Hiram Bithorn, a versatile competitor, helped Puerto Rico to garner a silver medal in volleyball and a bronze medal in basketball at the 1935 Central American and Caribbean Games. The next year he pitched for the Brooklyn Eagles before returning to manage the San Juan baseball club. In 1942 Bithorn became the first Puerto Rican to make a Major League debut as a pitcher, with the Chicago Cubs. In 1943 he won 18 games. Puerto Rico expressed its appreciation by naming the San Juan municipal stadium in his honor. Such memorials helped to construct a national history and a national identity apart from the dominant, imposed culture of the American administrators.[21]

Baseball assumed greater importance after the Cincinnati Reds held their spring training on the island in 1936, playing against American, Cuban, Mexican, and Puerto Rican contingents. Under the guidance of local organizers, Puerto Rico established its own professional winter league in 1938. The league featured eight teams by 1940, and fans established a close rapport with players, even feeding them in their own homes. Betting on baseball games, batters, or even pitches supplemented the gambling fascination that accompanied the cockfights, and new local heroes emerged, such as Cesar "Coca" Gonzalez and Perucho Cepeda, "the Puerto Rican Babe Ruth."[22]

At least one colonial administrator recognized the burgeoning nationalism and American ethnocentrism as the Depression drew to a close. In 1937 Theodore Roosevelt Jr., who had governed both Puerto Rico and the Philippines, wrote: "Being, on the whole, parochially minded, [we Americans] tend to fit our policies in the islands to our internal political opinions [and] persist too in thinking of all peoples, even those whose ethnological, social, cultural, and environmental background is totally different from ours, in terms of community life where we live."[23]

Forty years of Americanization brought limited acculturation to Puerto Rico, but it succeeded in establishing a consumer mentality. By 1940 a quarter of Puerto Rican homes had electricity; American companies owned more than half of the public utilities. Spending on home furnishings and recreation nearly equaled the expenditures on education. Like Hawaii, Puerto Rico exhibited noticeable differences from the U.S. mainland in racial practices. An army baseball team competed with Puerto Ricans and African Americans in a local league as well as in the professional winter league before the advent of World War II.[24]

World War II brought a fleeting prosperity to the island. The island's geographic location guarded the Caribbean shipping corridor and entry to the Panama Canal. Whereas 3,281 American military personnel had inhabited Puerto Rico in 1940, more than 21,000 were stationed there by 1942 in a multitude of hastily constructed bases. As in U.S. military quarters elsewhere, the government required separate units for African Americans, Puerto Ricans, and whites, reinforcing the established racial and social categories. When the significant shipping losses of 1942 (336 ships in the Caribbean region) dwindled to minimal numbers with Allied successes, Puerto Rico lost its military prominence. The recreational programs devised by military officers utilized local facilities and increased involvement with traditional American sports. Puerto Rican recruits particularly excelled in the track and field, softball, and baseball competitions. Neither the war nor baseball did much to change the dire poverty that afflicted most of the island. In the two decades after the war, more than a million residents, a third of the population, fled to the mainland.[25]

Those who remained won a greater measure of autonomy and a stronger sense of identity. Puerto Rico established its own Olympic team in 1948 when Julio Monagas, president of the national athletic federation, arrived with nine athletes, apparently unannounced, in London and won acceptance. Pole vaulter Jose Barbosa Muniz proved good enough to make the Olympic finals and later won a governmental position as secretary of sport. Puerto Rico got its own flag, its own anthem, and a separate official seal two years later. The U.S. government granted commonwealth status in 1952, allowing for a Puerto Rican constitution, legislature, and administration—in effect, home rule.[26]

Such developments allowed, and even encouraged, islanders to see themselves as a separate nation, particularly when engaged in athletic competitions. Puerto Ricans used their new status to declare Spanish the official language, although the United States still controlled external affairs and the economy. The latter influence allowed American businesses to operate on the island without paying taxes on their profits, while availing themselves of a cheap labor force and doing little to change the cycle of poverty over the next half century. American industrialization of the island resulted in the loss of agricultural land, which led to most food needing to be imported. More than two dozen drug companies operated on the island, testing their products on local inhabitants. The testing of birth control drugs and devices engendered particular concerns and controversies. A 1939 law permitted sterilization of poor women. At that time a third of the native women practiced birth control. After World War II the widespread poverty on the island fostered government fears of communism, and feminist scholars have charged that Puerto Rico became a laboratory for global policy on overpopulation in underdeveloped countries. Clarence Gamble described a 1947 research project of the Procter & Gamble Company that was "designed to discover whether our present means of birth control . . . can control the dangerously expanding population of an unambitious and unintelligent group . . . and [keep] our nation protected from an undue expansion of the unintelligent groups." Such pronouncements carried clear and overt racial overtones, and feminists have charged that the trials resulted in the mass sterilization of Puerto Rican women.[27]

Some Puerto Ricans sought drastic measures of retaliation. In 1950 two Puerto Rican nationalists made an unsuccessful attempt to assassinate President Harry Truman. Two police officers and one of the nationalists died in the ensuing gun battle. In 1954 an attack on the U.S. House of Representatives wounded five congressmen. Others transferred their nationalistic impulses to sport as the Puerto Rican national baseball team won the Caribbean championship in the 1953–1954 and 1954–1955 winter seasons. In 1955 Puerto Rico entered the Pan American Games as a separate team competing against the athletes of the United States. Many adopted a commuter strategy, traveling to New York in search of employment to support relatives on the island. The Nuyoricans brought their music, salsa dancing, culinary tastes, and baseball with them. More than a dozen Hispanic baseball leagues, most of them with Puerto Rican teams, formed in New York following World War II. An athletic federation of Hispanic leagues organized in 1954, and the city counted at least 190 Latin teams by the 1960s. As early as 1957 the *Revista Record* analyzed the embrace of the game on the Puerto Rican psyche when it stated: "Destiny disunites us but sport unites us."[28]

Sport offered hope for some and an opiate for others; by the late 1950s all could revel in new national heroes. Juan "Pachin" Vicens, the leading scorer in the Puerto Rican Basketball League, earned recognition as the best amateur player in the world at the international tournament of 1959. Carlos Ortiz ruled boxing's lightweight and junior welterweight ranks between 1959 and 1967, and Jose Torres won Olympic fame with a silver medal in 1956 and the professional light heavyweight crown in 1965. A host of baseball players emerged as stars in the Major Leagues, only to confront a bewildering racism in the United States. A comparative social study determined that "in the United States, a man's color determines what class he belongs to[;] in Puerto Rico, a man's class determines what color he is." Puerto Rico had eighteen different terms to designate one's skin color, while the United States saw only black and white.[29]

Vic Pollet faced the indignity of Anglophiles changing his surname to Power. In Florida he faced jail for challenging a white gas station attendant over the attempted purchase of a soft drink. Yet Vic Power persevered to win four Gold Glove awards as a top fielder in the Major Leagues. Orlando Cepeda, son of the great Perucho Cepeda, refused the dictates of a racist manager who forbade the speaking of Spanish in the clubhouse. He lived in quarters segregated from teammates and suffered in restaurants unwilling to serve him. When his father died, young Cepeda endured the pains of racism in order to support his mother. He triumphed in spite of the hurts, winning Rookie of the Year honors in 1958 and recognition as a home run champion, a two-time leader in runs batted in, and the Most Valuable Player in the league. Upon his election into the Baseball Hall of Fame in 1999, Cepeda's hometown of Ponce erupted into a spontaneous celebration of delight. Characteristically, his induction speech called for greater recognition of Latin players.[30]

The greatest of the Puerto Rican athletic heroes, Roberto Walker Clemente inspired a generation of Latin players in a long career (1955–1972) with the Pittsburgh Pirates. During that time Clemente amassed

3,000 hits, four batting titles, twelve Gold Gloves, and designations as both the World Series and the National League's Most Valuable Player. From humble origins, the son of sugar mill workers, Clemente attained legendary status as arguably the best right fielder in the history of baseball. Latin Americans cherished his humanitarian efforts as well. When an earthquake devastated Nicaragua in 1972, Clemente organized a relief mission. On this trip Clemente's plane crashed into the Atlantic Ocean, robbing Puerto Rico of its most beloved son. The newly elected governor canceled inaugural celebrations, and the island commemorated Clemente's lasting influence with the dedication of a $15 million sports complex. The Puerto Rican community in Chicago named its local high school after him, and in the New York area a state park and a hospital bear his name. As late as 1998 the National League named Clemente's widow as the honorary captain of that season's All-Star team. Rob Ruck, a Pittsburgh writer, has stated: "For those on the island, he is simply their greatest hero and legend . . . a pan-Caribbean sporting demigod. . . . Latin ballplayers breathe Clemente. He is of such historical significance to us. He transcends generations and borders. Tony Pena of the Dominican Republic keeps a portrait of Roberto displayed in his trophy room[;] Ozzie Guillen has a small altar for him in his home in Caracas. He is a god in Ozzie's religion." Nicaraguans renamed a ballpark in Clemente's honor and halt play for five minutes each December to remember his greatness and charity. In 1989 then Nicaraguan president Daniel Ortega bestowed his country's highest honor on Clemente posthumously.[31]

Despite such reverence and acclaim throughout the Latino Caribbean, American electors failed to select Clemente to baseball's all-century team in 1999. Amid charges of lingering racism, a Latino uproar ensued. Clemente, in fact, had received more votes than five other players who were awarded the coveted honor by the selection committee. Richard Lapchick, a sport sociologist, had already offered an explanation in his analysis that more than 95 percent of the sportswriters were white and that many were inclined to believe that stereotypical "natural" gifts rated lower than those gained by a disciplined work ethic. That betrayal proved yet one more insult to the Puerto Rican nation. Puerto Rico produced so many players of distinction that it founded its own Baseball Hall of Fame, further establishing a national identity separate from the United States.[32]

After Clemente's death other athletes assumed the cape of nationalism. In 1976 Wilfredo Benitez became the youngest boxer ever to gain a championship when he won the junior welterweight title at age seventeen. One of the Nuyoricans born in New York, Benitez made the reverse migration with his family, returning to Puerto Rico at age seven. He added the welterweight and super welterweight crowns in a stellar career.

Another Nuyorican, Butch Lee, star of the Marquette University basketball team, elected to play for the Puerto Rican Olympic team, which nearly upset the United States. Athletic controversies more directly affected Puerto Rican politics in 1979 when the island hosted the Pan American Games in San Juan. Governor Carlos Romero Barcelo, an ardent advocate for statehood, favored the flag of the United States over the Puerto Rican flag for the opening ceremonies. He suffered vehement, derisive, and immediate abuse for his choice, and in the next year's elections he lost more than fifty thousand votes. The situation exacerbated when, despite Governor Romero's objections and in defiance of the U.S. boycott of the 1980 Moscow Olympics, a Puerto Rican contingent traveled to Russia. When Cuba hosted the 1982 Central American and Caribbean Games, the governor refused to appropriate the expenditures needed to hold the event, but a populist fund-raising campaign among the masses secured the means for travel and competition. The four hundred Puerto Rican athletes, joined by hundreds who ignored the U.S. government's ban on travel to Cuba, responded by winning 105 medals, reinforcing the importance of sport to creating and substantiating a separate national identity.[33]

During the rest of the twentieth century, the flamboyant Hector "Macho" Camacho carried the Puerto Rican flag and the island's hopes throughout a long ring career, while Angel Cordero emerged as one of America's best jockeys. Cordero won the Kentucky Derby three times and claimed more than $121 million in prize money while earning election to the National Thoroughbred Racing Hall of Fame. Juan "Chi Chi" Rodriguez, son of a poor plantation worker, even became a star in the genteel circles of professional golf. Rodriguez learned to play as a caddie in his native land, then garnered more than $1 million on the professional tour in the United

States. His colorful play made him a fan favorite and even more successful on the senior tour, where his winnings topped $6 million. Women, too, found athletic success as the national softball team claimed the championship at the Central American and Caribbean Games in both 1982 and 1993. Gigi Fernandez won two Olympic gold medals in tennis before joining the professional tour.[34]

Still, baseball remained at the center of Puerto Rican life. When the Arecibo team won the Caribbean Series in Caracas in 1983, a cruise ship transported them home to a massive celebration. One of the players remarked: "It was like we won the World Series. We visited the governor's mansion and the roads from San Juan to Arecibo were lined two, three deep with people on our parade route."[35] During the rest of the century, Puerto Rican players excelled on the baseball diamonds of North America. Juan Gonzalez, Ivan Rodriguez, Edgar Martinez, Carlos Baerga, Benito Santiago, and Roberto and Sandy Alomar were only a few who became household names. Their success, however, could not transform the Puerto Rican economy.

In 1990 Puerto Ricans earned a per capita income of $4,117 annually, far below the average $18,660 of mainland citizens. American companies on the island still enjoyed a 35 percent profit margin during that decade, and 20 percent of island inhabitants remained unemployed. More than half subsisted below the poverty level. Nationalists continued to resist the imposition of the English language and the commercial development of the San Juan historic district and similar projects in Ponce, as strip malls and factory outlets littered other parts of the island. U.S. military training programs that had regularly bombed offshore Vieques Island met with a national protest and sit-in joined by mainland sympathizers. Puerto Rican resistance to Americanization continued in the adherence to a separate Olympic team and an independent entry in international beauty contests. On four occasions wild celebrations accompanied the choice of Puerto Rican women as Miss Universe pageant winners. A rally for boxer Felix Trinidad forced organizers to remove the U.S. flag from the stage, as fans claimed, "This is our victory."[36]

The Puerto Rican flag remains at the center of the debate over national identity and sport, particularly international endeavors that allow for its display. A Puerto Rican college professor acknowledged the symbolic importance of the opening Olympic ceremonies by stating: "It does not matter that we don't win anything[;] it's that procession that we have to have." Juan Garcia Passalacqua, a Puerto Rican intellectual with little affinity for sport, concurred: "Sport has become the most important single issue at the level of the masses with respect to the national identity, more important than language." Sport allows for the harmonious convergence of Protestant and middle-class values (such as individualism) and the communalism favored by Catholicism and Puerto Rican familial structures. Baseball, in particular, provides an opportunity for individual accomplishments within a team setting. Athletic stars and international competitions with a separate flag reinforce a sense of common identity, pride, and esteem.[37]

Puerto Rican pride and independence manifested itself through its athletes in the summer of 2004. When some Major League teams replaced the traditional song "Take Me Out to the Ball Game" during the seventh inning with the more patriotic "God Bless America" in support of the American war in Iraq, Puerto Rican star Carlos Delgado took a brave, and controversial, stand. He not only refused to rise to his feet for the homage but also indicated that he did not support the invasion. Moreover, he registered his disenchantment with the U.S. government's treatment of the people in Puerto Rico. At the Olympic Games that summer, Puerto Rican basketball players basked in their defeat of the U.S. team, as Elias Ayuso declared: "We're a small island with a big heart." Carlos Arroyo pulled at his jersey to accentuate the "Puerto Rico" on his chest for the television cameras, and Coach Julio Toro explained: "That was him telling his island of 4 million people he was very proud to beat the big collosal [*sic*] from the north."[38]

Still, Puerto Rico remains a conflicted, blurred, and fractured culture divided by politics, class, and identity. Americanization urbanized 70 percent of the island, a substantial increase over the 20 percent of 1898. Anglicization failed to gain a firm hold, yet tourism and casinos have greatly commercialized the society. Protestant proselytizers found little success, with only 10 percent of island residents converting. In some areas African Yoruba religious beliefs and bestial sacrifices retain their allure for animists. The YMCA failed to institute sabbatarian reforms, and its promotion of basketball and volleyball now herald national teams and native athletic stars. Internal differences pit Creoles against peasants, indigenous residents against Cuban and Dominican immigrants, and ardent nationalists against the contaminating influences of the Nuyorican culture. The latter is almost evenly matched, with the 2000 U.S. Census indicating 3.8 million island residents and 3.4 million in the United States. That diaspora has also transformed mainland popular culture with the acceptance of Latino music, salsa dancing, and Hispanic foods. Puerto Rican culture is not easily classified as Latin American, Caribbean, or American. A 1998 referendum underscored this ambiguity of identity. When given the choices of statehood, independence, or continued commonwealth status, more than half of Puerto Rican voters chose none of the above. It seems that after more than a century, baseball remains the strongest bond between the island and the United States as well as a major factor in preserving Puerto Rican national identity.[39]

Sport and Economic Retaliation in the Dominican Republic

The Dominican Republic had been a Spanish colony for three centuries before gaining its independence in 1844. American Protestants had begun settlements on the northeastern part of the island at Samana Bay twenty years before independence. The U.S. government desired the same location for a naval base by the mid-nineteenth century. The country fell under Spanish colonial rule again between 1861 and 1865 before the United States recognized its independence in 1866. Haiti, which won its independence from France in an 1804 slave revolt, occupied the western third of the shared island of Hispaniola and posed a constant threat to Dominicans, who sought a U.S. protectorate. The U.S. Senate rejected President Ulysses Grant's annexation attempt in 1870, but that hardly dimmed American intentions for a Caribbean naval station.[1]

Cubans settled on the island, bringing their love of baseball to the Dominicans in 1891. English-speaking blacks from the

West Indies also migrated to the country. They resided at San Pedro de Macoris and La Romana, east of the capital, where they established the traditional British sport of cricket. The two sports competed for Dominicans' attention over the next generation.[2]

The case for baseball grew with American intervention on the island. U.S. interests in safeguarding American shores as well as the Caribbean entry to a proposed canal in Central America intensified by the end of the century. The British Navy still ruled the seas, and the growing German fleet and its Caribbean activities posed a particular threat to U.S. interests in the region. The assassination of Dominican dictator Ulises Heureaux in 1899 left his country bankrupt and in debt to New York and European financiers. Consequent insurrections provided a viable excuse for intercession by the United States. U.S. Marines landed in the country in 1905 to establish security for the commercial enterprises and to assume control of the Dominican customs house and finances in order to pay off the debt. Rear Admiral Charles Sigsbee, the Caribbean squadron commander, voiced his opinion of the Dominicans: "The Spaniard has intense and aggressive pride. . . . The Negro is highly imitative and lacks a sense of proportion. Cojoin these qualifications and we have the Hispano-Negro, with his lofty declarations and his poor performance."[3]

President Theodore Roosevelt shared Sigsbee's view of the Dominicans as immature, less civilized, and in need of guidance. The perception carried over to the mixed races of other Caribbean nations, and fearful of their submission to European powers, Roosevelt issued his corollary to the Monroe Doctrine. In it he justified American police powers throughout the region as a duty to civilized nations, part of the "white man's burden." Under such guise U.S. presidents kept the sailors and marines busy in the region over the next three decades; wherever the navy intervened its bats and balls soon appeared.

During the administration of President William Howard Taft, American capital flowed into the Dominican Republic. With the assassination of President Ramon Caceres in 1911, U.S. Marines moved in to protect U.S. property and supervise the necessary election. The United States tried to secure its own interests by installing a reluctant and ineffective local archbishop as president. His quick departure required another election in 1914, in which the United States increased its hold. A civil war ensued in 1916; when no Dominican proved willing to preside as an American puppet, the marines established a military government that lasted until 1924.[4]

Baseball served as a useful means of social control. As early as 1913 James Sullivan, the U.S. minister to the Dominican Republic, wrote to Secretary of State William Jennings Bryan:

> *I deem it worthy of the Department's notice that the American game of baseball is being played and supported here with great enthusiasm. The remarkable effect of this outlet for the animal spirits of the young men, is that they are leaving the plazas where they were in the habit of congregating and talking revolution and are resorting to the ball fields where they become wildly partizen [sic] each for his favorite team. The importance of this new interest . . . should not be minimized. It satisfies a craving in the nature of the people for exciting conflict, and is a real substitute for the contest in the hill-sides with rifles, if it could be fostered and made important by a league of teams . . . it well might be one factor in the salvation of the nation.*[5]

Sullivan failed to recognize that although baseball might pacify the Dominicans it could also assume resistive and retaliatory elements. A year later Enrique Hernandez, a pitcher for El Club Nuevo, threw a no-hitter as the Dominicans defeated the sailors from the USS *Washington*. Thereafter relations deteriorated precipitously. Sullivan, who had been a gambler and a boxing promoter before his assignment to the Dominican post, caused a scandal in 1915 when the *New York World* exposed his bribe and kickback scheme in collusion with the Dominican president and its national bank. By 1916 the marines battled natives in armed struggles. When the United States canceled the scheduled 1917 election, the national legislature and the president resigned in protest. Marine officers with little legal expertise served as judges of provost courts in the military districts, often meting out harsh punishments. The United States effected martial law and censored the press. In establishing a national constabulary in 1917, a marine officer indicated that race continued to play an overriding factor in judgments: "As a general rule, the degree of intelligence increased with the decrease of the ebony tinge. . . . All of our best non-commissioned officers were either of

Porto Rican descent, or had a larger proportion of Spanish than of Negro blood in their veins."[6] White marine officers ensured that leadership roles within the constabulary remained in Anglo hands.

A guerrilla war ensued after 1916. As General Edward Craig admitted: "The natives had no liking for the Marines."[7] Admiral William Caperton shared more explicit feelings: "I have never seen such hatred displayed by one people for another as I notice and feel here. . . . We positively have not a friend in the land."[8] Wealthy families refused to let their sons join the constabulary, while peasants actively aided the native combatants. The U.S. troops initiated public schooling, but those who could afford it sent their children to private schools. Another American, a southerner, created a faux pas upon attending a state ball. Assuming a mulatto to be the waiter, he ordered a drink, only to discover the purported server to be the Dominican secretary of foreign affairs. Such racial attitudes permeated American relations and fostered long-held resentments.[9]

By 1918 the Dominican warriors were engaged in a crusade for national emancipation, which the Americans blamed on their World War I foe. Colonel George Thorpe wrote to his superior General Joe Pendleton: "He is certainly getting a lot out of the niggers. . . . It shows the handwork [sic] of the German."[10] The conflict continued after the armistice, however, with 116 combat incidents in 1920 alone. Between 1917 and 1922 the marines recorded 370 such occurrences, which required reinforcements and the employment of an air squadron. Baseball continued despite the hostilities, serving a surrogate purpose when natives met marines on the diamond. In urban areas such confrontations only spurred Dominican nationalism, and the local media extolled players as folk heroes. Fellito Guerra, one of the country's star players, even refused to play in the United States while his country labored under American occupation.[11]

While Dominican culture resisted Americanization, the United States secured its grip on the economy in the 1920s. By that time 95 percent of Dominican sugar went to the States and twelve American companies owned 75 percent of the sugar acreage. More than half of the Dominican imports arrived from the capitalist giant. Baseball superseded cockfighting as the national sport, while Dominicans used the game to promote their own dignity and national pride. Rob Ruck asserted that "Garveyism swept through the ingenios and San Pedro during the United States Marines' occupation."[12] Marcus Garvey, a militant Jamaican operating from the United States, preached black nationalism, colonial independence, and self-help. He, too, lost his battle with the U.S. government, which indicted him for mail fraud in 1923, then imprisoned and deported him.

Amid the turmoil a strong and ruthless Dominican leader emerged. Rafael Trujillo rose to power through the ranks of the Dominican constabulary, serving as a commander in 1928 and assuming the presidency in 1930. Trujillo presided for thirty years, maintaining close ties with the United States while also promoting Dominican nationalism, particularly through his use of baseball. Trujillo organized teams and built fields for the sugar cane workers in conjunction with their American employers, who viewed the game as wholesome recreation. Poor Dominicans perceived it as a means of social mobility as teams from Puerto Rico, Cuba, and Venezuela began hiring the top talent. Baseball also recognized and accentuated one's physical prowess, a prevailing factor in the concept of machismo.[13]

The Trujillo era also fostered the Latin concept of *bèisbol romantico*, in which Dominicans developed their own style of play. Whereas American teams, like the American military, emphasized power, Dominicans favored flair, grace, speed, and hustle, the qualities of an artist rather than a behemoth. Fans developed deep loyalties to their regional teams, and Trujillo ensured that his favorite, Escogido, was well stocked with outstanding players, including stars from the American Negro League.[14]

The 1937 season carried particular political importance as Trujillo decided to use the game to improve his standing with the populace. His political opponents owned top teams in the Dominican League and spared little expense to attract the best players from around the Caribbean as well as several African Americans from the United States. Trujillo's brother, a baseball zealot, bankrolled the Licey team, but Escogido and Licey combined forces as the Ciudad Trujillo Dragons in quest of the national title and political favor. Moreover, given the stacked rosters of their opponents, the Trujillos lavished enormous amounts of cash on legendary stars in the Negro National League to obtain their services. The defectors included Satchel Paige, Josh Gibson, and "Cool Papa" Bell, among others, and their departure crippled the Pittsburgh Crawfords team, which had to forfeit its own pursuit of a championship. Many considered Paige to be the game's greatest pitcher, Gibson inspired awe as the "black Babe Ruth," and Bell was baseball's premier base stealer. For good measure Trujillo added Puerto Rican superstar Perucho Cepeda. Despite their talents the Dragons trailed in the deciding series. Trujillo allegedly jailed the Americans to ensure their safety and suitable physical condition for the championship. Armed guards accompanied their transfer to games; one particular loss resulted in a discharge of their weapons, which Paige took as a warning. He later exaggerated such stories as a death threat, but in any case he rallied from behind for a 6–5 win in the championship game.[15]

The overwhelming expense of the 1937 season decimated the Dominican professional league until midcentury. The reckless spending on imported players left little for the locals in the aftermath. Even Licey and Escogido returned to semipro status, which only spurred regional rivalries within the country. With the top players conscripted by other Caribbean teams, the situation gave rise to a new generation of young stars, many from the area of San Pedro de Macoris. Sugar mills funded teams, hoping to provide wholesome recreation during slack periods. Baseball provided much more for the players and fans. As one player stated: "These games [between refineries] were bigger than the World Series to us. . . . Baseball was the only thing. . . . There was no movies . . . everybody was on the field. So when you [lost] a game, everybody [was] crying or . . . fighting."[16] The passion and excitement of sport compensated for the dreary labor of the cane fields.

The local passion for baseball transferred to nationalism when the Dominican Republic faced Cuba in a 1944 series. Over the previous two decades, Cuba had claimed the Caribbean tournament title in all but two years. Nevertheless, the Dominicans stunned the Cubans, winning 5 of the 7 games. Such triumphs stirred patriotism, provided a showcase for talented players to exhibit their skills to professional bidders, and allowed the country to measure itself against Caribbean rivals. The last proved particularly important for national self-esteem as Cubans and Puerto Ricans often derided Dominicans as poor cousins and country bumpkins.[17]

The resurrection of the Dominican professional league occurred in 1951 with four teams. The summer schedule coincided with that of Major League Baseball in the United States, but the Dominican League did not yet have American ties and so remained locally controlled. The switch to winter league play in 1955 brought many more American players to Dominican shores in search of supplemental pay. Many Major Leaguers at that time derived from working-class families, and the reserve system tied them to one club and restricted salaries before the era of free agency. The influx of Americans also brought greater interest in Dominican players after Jackie Robinson's breakthrough relaxed the racial ban on blacks in the Majors. Dominicans represented a new and cheaper labor force for American teams. Ozzie Virgil, signed in 1953, became the first of the islanders to arrive in the Majors with the New York Giants.[18]

Trujillo's son, a military general, noticed the talent of a young pitcher named Juan Marichal. Within days Marichal got his air force draft notice. His assignment appointed him to the general's favorite baseball team, where the game was taken quite seriously. After losing a doubleheader, for example, the players endured five days in jail. Marichal won the approval of the younger Trujillo and signed a contract with the New York Giants that included a meager $500 bonus. Marichal pitched a one-hitter in his Major League debut, an auspicious start in a Hall of Fame career. Dominicans adored him as a national hero, and a record-setting crowd witnessed his 1965 homecoming start in winter league play. Dominican players considered such off-season work a national obligation to their countrymen. Upon induction into the Baseball Hall of Fame in 1983, Marichal stated that "the triumph of getting in the Hall of Fame wasn't just for me[;] it was for all the people of the Dominican Republic."[19]

Dominican players, like the Cubans and the Puerto Ricans before them, bore the burdens of racism in the United States. Jesus Alou, one of three Dominican brothers to make it to the North American ranks, had to Anglicize his name to Jay because his real name offended some religious sensibilities. Felipe Alou paid a fine for simply talking to his brother Matty, a member of the opposing team, before a game. Fraternization with the enemy overruled family loyalty. Authorities had little to fear as Matty led the league in batting in 1966.[20]

The Cuban Revolution of 1959 curtailed the flow of players from Cuba, while the assassination of Trujillo in 1961 increased the interest in Dominican players. Political events, however, disrupted the baseball migration. More than twenty-two thousand U.S. Marines landed in 1965 to suppress a left wing political movement. Despite their efforts the Dominican Revolutionary Party took office, and the American occupying force soon left amid graffiti that entreated "Yankee Go Home."[21]

However, baseball brought the Americans back to the island in search of talent. By the 1970s both the Toronto Blue Jays and the Los Angeles Dodgers had opened baseball academies on the island, and other teams, including the Japanese, followed. Such institutions avoided the draft of players in North America and procured players at a young age at minimal cost to the teams—but also caused the individuals to forfeit their educations. While criticism has led to improvements at such institutions, most young players learn baseball and little else, hardly preparing the majority of "students" who will never make it to Major League status for life outside of baseball. Furthermore, the recruitment of young players, which meant removing them from the ranks of local organizations, brought a deterioration of national play. Those who attain star status at the Major League level are often discouraged or prohibited from playing before their homeland fans in the winter league by team owners who fear an injury and thus the loss of their valuable property. That issue has driven a wedge in Dominican society and disrupted the nationalistic bond between players and fans.[22]

The loss of their baseball players struck a severe blow to Dominican pride. Manny Mota, a former Major League player, asserted: "If you ask any Dominican what he is proudest of, he will read you a list of ballplayers. This country doesn't have much, but we know we are the best in the world at one thing (baseball)."[23] Mota made no idle boast. By the turn of the twenty-first century Dominicans comprised the largest number of all Major League Baseball (MLB) players born outside the United States. Yet the typical Dominican, who lived vicariously through baseball, made only $79 per year in 1989. The 125 U.S. companies operating in the Dominican Republic did so with tax-exempt status yet paid workers less than a minimum wage. Baseball had to soothe the soul, if not the palates. As Alan Klein has stated: "There are no cultural heroes with a machete in their hands."[24]

Baseball players are one of the Dominican Republic's main exports. At the start of the 2000 MLB season, Dominicans comprised nearly 10 percent of the rosters of Major League teams. The previous year North American professional teams signed 860 foreign players to contracts—473, or 55 percent, of them from the Dominican Republic. Carlos Bernhardt, the Baltimore Orioles' director of scouting in Latin America, claimed: "Everybody wants to become the new Sammy Sosa. Everybody wants to become the new Pedro Martinez. Everybody wants to become the new Manny Ramirez. Everybody has the dream." Criticisms of conditions in the baseball academies and exploitation of the young players led MLB to enact a rule prohibiting professional teams from signing anyone before he had reached the age of sixteen years and nine months. Independent sports agents, however, face no such restrictions, and they recruit children as young as age twelve.[25]

Agents may also exploit young players, but they have provided Dominicans with greater negotiating power at the contract table. Whereas Texas had originally signed Sammy Sosa, (who has since hit more than 500 home runs) for only $3,500 in 1985, such bargains are no longer the case. In 1988 the Dodgers got Pedro Martinez, a dominating pitcher, for only $8,000, but by 2001, a sixteen-year-old outfielder named Juan Severino, who had an American agent, could expect at least a $100,000 signing bonus in addition to a lucrative contract. Even young players have recognized their own power to assume greater control of their futures. Joe Kehoskie, Severino's agent, stated: "It's shocking, but it's not unusual to see a 16 year-old kid already on his third agent." Relatively uneducated Dominicans soon grasped the elements of high finance economics.[26]

Former Dominican employees of the Major League academies have rebelled as well, establishing their own independent baseball schools under local and native direction. The young players have found other means to manipulate the system to their advantage, such as by falsifying or presenting fictitious birth certificates that declare them to be younger than their actual age and therefore more valuable in potential years of service. Still other Dominicans have made a handsome living as "bird dogs" who hunt the island in search of future stars for the Major League teams.[27]

Bud Selig, the MLB commissioner, hopes to enact a worldwide player draft to reassert the team owners' economic advantage. If the draft were effected, all drafted players would be subject to contracts offered only by the drafting team, essentially ending their free agent status, as is already the case for American and Puerto Rican hopefuls. Victor Garcia Sued, a Dominican politician and founder of an independent baseball academy, has vowed to fight such a move by organizing opposition in his own country and other Latin American nations. While Garcia may have personal reasons for attacking the American economic hegemony, he has also identified the one viable means of Dominican resistance—baseball. Dominican players have allegedly taken matters upon themselves as well by playing poorly to discredit American managers sent to the island by parent organizations in the states.[28]

Reminiscent of the military occupations of the past, American baseball interests descended on the island in the late twentieth century in search of cheap labor. After initially losing control to these impresarios, Dominicans have begun to reassert themselves by resisting such outside influences. Unlike the Cubans who use sport as a political equalizer in the Communist struggle with capitalism, and unlike the Puerto Ricans who have suffered an identity crisis through their long association with American culture, the Dominicans have chosen a middle road. They continue to revel in their local culture, adhering to merengue in the face of American popular music. Baseball may have replaced cockfighting as the national sport, but Dominicans have learned to turn exploitation of their human resources into individual and national gain, as wealthy professionals typically maintain island homes and lifestyles and contribute to community services as a civic responsibility, thereby bringing American dollars to the local economy. The United States no longer deploys troops or maintains any military bases in the country, long since finding it cheaper to dominate the island economy instead. Like the American companies, the baseball team owners found a source of cheap labor, but the Dominicans have learned to fight back. In San Pedro de Macoris, the most prolific supplier of Major League stars and the home of Sammy Sosa, who now commands a salary equivalent to the top American stars, the hospital presents a baseball glove to all newborn male babies.[29]

The Outposts of Empire

Samoa

A Dutch explorer noted the Samoan islands in 1722. In 1782 the French lost a dozen sailors, killed by the inhabitants when trying to land there. British missionaries had settled the region by 1830, establishing Christian schools and attempting to end the tribal warfare that afflicted Samoan society. Whaling ships increased Anglo contact during the 1830s. In 1838 the United States sent an exploratory expedition to the South Pacific under the command of Captain Charles Wilkes, which arrived in Samoa the following year. The export of copra to America began in 1842, and American missionaries soon set out in search of souls. There they found a polytheistic and patriarchal society headed by an elected chief and a communal ownership of land. Family honor ensured that no poverty and only limited crime existed, as each clan held responsibility for its individual members.[1]

Missionary influences, with their Anglo emphasis on individualism rather than communalism and the clerical habit of wearing cumbersome clothes despite the salubrious climate, conflicted with traditional Samoan lifestyles. Samoan girls who failed to adhere to Western standards of decorum faced corporal punishment. The missionaries also espoused the superiority of their written word over the oral culture of the local population. The transformation of Samoan leisure culture evolved similarly. Chiefs traditionally hunted sacred but inedible pigeons for sport, but missionaries prohibited the pastime because it interfered with church attendance. The introduction of firearms eventually decimated the pigeon population. The Anglos also levied fines as high as $5 when adolescent boys and some young women tattooed their bodies as a customary sign of maturity. Various ball-and-stick games developed into intervillage competitions for food prizes, which the English converted to cricket matches. The combative sports of boxing, wrestling, spear throwing, and battling with war clubs, as well as the aquatic pastimes of surfing, sailing, outrigger canoeing, and swimming, resisted the religious mandates. A German surgeon reported during his 1890s sojourn in the islands: "Playing games is [still] very popular."[2]

The Germans, British, and Americans all showed interest in the islands by the late nineteenth century as trade increased with Australia and New Zealand. President Ulysses Grant sent a mission to Samoa in 1872, with Grant's friend Colonel A. B. Steinberger as a special agent. Steinberger returned to the archipelago in 1875 and effected a conspiracy with a German trading company in which he proclaimed himself to be the premier with ultimate powers. A brief five-month reign resulted in Steinberger's imprisonment by the British on the island of Fiji. The United States secured rights to a coaling station and a commercial treaty in 1878, then defended the natives, whom the Germans attacked in 1885. An 1886 tripartite mission of the Anglo-Saxon powers determined that the Samoans were incapable of self-rule. Then, to the consternation of American commercial interests, the Germans established a colony. A Berlin conference in 1889 reached consensus relative to a triple protectorate by the Western powers.[3]

An 1899 civil war between Samoan chieftains brought Western intervention and the establishment of a provisional government. In the deliberations, Great Britain agreed to withdraw from the islands in exchange for suzerainty over Tonga, while the Germans retained possession of Western Samoa. The eastern islands became American Samoa. Because of its fueling station at Pago Pago, the U.S. Navy assumed responsibility for governance. Within a short time twenty chiefs had ceded half of the territory to the United States. President Theodore Roosevelt acknowledged their gift with a present of medals and inscribed watches in 1904, but Samoans had already been denied a commercial permit to operate an interisland ferry on the grounds that they were not American citizens. Thereafter the American administrators promoted and assisted business groups from the mainland rather than local native islanders.[4]

One of the first undertakings was the construction of a mansion for the naval commandant in 1903. Perched prominently on a hilltop overlooking the bay at Pago Pago, the edifice dominated the landscape as a symbol of American might, not unlike the later prominence of Baguio in the Philippines. The navy transformed more than the natural environment, however. It replaced the traditional barter economy with wage labor and undermined the power of the local chiefs by instituting judicial courts. Commander B. F. Tilley established a system of public schools that required English-language instruction, thus denigrating the local dialect. Boys received vocational training for the new capitalist workforce, while girls were relegated to unequal roles in domestic science classes. To ensure greater productivity the navy prohibited the traditional *malaga*, a show of hospitality for large group visits, deeming the time and expense a detriment to disciplined work schedules. Henceforth the government limited visiting parties to no more than eight persons. By 1909 three schools operated in the islands; two years later Governor W. M. Crose attempted to introduce moral training into the curriculum. When a lack of federal aid thwarted his organization of the schools, Crose sent some boys to Hawaiian boarding schools.[5]

The United States neglected Samoa in other respects as well, including its refusal of a request for an experimental agricultural station in 1905 (it was finally granted in 1946). Samoans did not take kindly to the rapid transition in lifestyle, refusing to work on the labor-intensive cocoa plantations, which required the importation of Chinese laborers to the islands.

The chiefs further protested in 1920, a year after the governor enacted a ban on interracial marriages between American sailors and Samoan women without gubernatorial consent. Government impositions included Western notions of hygiene, requiring village latrines and fines for dilatory inhabitants. A patrolling inspector of sanitation enforced the edict. The racial, class, and paternalistic connotations proved obvious to the natives. When the Samoan chiefs lodged a formal protest against the governance and their own high chiefs' acquiescence in the submission, the recalcitrant leaders were imprisoned for heading an insurrection.[6]

New Zealand had seized Western Samoa from the Germans at the outbreak of World War I. When the Mau movement, aimed at securing greater political rights, emerged throughout the islands during the 1920s, the Anglos brutally suppressed it. More diplomatically, the American Samoans requested a de-emphasis on Americanization in the schools as their traditional culture waned. They had little recourse when ignored, however. The New Zealanders demonstrated Anglo might on December 28, 1929, known as Black Sunday in Western Samoa, when soldiers machine-gunned a peaceful Mau parade, killing the head chief. Colonel Stephen Allen hardly lamented the loss of life as he characterized Samoans as apes. In American Samoa the United States declared martial law and exiled Mau leaders, while the navy adhered to its racial segregation practices in public places. The Mau could retaliate only by refusing to pay their taxes. Such demonstrative Anglo perceptions of white superiority lingered for years in the islands.[7]

By World War II the Samoan children attended nineteen schools but were prepared only for menial labor because no high school was erected until 1946. Income levels in the South Pacific actually increased under Japanese occupation during the war. In 1951 the U.S. Navy relinquished control to the U.S. Department of the Interior, which appointed a governor; the Samoans also finally got some elected officials.[8]

As in Puerto Rico, the adoption of American sport forms has enabled Samoans to resurrect pride in their national identity. In 1963 Samoa sent a tennis team to the first South Pacific Games, in Fiji. Five years later Tony Solaita became the first Samoan to make it to Major League baseball, with the New York Yankees. His fellow citizens took satisfaction in a career that lasted until 1979. The increasing Americanization of Samoan culture came with a price, as greater commercialization also brought increased tourism to the islands. Property values increased, but so did absentee owners and many Samoans proved unable to afford the real estate in their own land. Commercialization reduced traditional farming to the extent that native tropical plants had to be imported by the end of the century. Samoans lost a greater share of their independence and self-sufficiency. By 1990 their per capita income stood at $2,302 per year, about a quarter of that for residents of the Virgin Islands or Guam, and half of what Puerto Ricans made. More than half of the native population lived in poverty, and only 10 percent earned college degrees. Samoans gained universal suffrage in 1977, but little of their culture remained by that time. The English language, American media, schools, the YMCA, mainland fraternal organizations, and the chamber of commerce presented a mainland appearance in a tropical setting.[9]

Samoans continued to resist the cultural disintegration by adhering to *matai*, the chief system, in lieu of a formal government, although a territorial assembly has met since 1950. A vast amount of Samoan land is still held in communal trust, and children maintain a great respect for elders. Samoans have learned to adapt American sports to coalesce with their own cultural values. Baseball merges teamwork with American individualism, while communal team sports like rugby and American football allow males to assert their masculinity through demonstrations of physicality. Samoans have succeeded notably on college gridirons and in the professional ranks of the National Football League.[10]

While such accommodation brings the disparate cultures closer together, the formation of independent athletic teams reinforces a sense of a separate national identity. Samoa continued to send a tennis team to subsequent South Pacific Games competition after 1963. In 1981 its basketball team competed in the first Oceania regional tournament, in Fiji, and it has since secured developmental funding from the International Olympic Committee (IOC). In 1985 Samoans established their own national Olympic committee, further enhancing their self-esteem and separate cultural identification. In 1997 Samoan Little League baseball players toured New Zealand, winning all of their nine games, a more restrained athletic retribution for the horrors of Black Sunday.[11]

Sport has achieved even greater prominence as a way to accommodate with the commercial capitalist culture as high school athletes earn college scholarships in football and softball. In 2001 Samoa conducted its first American Samoa Games, and its best basketball players joined others from Fiji, Vanuatu, New Caledonia, and the Solomon Islands in an all-star contingent for competition in Sydney, Australia. The regional alliance signaled a growing sense of difference even as the globalization of sport brought distinct cultural groups together in a common purpose. That distinction and the playful nature of Samoan culture became evident at the World Track Championships held in Edmonton, Canada, in 2001. Trevor Misapeka, who had attended American universities as a three-hundred-pound football player, represented Samoa as a shot-putter. When the International Amateur Athletic Federation (IAAF) abruptly changed the rules that had allowed two automatic qualifiers in the field events in favor of permitting two participants in the running events instead, Misapeka switched his entry to the one-hundred-meter dash. Despite the seriousness of the occasion, the IAAF had to conform to its own dictate. Misapeka treated spectators to the sight of his lumbering frame adorned in tattoos and covered in a sleeveless black T-shirt. His ordinary gym shoes propelled him down the track to a time of 14.28 seconds, nearly 4 seconds behind the heat winner. The sportswriters labeled him "Trevor the Tortoise," but Misapeka claimed a personal best and Samoans reveled in his new celebrity. Sports had allowed them the final laugh and the chance to poke fun at the staid Anglos who had controlled them for more than a century.[12]

Guam

Guam, a long-held colony of Spain, accrued to the United States on December 10, 1898, with the Treaty of Paris, which formally ended the Spanish-American War. The transformation to American dependency began almost immediately as administrators replaced the Spanish and native Chamorro cultures. English supplanted the Spanish language, and American holidays unseated the traditional local festivals on the social calendar. The village chiefs, who had retained their powers under the Spanish, lost their control. The new governor expelled Catholic friars from the island and prohibited religious processions. The prohibitions extended to leisure as well, including a ban on cockfights and even on public whistling or serenading. The U.S. Navy imposed its own standards of morality to the extent of regulating the length of women's dresses. As in Samoa, the Chamorro society revolved around communal settlements of extended family. Such cohesion fragmented with the U.S. emphasis on individualism and the navy's confiscation of Chamorro lands for its own recreational uses. As in the other colonies of the growing American empire, the navy practiced a policy of racial exclusion, denying the locals access to the beaches that served military personnel. The natives had little recourse; the insular cases of 1900–1901, decided in the U.S. Supreme Court, determined that territories were not states and therefore that residents lacked the same constitutional rights.[13]

By 1922 Guam had adopted the curriculum of the California public schools. The American authorities determined that "English will bring to the people of Guam, through the public schools, a knowledge of sanitation and hygiene . . . knowledge of fair play and a keen sense of honor . . . [and] a natural love for labor and industry by those who come to think themselves educated." The denigration of Chamorro health, honor, and lifestyle could not have been much more complete. In such ways did the white government establish its own perceived superiority and dominance. However, not all of the locals accepted the whites' view of the Social Darwinian hierarchy; some residents formed the Chamorro Nation Traditional Council as a formal means of resistance to the Americanization efforts.[14]

Sport provided a less formal but clearly visible means of reclaiming lost honor. The U.S. Navy initiated a sports program to serve as a prophylactic device against the suspected physical and moral degeneracy of the tropics, of which they accused the natives. Much to the surprise and embarrassment of the naval personnel, the lone native team in the baseball league, known as the Carabaos, defeated the officers' team in the championship. Labeled "the Great White Hopes," the military brass supposedly represented the best of American manhood.[15]

The navy surrendered governance of the island to the U.S. Department of the Interior, but erosion of the native culture continued. The importation of Filipino workers further rent the social fabric, pitting the immigrants against the indigenous population, to the benefit of employers. The traditional lifestyle continued to disintegrate, as men left agricultural plots for government jobs. The U.S. government claimed almost two-thirds of the island by the end of World War II. The Japanese held Guam during the war, but upon its conclusion the island entered into the tourism industry, becoming one of the most popular destinations for Japanese tourists. As in Hawaii and Samoa, tourism brought greater commercialization and enhanced property values, but at a loss of local ownership. The introduction of Asian workers for the service economy further fragmented the society, and the natives began to fight back. In the postwar years the residents of Guam acquired U.S. citizenship but not complete constitutional rights. They elected their own governor and legislature, but even that proved deficient. A nationalist party emerged in the 1970s, and the Chamorros' sense of identity often pitted itself against non-Chamorro "others," such as the Filipinos, Chinese, and Japanese who had also come to inhabit the island, reducing the indigenous population to less than half.[16]

The resistance movement attempted to regain native lands and produced a backlash against the use of English. Using the native language was forbidden, and Chamorro dictionaries had been collected and burned. Yet the practice continued in secret. Ironically, children learned their native language in the schools and playgrounds designed to assimilate them with mainland culture. Both the defiant use and the resilience of the language succeeded. Whereas previous usage of the Chamorro language incurred a fine, it is now taught in the elementary schools.[17]

Schools and playgrounds also provided the instruction in American sport forms that helped to resurrect a multicultural union and pride in the pluralistic culture that has evolved on the island. Originating in 1947 a military football league proposed to transfer interservice rivalries and animosities to the athletic field and so build better community relations with local civilians. Intended to modernize and Anglicize the natives, team sports like baseball and football also reinforced the communal lifestyles of the diverse Asian populations. Coaches served as father figures in the team "family." When the U.S. military organized a youth football league in 1966, it provided for one civilian team for the children of its Hawaiian employees. Football linked the authority and discipline of the military with the masculinity and physical performance aspects important to Hawaiian culture and adolescent boys. The Hawaiian coaches, raised on the rugged barefoot version of the game as practiced in Hawaii, instilled pride, toughness, and a warrior tradition in their Tamuning Eagles. Practices even incorporated Hawaiian songs and language. The Eagles conquered their opponents in 125 consecutive contests over the next fifteen years. By beating the colonizer at its own game, the coaches and players also destroyed the myth of Anglo superiority and reestablished much racial, ethnic, and class pride. In 1999 the Guam Raiders solidified intra-island esteem when they defeated a team from Russia, a former world power, in the World Youth Super Bowl in Orlando, Florida. The athletic successes of the polyglot teams from Guam have restored respect, dignity, and confidence to the subordinate groups who previously labored under white Anglo domination.[18]

Haiti

The history of Haiti is mired in race and revolution. On this island that had been a French colony since 1697, black slaves greatly outnumbered their white owners. Inspired by the French Revolution, black Haitians overthrew the French, freed the slaves, and declared their independence by 1804. Internecine quarrels soon followed and continued throughout the 1800s. The Haitians fought one another as well as the Spanish colonials, with the former claiming the entire island of Hispaniola in 1822. Santo Domingo conducted a successful secession in 1844 and sought a temporary protective annexation by Spain, as the Haitians returned to internal feuds. Despite the continual political turmoil, the country's rich natural resources attracted American businesses. With the construction of a canal in Central America, Haiti would assume greater importance as a refueling station for European ships, whose operation in the Caribbean concerned the United States. In 1908 an American company secured a contract to build a railroad in the country, despite the opposition of the black Haitians, known as Cacos. The Haitian American Sugar Company, composed of American and European investors, assumed a large role in the Haitian economy; in 1910 Americans moved to take control of the Banque Nationale of Haiti.[19]

The U.S. government depended on American business concerns for its intelligence network in Haiti and throughout the Caribbean. As expected, their reports emphasized economic opportunities and potential profits while neglecting any thorough understanding of the local culture. Haiti thus presented an enigma to white Americans, who perceived the independent, black, French, Catholic nation as a land of illiterate but pompous buffoons who practiced voodoo and cannibalism. A *National Geographic* article claimed that "the army officers of Haiti were as fond of gold lace as a mountain girl of bright colors. . . . The soil is wonderfully fertile and nothing but sheer lack of initiative and industry keeps them from being rich. . . . [The lack of] roads furnish[es] eloquent testimony as to the economic backwardness of this land of potential riches."[20]

Haitians resented such characterizations, particularly the wealthy and refined citizens who had been educated in France. The poorer Cacos confronted their adversaries with arms, adding to the political instability of the country. Between 1911 and 1916 Haiti went through a succession of six presidents—two of them deposed and three assassinated. In December 1914 U.S. Marines confiscated $500,000 in gold from the national bank, allegedly to safeguard it from the Cacos. The Haitian ambassador in Washington, however, termed it "a flagrant invasion of the sovereignty and independence of the Republic of Haiti."[21]

Another revolt ensued in 1915. Fearing that European powers would occupy the country to settle their debts, the United States offered to intervene, a move rejected by the Haitians. With World War I raging in Europe, President Woodrow Wilson invoked the Monroe Doctrine as the United States invaded Haiti in July 1915, overthrowing the president, establishing a puppet government, and securing a treaty that established the country as an American protectorate. The U.S. seizure of the customs houses provided effective control of the national finances, and U.S. investments proceeded under the veil of modernization. The United States rationalized the seizure on several counts. Strategically, Haiti controlled the Windward Passage between it and Cuba, and it rested only six hundred miles from Florida. Politically and economically the United States assumed it could bring Haiti into the international capitalist economy and stabilize the country and the region, all under the beneficence of the "white man's burden." *National Geographic* supported such justifications with this statement: "It is, indeed, a region where nature has lavished its richest gifts, and where a simple population, under a firm yet gentle, beneficent guidance, may realize the blessings of tranquil abundance."[22]

Haitians failed to see any charity in the U.S. intentions. Revolutionary forces under Rosalvo Bobo, a doctor, opposed the American military forces. Snipers fired on the marines as they marched to the capital. Two American sailors and six Cacos lost their lives. Marine reinforcements arrived in August, only to be pelted with bricks by the local populace. In the larger towns riots ensued when natives refused to accept the U.S.-installed government. At Port de Paix, the Cacos "declaimed in loud defiance their hatred for the United States, and summoned all Haitians to a patriotic revolt."[23]

Haitian writers mounted a literary protest that belied the racial overtones. One writer, Roger Dorinsville, asserted: "The white soldiers had come to defile our independence."[24] A U.S. Marine described his black adversaries as follows: "All were but slightly clad, and each was armed with a musket, a pistol, a sword, and a long, vicious knife. . . . Each man looked to be a diabolical devil."[25] The Cacos refused to surrender their weapons despite a declaration of martial law. Skirmishes and battles eventually erupted into a full-scale uprising known as the First Caco War in an occupation that would last until 1934.[26]

The Americans banned voodoo, yet the practice continued as a clandestine form of resistance. One American writer stigmatized the folk religion by claiming that "in the frenzy of the snake dances the worshipers refuse to be content with anything less than a sacrifice of . . . a living child." Another reiterated that "in the heart of them has revived the old idolatry of the Gold Coast, and in the villages of the interior, where they are out of sight and can follow their instincts, they sacrifice children in the serpent's honor after the manner of their forefathers."[27] Such speculations only reinforced negative stereotypes and rationalized the need for white moral guidance.

American missionaries assumed the superiority of their own beliefs and deplored the physicality and inherent sexuality of the Haitian dances. One missionary, Samuel Guy Inman, described the dances as having "the abandonment characteristic of animals. . . . Body and song alike exhibit brazen proposals."[28]

The U.S. military endeavored to clean up the corporeal as well as the spiritual. Sanitation laws addressed public urination and excretion, garbage disposal, and unleashed animals, all issues to be policed by sanitary engineers and a quickly established national police force. The American agenda and organization of such law enforcement groups in the more recent occupations of Afghanistan and Iraq have followed similar patterns.[29]

Established in September 1915, the gendarmerie regulations stipulated that the local forces would be commanded by white officers drawn from the ranks of the U.S. Marine Corps and that drills would be conducted in English rather than the native French. Drawn from the ranks of the working class, often from the South, marine officers appeared coarse, rough, and unrefined in comparison to the gentlemen officers of the navy. One marine commander, Colonel Littleton W. J. Waller, wrote to assistant commandant John Lejeune: "I know the nigger and how to handle him." Waller's family had been southern slaveholders. Waller had been indicted for brutal executions of Filipinos during his service there, but despite substantial evidence against him he won acquittal. Waller served as the best man and mentor to Smedley Butler, a legendary marine hero, conqueror of the Cacos, and first commander of the Haitian constabulary.[30]

The U.S. treaties with Haiti made no provision for educating the populace. The Americans did initiate schools and brought some improvement to the literacy rate, but education focused on vocational training. The American teachers spoke no French, many came from the South and carried its racial attitudes, and none were black. Moreover, marines conscripted Haitians in forced labor campaigns that sometimes resulted in death. Haitians perceived such impressment as the reintroduction of slavery and resisted the inductions.[31]

The resistance escalated into the Second Caco War, from 1918 to 1920. Although the marines killed the resistance leader, Charlemagne Peralte, by bribing a traitor and effecting a ruse, the revolt continued. The marines declared 1919 an "open season" for "hunting Cacos," resulting in random killing. The guerilla fighters found allies in the United States. The National Association for the Advancement of Colored People (NAACP) protested the American occupation, missionaries deplored the violence, and Eugene O'Neill's 1920 play, *The Emperor Jones*, harpooned imperialism.[32]

The Haitian government tried and failed to regain control of the constabulary in 1919. In 1921 an American lieutenant in the gendarmerie commented that "the entire population it is thought does not like white people down in their heart and especially a white race maintaining military rule over them." A year later the United West Indies Corporation was out of business and the Haitian American Sugar Company was in receivership.[33]

American concerns revolved around commercial and strategic interests relative to Caribbean Sea passages. The general black population was held in disdain and wallowed in poverty. While the population suffered, marine officers cavorted in segregated facilities on the polo field or pursued golf, basketball, or boxing. Social relations with the natives often proved hostile or carnal. Enlisted men played baseball or found pleasure in nearly 150 brothels in Port-au-Prince in the 1920s. Military authorities provided adequate recreation facilities lest men in the tropics succumb to the immoral influences, blaming the environment rather than American manhood. As with the Filipinos in Manila, the use of Haitian women as sexual commodities found acceptance as a necessary evil.[34]

Shooting competitions provided sport both in garrison and in the field. Paternalistic American tutors evinced pride when their Haitian trainees in the constabulary performed well in the rifle matches. One marine described killing while on patrol as sport: "I steadied down to my job of popping at black heads, which appeared very much as those behind the 'hit the nigger and get a cigar' games at American amusement parks." Such marine brutality extended beyond individual encounters, as soldiers torched villages in guerilla areas and even murdered a voodoo priest who had been jailed for practicing his banned religion. The killings became so widespread as to engender courts-martial and a formal investigation.[35]

In 1929 Haitians retaliated against the occupation in a general strike. Students at the Central School of Agriculture revolted, successfully removing the school's American superintendent. Americans encountered beatings by the natives, and when marine reinforcements arrived to quell a crowd they suffered twelve killed and twenty-three. In 1930 President Herbert Hoover convened a special investigation committee, headed by

W. Cameron Forbes, former governor general of the Philippines. Forbes recommended a troop withdrawal, which was finally completed in 1934; the United States continued to control the Haitian economy for another eight years.[36]

During the occupation, educated Haitians escaped to New York, establishing a colony similar to that of the Nuyoricans. With the U.S. exodus Haiti slid into dictatorship, as nineteen years of American influence failed to take hold. Unlike in the Philippines or other areas of extended occupation, sport had little effect in cultural transition. A virulent racism clearly played an important role in the lack of integrated pastimes that had incorporated some common values in the Philippines, Hawaii, Samoa, Guam, Cuba, Puerto Rico, and the Dominican Republic. The Haitians proved to be too black, too proud, and perhaps too poor for assimilation. When the poverty-stricken Haitians fled to Florida in 1994, the U.S. government refused to accept them as refugees, sending troops to restore Jean-Bertrand Aristide to power. Ten years later the United States ousted Aristide in yet another upheaval.[37]

Nicaragua

American adventurers and entrepreneurs espoused a long-held interest in Nicaragua. William Walker invaded the country on several occasions in the mid-nineteenth century in an ill-fated attempt to establish a slave republic. His exploits finally ended in front of a Honduran firing squad. Cornelius Vanderbilt contracted to construct a passage across the country, and the United Fruit Company, founded in 1889, operated throughout Nicaragua and other Central American and Caribbean nations. Competitors, such as the Bluefields Banana Company and the Atlantic Fruit and Steamship Company, soon followed. Such American business and political interests brought U.S. troops to Nicaragua in 1911–1912 and 1926–1932, and in a clandestine operation in the 1980s.[38]

Baseball arrived with the banana companies. The English-speaking residents of Bluefields, a British settlement on the Caribbean coast since the 1840s, had already been engaged in cricket when an unknown American suggested a change. Within two years the American national pastime appeared in the western urban areas of Managua and Granada. Nicaraguans who had attended schools in New York and learned the game there returned to their homeland and organized baseball clubs. The game spread thereafter with enough teams to organize a league in Managua during the 1911–1912 season.[39]

American influences proved less benign during the Central American wars of 1907–1911. After a long-sought Central American union of Nicaragua, Honduras, and El Salvador disintegrated in nationalistic and personal rivalries between the countries' leaders, a series of territorial invasions ensued, with American soldiers of fortune fighting on opposing sides. A court of justice negotiated by Mexico and the United States failed to settle disputes, as Nicaraguan president Jose Santos Zelaya proved a thorn in the American efforts. After the United States secured a canal deal with independent Panama, Zelaya pursued possibilities for a Nicaraguan canal with interested parties in Europe and Japan. In 1909 Zelaya executed captured American mercenaries who had fought in opposing ranks. The *New York Herald* portrayed the deaths as assassinations of freedom fighters, stating that Zelaya delighted in "Yank[ing] Mr. [President] Taft by the ear."[40]

Once again, race mattered in such deliberations. One New York businessman inquired of Secretary of State Philander Knox: "How long will our chicken-livered government continue to allow those damned Nicaraguan 'niggers' to insult, humiliate and injure Americans and their interests."[41] Zelaya responded to such vituperation by stating: "It is better to die than to submit being sold to slavery." Zelaya soon died a political death as the United States backed his conservative opponent and sent a military contingent of its own. Zelaya resigned after eighteen years in office but named his own successor, Jose Madriz. The new president faced a civil war, as Juan Estrada, governor of the Bluefields sector, mutinied, backed by four hundred American mercenaries. Still, Madriz prevailed until a U.S. Marine battalion arrived from Panama to "protect American interests" and U.S. Navy ships patrolled the Bluefields coast to harbor Estrada.[42]

With such support Estrada gained the presidency in 1910, but he too soon lost favor and was supplanted by the more conservative Adolfo Diaz after another civil war. This time the U.S. Marines established a legation in Managua, with the United States assuming control of the Nicaraguan customs houses. When Luis Mena, the Nicaraguan secretary of war, effected another uprising in 1912 to oppose the U.S. occupation, 1,100 more marines arrived to ensure U.S. control of the government. In 1914 the Bryan-Chamorro Treaty gave the United States rights to a Nicaraguan canal and naval bases, guaranteeing a military presence.[43] Elliot Northcutt, American ambassador to Nicaragua, reported "an overwhelming majority of Nicaraguans . . . antagonistic to the United States."[44]

Sport provided some rapprochement as well as retaliation. By 1915 Managua featured an enclosed baseball stadium, establishing the game on a commercial basis with paid admissions. A national league organized that same year, and by 1918 the Nicaraguans met the U.S. Marines team in a series of games. The marines gained entry into the national association in 1919. A joint Nicaraguan-American tennis tournament took place in 1917, followed by the start of an integrated national tennis association. When political issues frayed relationships again, the Nicaraguans redeemed their honor at the ballpark, defeating the Americans in all 4 games in 1919 and taking 3 of 5 in 1920. In 1921 U.S. Marines plundered a newspaper office and killed six Managua police officers in separate incidents to offset any harmony won through sports. In 1922 American naval ships anchored in Nicaraguan waters and sent their baseball teams for an encounter with the Titan II club of Chinandega. The first game ended in a 3–3 tie. A newspaper in Managua described the second match with the USS *Galveston* leading 15–9 in the ninth inning: "The huge crowd is sad; not a happy voice is heard. Titan seems defeated; but the nine Nicaraguan boys, as if in a war between races, exalted by their Nicaraguan pride, as though influenced by powerful Indian blood, entered the bottom of the ninth with an enthusiasm spurred on by the screams of the crowd."[45] To the delight of the local crowd, Titan II emerged with a 16–15 victory, and the newspapers left no doubt as to the racial connotations of the contest.

The confrontations got even more personal in boxing matches, which appeared by 1916 and gained considerable popularity thereafter. By 1922–1923 the boxing matches preceded the baseball games as a commercialized athletic spectacle. Athletic triumphs bolstered nationalism and Nicaraguan pride, and they soon expanded their endeavors to regional competitions. Nicaraguans returned from Costa Rica in 1917 with the game of soccer and began competing with their southern neighbor and British sailors soon thereafter. Women, too, engaged in physical pastimes, starting a basketball club in 1917. Nicaraguans began competing in the Second Central American Games, held in San Salvador in 1923. A year later Nicaragua defeated Panama for the baseball championship. In such regional challenges sport compensated for more deadly wars, and as in the Caribbean nations, fostered the burgeoning construction of a national identity.[46]

Most sports, introduced or practiced by the social elites or commercial bourgeoisie, assimilated aspiring Nicaraguans into the international capitalist culture, which promoted the parallel values of discipline, work ethic, and respect for authority. Regional sport associations brought such like-minded people together in their shared beliefs and values even as they fueled nationalistic fires. In contrast, the working classes adhered to the traditional pastimes, gambling on horse races, cockfights, and bullfights, while also adopting boxing as a means to demonstrate the traditional qualities of machismo. A brief flirtation with female boxers soon lost its appeal. By the mid-1920s Nicaraguan boxers also carried the nationalistic mantra for the working classes, engaging in bouts with their Guatemalan and El Salvadorian counterparts.[47]

A resurgence of Nicaraguan pride spurned American efforts to control the national guard in 1925, the same year General Emiliano Chamorro enacted a coup. The resultant civil war against liberals under General Augustino Sandino brought U.S. intervention. The American troops, navy, and an air squadron secured the government for the conservatives. U.S. Marines took charge of the constabulary as Sandino persisted in a guerilla war that lasted until his death in 1934. During the insurrection the marines commandeered a cherished Managua ball field for a landing strip, and Sandino framed the struggle in nationalistic rather than internecine terms: "This is a struggle for the Nicaraguan people in general, [not a civil war] to expel the foreign invasion of my country. . . . The only way to put an end to this struggle is the immediate withdrawal of the invading forces from our territory . . . and supervis[ed] elections by representatives of Latin America instead of by American marines."[48]

The United States did supervise the 1928 elections, won by liberal Jose Moncada. Sandino spent 1929 in Mexico decrying "foreign intervention and the exploitation of the country by the money powers of Nicaragua and Wall Street." He got some support from the All-American Anti-Imperialist League in the United States, but his revolutionary quest ended when Juan Sacasa, the new president, drew him into a truce in 1933. The U.S. Marines withdrew after a six-year occupation that entailed 150 combat incidents and cost 136 American lives. After a 1934 dinner with Sacasa, Anastasio Somoza, head of the national guard, killed Sandino. He then deposed Sacasa in 1936 and assumed dictatorial powers.[49]

Somoza, a former umpire, recognized the power of baseball, by then already the Nicaraguan national game. He built a thirty-thousand-seat stadium in Managua and attached his own name to it. Lest anyone forget, he also adorned the entrance with a statue of himself on horseback. The Sandinista movement got its revenge by overthrowing Somoza's offspring in 1979, but they too attached sport to politics, sponsoring a baseball team in the national league, winners of the championship in 1988.[50]

A former Sandinista, Alexis Arguello, carried the international athletic fortunes of Nicaraguans into the boxing ring. Arguello defeated Alfredo Escalera of Puerto Rico for the World Boxing Council super featherweight crown in 1978 and proceeded to gain the World Boxing Association featherweight, junior lightweight, and lightweight titles in a distinguished career. Ironically, the Sandinista government banned boxing and Arguello in an attempt to promote baseball. Throughout the 1980s the Central Intelligence Agency of the United States conducted a clandestine guerrilla war against the Marxist Sandinistas. With the collapse of the Sandinista government, Arguello returned to his homeland in 1990. By then Nicaraguans had found a new athletic hero, Dennis Martinez, a native baseball star with the Baltimore Orioles and Montreal Expos. Upon his retirement in 1998, Martinez declined to run for the presidency of Nicaragua; the citizens of Managua deferentially renamed the baseball stadium in his honor.[51]

At the close of the twentieth century, Arguello and Martinez represented the accommodation reached between Nicaragua and the United States. After more than a century of tension, protection, occupation, exploitation, and animosity, sport began to heal old wounds.

Panama

Panama owes its independent status as a country to the United States, which orchestrated its secession from Colombia in 1903. The United States had long been involved with the region before that insurrection, however. An American company contracted to build an isthmian railroad across the narrow passage in 1849 with a ninety-nine-year lease. Americans operated at risk in the territory throughout the remainder of the century. Riots and civil wars caused American deaths and brought the U.S. Navy and Marines to the area in 1856 and 1885. The Colombian government requested U.S. intervention during the civil war of 1899–1902. The U.S. government secured a peace treaty but maintained its desire for regional control of the unfinished canal, as the original French construction company had gone bankrupt. President Theodore Roosevelt characterized the racial nature of American frustrations: "To talk of Colombia as a responsible Power to be dealt with as we would deal with Holland or Denmark . . . is a mere absurdity. The analogy is with a group of Sicilian . . . bandits. You could no more make an agreement with the Colombian rulers than you could nail currant jelly to the wall."[52]

The original U.S. offer to Colombia for canal rights fell far short of the annual income derived from isthmian business even during the civil war period. When the Columbian Senate unanimously repudiated the treaty, Panamanian politicians, backed by eight U.S. Navy ships and a contingent of U.S. Marines, declared their independence. The U.S. government recognized the new nation only three days later, on November 6, 1903. On November 18 the new, independent government of Panama granted the canal zone to the United States in perpetuity, and the Americans guaranteed sovereignty but reserved the right to intervene in Panamanian affairs. Even the New York newspapers disparaged the blatant usurpation of power as "a vulgar and mercenary venture" and "the path of scandal, disgrace, and dishonor."[53]

The Panamanian workforce soon took on a distinct racial cast. The United Fruit Company employed more than six thousand laborers—mainly blacks imported from Jamaica—over 170 square miles of territory. One American writer explained: "It is almost impossible to tempt the average native of Central America to work, and many of them are physically incapable of sustained manual labor. . . . The lowest classes are Indians of innumerable tribes and varying customs, but a considerable portion of them obey the latent instinct of hatred for physical labor."[54] The writer further attributed any progress or civilization to "Caucasian initiative and eventual supremacy."[55]

Progress on the canal construction, however, rested primarily on a multinational but largely nonwhite labor force. Teddy Roosevelt handpicked George Shanton, one of his former Rough Riders, to command the Canal Zone police force. Shanton regulated the lives of as many as forty-five thousand workers at one point. The labor force was split into two color-coded categories, clearly marked by race, skill levels, and citizenship. Skilled, white American employees earned their salaries in gold, while unskilled blacks from the Caribbean islands got paid in silver. Employees on the silver roll got lower pay, substandard housing, and inferior food. The U.S. government labeled Spanish, Italian, and Greek workers as semiwhite, placing them in a liminal status. Such placement led to militancy, with the Spanish leading an anarchist movement in 1911.[56]

An American claimed: "Here [Panama] is a practically unknown paradise for the hunter, fisherman, and the devotee of the beautiful."[57] Few on the silver pay scale experienced such pastimes, while white workers, who were encouraged to bring their families, got free housing and furnishings, free schooling for children, recreational facilities, and annual leaves back to the States. Roosevelt requested that the YMCA provide "moral sanitation" for workers, which it did with seven stations along a twenty-eight-mile route; however, such facilities catered only to white men. White employees received free travel privileges throughout the Canal Zone, musical entertainment, and access to sports facilities, including tennis courts, pool tables, bowling alleys, gymnasiums, clubhouses, and baseball fields. By 1912 Panama had enough teams for an amateur baseball league. Meanwhile, black workers got no amenities and even faced a 9:30 p.m. curfew each night. Those with semiwhite status had to endure the long lines reserved for "coloreds" at the post office.[58]

Work, too, became a segregated contest as the United States pitted segregated national crews against one another to achieve maximum productivity. Whites and semiwhites served as supervisors and labor bosses, adhering to a strong racial hierarchy. The completion of the canal, which opened in 1914, firmly established the technological dominance of the United States on the world stage. It had succeeded where the French had failed, and the whole world bore witness to American preeminence.[59]

In ensuing years the United States moved to assume even greater domination in Panama. It established a national guard that became a political force for dictators friendly to the United States. American troops manned Panamanian bases until 1948. By the 1920s many Panamanians had found their own sense of nationalism through sport. Panama Al Brown, a slender five-foot ten-and-one-half-inch boxer with a seventy-six-inch reach, whom whites derisively referred to as a "tall, skinny freak," became a world champion. Brown started his boxing career in Panama but worked as a New York busboy as a flyweight in 1922. He grew into a bantamweight contender by 1925 and won that title in 1929, holding the crown until 1935. During that time Brown and his good friend Kid Chocolate, the Cuban featherweight champ, refused to fight each other, demonstrating a cultural solidarity that chagrined white fans and promoters. Brown demonstrated remarkable resilience and endurance, fighting until 1944. After his death from tuberculosis in 1951, his body was returned to his homeland for burial in Panama City.[60]

Brown's career coincided with the realization of Panamanian identity and the rise of nationalism. Panama began to question U.S. sovereignty in the Canal Zone in 1926, and the debate only heightened in the 1930s, resulting in a new treaty in 1939 that limited America's role. Still, Panamanian concerns lingered until 1964 when rioting followed an American failure to fly the Panamanian flag in the Canal Zone, and the local government severed relations with the United States until its demands were met in a new treaty.

As squabbles between the two countries continued throughout the latter part of the twentieth century, Panamanians found a new hero in another boxer, Roberto Duran. A poor street urchin, Duran became a professional fighter in 1967, at age sixteen. In his first thirteen years as a professional, Duran amassed an amazing record of 72 wins and only 1 loss. He shared his winnings with poor supplicants and assumed heroic status in the country where "everybody bet on him."[61] Duran once remarked: "I understand the importance my life holds for people who are poor and have nothing." Throughout his career Duran exhibited both a cultural and a class awareness despite his lack of education. In his leisure time he played Panamanian instruments and sang native songs, eschewing the bright lights of New York City for his homeland.[62]

In the ring Duran fought with a ferocious intensity and a toughness that overwhelmed his opponents. Still, the television networks paid him less than his worth and below other boxers of distinction, a situation that reflected Panamanian deliberations with the Americans. Duran secured the lightweight championship of the world by age twenty-one and returned to Panama amid flowing champagne on the presidential plane. Upon his arrival he slept at the presidential palace. He went on to garner the welterweight, super welterweight, and middleweight titles as well, then defeated the seemingly invincible Sugar Ray Leonard, America's premier boxer and Olympic champion, in 1980. Duran assumed godlike status in Panama, at least until the rematch. In that celebrated affair a frustrated Duran, unable to effectively hit a taunting Leonard, quit in disgust midway through the fight. The aftermath exhibited the extent to which Panamanian pride rested in the machismo of their national hero. Graffiti in his homeland labeled him a traitor. Duran admitted: "The only thing they didn't call me was a maricon [homosexual]. The most common cry was 'Vendi patria' [you sold out your country]." Duran continued to fight to restore his tarnished image and national pride until a car crash forced his retirement at age fifty. In 1997, when he was forty-six, Panamanians named him their boxer of the year.[63]

As Panamanian relationships with the United States deteriorated into a state of war, the glory of Duran held an even greater importance for his fellow citizens. The United States had supported General Manuel Noriega when he was a corrupt dictator, but by 1988 a Florida court had indicted him as a drug dealer and a duplicitous double agent. When a coup failed to replace Noriega, he had the Panamanian assembly declare war on the United States and attacked American military personnel in the Canal Zone, resulting in a U.S. invasion and his downfall. The United States had once again asserted its authority, but Panamanian pride took refuge in its athletes, including Roberto Duran and more than two dozen Panamanian baseball players who had made it to the Major Leagues. In a country dominated by an American political and military presence, Panamanians sought compensation in their sports stars, in whom they saw images of themselves—poor but tough, gritty, and proud, able to compete with the Americans on a level playing field. By 2000 Panama had regained national control of the Canal Zone in a jubilant celebration that signified they had more than athletes to offer the world.[64]

The Globalization of Sport

Sport has figured prominently, if more subtly, in the imperial process. Colonial powers subdued or subverted nationalistic impulses by authoritarian, often harsh and militaristic, means that often met resistance. Sport proved a less overt means of instilling belief in a dominant system's values and principles. Spaniards brought bullfighting and cockfighting to far-flung colonies in Asia and Latin America, while the British promoted soccer, cricket, and amateur ideology throughout the world during the nineteenth century. The United States continued the emphasis initiated by the British but substituted its own games, particularly baseball, football, and basketball thereafter. In the American case, sport not only followed the flag but often preceded it as religious missionaries, expatriates, and foreign students introduced American sport forms to other nations previous to U.S. administrative control or military occupation of the territory. Capitalism, commercialism, bureaucracy, standard-ization of rules, the rationalization of sport and leisure, and its commodification produced a more homogeneous sporting world, with the United States resting at the hegemonic apex of a Western-dominated authority by the end of the twentieth century.[1]

Although Washington DC imposed its military might on Europe and the Mideast, New York dictated financial markets, and Los Angeles effected popular culture on a global scale, the process remained incomplete and less than unilateral. Cultural flow moved in multiple directions, and the resiliency of local, native, ethnic, religious, and racial influences transformed American society as well. Musical, dance, and fashion styles drew from Caribbean rhythms and urban black culture, while sport assumed particular manifestations of class, race, and nationalism that thwarted a hegemonic homogenization. While a transnational, global, capitalist culture has seemingly emerged from the power struggles of the past, a more pluralistic culture lurks below the surface. Joseph Maguire asserted: "The hegemonic position enjoyed by specific sports within this global media–sports complex requires less powerful sports to conform to the style and form in which the dominant sports are displayed. The glitz and spectacle of the NFL and the NBA became the benchmark by which other sports are judged." That contention rings only partially true and must be tempered by the fact that such sports have also assumed "styles" perpetrated by independent actors that counter the wishes of the governing bureaucracies and do not always fit WASP norms and value systems.[2]

The United States may have assumed the imperial "white man's burden" from the British, but the load is shouldered with some distinct differences. Like Great Britain, the United States exported its people, commerce, sport, and ideology, but the American dream also brings millions of immigrants to the host culture who gradually elicit some change in the dominant norms and values. In the Southwestern United States the growth of the Hispanic population has even endangered the English language. On the baseball field Latin American players now dominate what was once America's national game. In the 2003 season more than 25 percent of Major Leaguers hailed from outside the United States. On the courts of the National Basketball Association, American children find athletic heroes from a multitude of nations in a game that features a distinct African American urban style of play. Unlike Great Britain, the United States is bound to a democratic ideology, at least in rhetoric if not in practice. While the American imperial crusade benefited American commerce first and foremost, it did so while espousing the tenets of liberty, freedom, and democracy that colonized or subject peoples came to expect. For such groups sport became a political tool of accommodation or resistance to the dominant power or a means to greater nationalistic identity.[3]

While subject nations could not prevent American commercial enterprise, they could reject the religious and racial impositions that accompanied imperialism. Such impulses clearly raised the ire of the Japanese, whose baseball triumphs over American teams in the 1890s and athletic successes against both white and Asian rivals thereafter spurred a nationalistic pride and confidence that challenged notions of Anglo world leadership. A century later America's best teams import Japan's star players in acknowledgement of their abilities.[4]

Filipinos labored under a long American occupation, accepting American tutelage and sport forms yet denying complete assimilation. Ultimately they rejected English in favor of Tagalog and a variety of local dialects, the Filipino government retained its traditional elitism despite the trappings of a democratic structure, and Catholicism remained intact against the widespread influence of the YMCA and Protestant missionaries. Filipinos eventually eschewed baseball and football, choosing basketball as their national sport. They adapted the Americanization efforts to their own needs and values to produce a new hybrid culture similar to yet distinct from that of the United States.[5]

The annexation of Hawaii and its eventual statehood subsumed and nearly exterminated native culture. Sport, however, helped to preserve remnants of the traditional lifestyle, such as surfing and outrigger canoe racing. The incorporation of Hawaiian athletes, such as Duke Kahanamoku, into the dominant sporting culture brought a reverse cultural flow that transformed even the American sporting scene. By the 1960s surfing had become integral in California's image, music, and fashions. Beach Boys songs, clothing, and hairstyles proliferated among eastern urban youth who had never seen the West Coast, and by the end of the century even landlocked European youths sported surfing attire. Sport also served to bring the polyglot Hawaiian labor force closer together as segregated plantation workers, African American soldiers, and Asian immigrant families found a common purpose in baseball leagues. Natives adapted American football to fit their own cultural and geographic requisites, and by the mid-twentieth century native Hawaiian culture had experienced a renaissance.

In the Caribbean, Cuba experienced less formal occupation of its territory but continual American influence until the Castro revolution. Baseball had preceded American interventions and remained a mainstay in Cuban culture as a resistive force. Black Cubans found in the game a means to assuage racial hurts, establish their masculinity via physical prowess, and eventually gain greater socioeconomic status as professional players. Under the Castro regime, sport gained primary importance as a political weapon against capitalist forces, especially against the regimes principal nemesis, the United States. Olympic athletes from the tiny island nation symbolically slew the representatives of the oppressive Goliath lurking nearby. Cuban boxers delivered political black eyes on a regular basis, and the Olympics provided a world audience when the Cuban baseball team beat the United States at its own game. In a land sanctioned by an American economic embargo and mired in poverty, sport provides a measure of hope, dignity, and pride.

Puerto Rico suffered a fate more unkind than that of Hawaii. Annexation and a long occupation failed to produce the benefits of statehood. Lack of political power has left the territory a U.S. bombing range and a pharmaceutical testing laboratory. A strong resistance to full Americanization has resulted in a healthy national identity and the predominance of the Spanish language and traditional Catholicism. The YMCA installed its sport forms but failed to achieve its religious goals. As Puerto Ricans established a migratory culture between stateside urban centers and the island, indigenous boxers and baseball players promoted a nationalistic pride that separated them from other American citizens. They accentuated that difference in the selection of their own flag, their own anthem, and their own Olympic team. They revel in their own athletic heroes, who have demonstrated an excellence worthy of any independent nation, and baseball provides perhaps the strongest cultural bond with the United States.

Although the Dominican Republic escaped formal annexation by the United States, multiple and lengthy occupations of the country produced a close interrelationship and cultural exchange. Dominican nationalism befuddled Americans' half-hearted efforts at assimilation, and islanders openly breached stateside racial practices. Dominican promoters not only accepted but ardently sought African American baseball players for their teams in an era when segregation prohibited them from interracial competition in the Major Leagues. A passion for the game earmarked Dominican culture, arguably surpassing even that of the Cubans. The success of Dominican players had made them one of the country's most valuable exports by the 1960s, a widespread distinction that renewed American baseball team owners' interest in the nation as a source of cheap labor. Baseball academies proliferated throughout the country in search of young talent that could be easily exploited. Only recently have Dominicans reasserted some authority over their own baseball destinies by establishing locally owned academies and employing bargaining agents to yield equitable contracts. Dominicans adopted an American sport form, but they have used it to promote their own human resources, to bring capital to the country, and to glory in the national prestige accorded by baseball.

The relative neglect of American Samoa did not safeguard it from the American sporting culture. Samoans both adopted and adapted those sports that corresponded to their native values. Communal team sports complement traditional lifestyles, and the physical toughness demanded of contact sports allows young men to assert their masculinity. By appearing on intercollegiate and professional gridirons, numerous Samoans have used football as a vehicle to an education and greater wealth.

American governance in Guam brought a decline in the traditional Chamorro culture. The importation of Filipino, Hawaiian, and other Asian workers created ethnic rifts in the labor force akin to the situation in Hawaii. Like Hawaiians the residents of Guam found in sport the ameliorative means to build a heterogeneous community. Baseball and football teams brought disparate groups together, and their successes restored pride and engendered a new sense of identity within the American empire.

Race proved a decisive factor in the long subjugation of Haiti. Despite a long American presence in the country, Haitian pride and American racial policies of segregation and denigration fostered little interaction. The commodification of Haitian bodies, both in brothels and as hunted prey, represented an entrenched bigotry that exceeded white reservations in the other colonies. Americans failed to share their pastimes with the native population to any great extent, and Haitians rejected those pastimes, adhering to the French language and cultural influences despite their own geographic proximity to the United States.

Episodic intrusions into Nicaraguan territory eventually brought such Western sport forms as cricket, baseball, and boxing to that country. Unlike in Haiti, the U.S. Marines and sailors engaged the local populace in sporting ventures despite racial overtones. Like the Cubans, Nicaraguans adopted some American sports (as well as soccer) but used the activities to build a greater sense of nationalism. Particularly after the Sandinista revolution of 1979, the Marxists utilized sport as a political weapon. With the downfall of the Sandinistas, Nicaragua returned to the capitalist world system of sport; rather than be subsumed by it, however, Nicaraguans reached an accommodation, extolling their national heroes who had triumphed in the Anglo world.

Panama followed a path similar to Nicaragua's. The country owed its existence to the United States but forfeited much of its liberty as a result. As in Haiti, recreational facilities and YMCA programs restricted activities to white patrons—in this case, to whites in the Canal Zone labor force. Like other Caribbean nations the Panamanians asserted their nationalism and developed a self-identity through sport. With the Panamanians unable to contest political issues with the United States on equal ground, Panamanian boxers carried the weight of national pride into the ring. Their victories brought a greater sense of confidence in political confrontations as well. Although an American military force overthrew General Noriega, the Panamanian strongman, the country ultimately won the return of the Canal Zone to the people of Panama.

In a world of increasing capitalist domination, sport provided one means for smaller nations to retain their national culture or at least portions of it. It allowed for the expression of national identities as colonial powers attempted to fashion subject populations in their own images. It promoted national heroes, national pride, and national self-esteem, if not equality, within the imperial process. Between 1950 and 1973 worldwide trade grew by almost 10 percent per year, but Europe, Japan, and the United States dominated that growth. By 1997 more than two-thirds of the multinational corporations were centered in those regions. The globalization and homogenization of business and sport have coincided since the British employed games to teach the values of "civilization" to their subject peoples. The United States assumed the imperial mantle and invoked a similar, if somewhat more subtle, athletic crusade by the end of the nineteenth century.[6]

John Bale has identified the process of globalized sport as it proceeded throughout the twentieth century. By the latter half of that period, it revolved around the increasing importance of telecommunications networks and conglomerates, an international labor force that produced products for worldwide consumption, international sports governing bodies that standardized rules and procedures, international sport management firms, the promotion of national leagues and even of local teams or individual athletes abroad, the international migration of athletes, and the professionalization of previously amateur sports.[7]

The proliferation of the American sporting culture via telecommunications might be traced to the development of cable station ESPN, which originated in 1979. Numerous spinoff stations, sports radio, and sports Web sites mushroomed thereafter. By the turn of the century ESPN broadcast to 150 million households in more than 180 countries in twenty-one different languages. ESPN Radio provides twenty-four-hour-a-day sports coverage, and the megastation has now branched out into magazine publishing, merchandising outlets, and sports-themed restaurants. The entire organization was bought by the American Broadcasting Company (ABC), which is now owned by the Disney Company (owner of theme parks, a third of the Eurosport Channel, the Anaheim Angels baseball team, the Los Angeles Kings basketball team, and the Anaheim Mighty Ducks hockey franchise). The package presents a sporting empire with global ramifications. A rival organization, the National Broadcasting Company, also controls Europe's Superchannel, with its 60 million viewers. Nearly 80 percent of European programming originates from the United States, greatly expanding English-language cultivation at the expense of national languages and cultures, a process that has been termed "financial and intellectual imperialism."[8]

Rupert Murdoch—the Australian media magnate who owns the BSKYB network, Europe's most profitable, and the American Fox network, and who is Disney's biggest competitor for global supremacy—"believes that sport absolutely overpowers all other programming."[9] Murdoch also owns sports franchises in New York, Los Angeles, and Great Britain that provide ready programming for his stations. The resultant proliferation and promotion of American sport forms on a global scale has also produced a particular homogeneous packaging of sport for consumers, with an emphasis on editing, particular camera angles and focus, slow motion replays, graphics, music, interviews, and "expert" analysis that interprets sports with an American perspective and bias for a global audience.[10]

American football began televising its games in Great Britain in 1982, and by the end of the decade Super Bowl XXII drew more than 6 million viewers in that country. Anheuser-Busch, the American brewery, sponsored an American football league in Britain in 1983, known as the Budweiser League to provide name recognition for its product and a tie to sport. In 1986 the Chicago Bears and Dallas Cowboys professional football teams played an exhibition game labeled "The American Bowl" in London's Wembley Stadium to a sellout crowd of eighty thousand. The next year the Budweiser League featured 105 British teams, and it soon spawned a rival league with another 72 teams. In 1990 the American National Football League initiated the World League of American Football, later renamed NFL Europe, with its reserve players. Offered as a springtime alternative on television networks, it posed no threat to the regular schedule of college and professional games in the fall season, and it also promoted both the game and a new market for goods, clothing, and media.[11]

The game of football has since expanded to Germany, the Netherlands, Austria, Italy, Spain, Russia, Finland, Japan, Mexico, and Australia, and the NFL broadcasts to more than 190 countries in twenty-six different languages. A 1994 NFL game in Mexico City attracted 112,000 fans. The NFL moved its American Bowl to Sydney, Australia, in 2000 and planned to introduce the game to China as well. With designs on the most populous market, Super Bowl XXXVIII was broadcast to China in conjunction with a new Web site that promotes the particularly American sport form in Asia. NFL commissioner Paul Tagliabue, in an attempt at humor, even speculated on a future Chinese quarterback who might be named Yao Fling (a reference to the popular Chinese player Yao Ming in the NBA). Just as cricket personified the qualities of the British empire, American football has replaced baseball as the national game. It symbolizes a tough, aggressive, even sometimes brutal, competitive, and commercial American masculine character in its quest to achieve a global hegemony.[12]

While football has surpassed baseball in popularity in the United States, the latter has a longer history abroad. The Spalding world tour of 1888–1889 might be considered the first concerted effort to attract a global audience for commercial purposes. By spreading the game of baseball and its values, Spalding hoped to increase sales for his sporting goods firm as well as promulgate particular values that he believed to be distinctly American in nature. While Spalding espoused democracy (although not for players), he expressed particular pietistic, middle-class, WASP concerns regarding gambling, drinking, and rowdyism. Caribbean and Central American countries adopted the game but used it to reinforce their own cultural values and a greater sense of nationalism.[13]

Numerous globe-trotting American teams, missionaries, expatriates, and American-educated nationals brought baseball to other countries in Latin America, Asia, Europe, and Australia. The International Baseball Association counts more than eighty members and 100 million worldwide participants. Pepsi sponsors the Australian Baseball League, and Major League Baseball sells its products in 109 countries, while it broadcasts to 215. Baseball academies have expanded not only in the Dominican Republic but to Venezuela as well, where half of the Major League teams have opened schools to exploit a cheaper labor force. At the turn of the century at least 25 percent of the players on Major League rosters hailed from countries other than the United States; the Colorado Rockies paid a signing bonus in excess of $2 million to a Taiwanese pitcher. In the 2003 All-Star Game, twenty-four players had been born outside the United States. A multitude of Latin and Asian stars have popularized the game abroad despite its labor struggles at home, from Fernandomania to Ichiro madness to Matsui fever. Such heroes have brought a measure of accommodation among previous rivals.[14]

After its creation at Springfield College in Massachusetts in 1891, basketball presented perhaps the most explosive growth of the American sport forms. Within three months the game had spread to nearby Smith College for women. The YMCA vigorously promoted basketball in its stations throughout the world. R. William Jones, a graduate of Springfield College, served as cofounder and executive secretary of FIBA (International Federation of Basketball) upon its organization in Europe in 1932. Frank Lubin, captain of the 1936 U.S. Olympic team and the son of Lithuanian parents, staged clinics in that country in 1938 and played for its national team, European champions in 1939. Basketball has remained popular in Eastern European countries ever since. In England a national league formed in 1972 with only six teams; by 1988 it had fifty-two. By the late 1980s more than four hundred American players appeared in western European leagues. Japan soon retaliated by banning American women from its league, but the cultural flow proceeded in both directions for the rest of the century. By 2001 American professional teams in the NBA included players from twenty-eight different countries; the following year the teams chose sixteen foreign players in the first two rounds of the draft. The top pick, Yao Ming from China, soon became an international celebrity.[15]

The inclusion of such players on American teams, the recruitment of African American men and women for leagues overseas, and the play of an American Muslim for an Israeli team have fostered a greater democracy than baseball's originators ever perceived. During the decade of the 1990s, the number of German players doubled to two hundred thousand. The Women's National Basketball Association's games reached 125 countries and were transmitted in seventeen languages. The NBA Finals, which had reached televisions in 35 countries in 1986, found eager reception in 175 by 1996. Only three years later youth in 206 countries played the game, surpassing even the number of countries playing soccer.[16]

If basketball carries with it democratic tendencies, it also bears capitalistic intentions. The NBA sponsors youth leagues abroad and has eleven offices outside of North America, while NBA teams have played in such places as France, Mexico, Israel, and Japan. Such ventures are not humanitarian gestures. The NBA earns 15 percent of its revenue from merchandise sold outside of the United States, and its sponsors profit accordingly. After more than one hundred NBA promotions in forty-seven countries over a four-year period for Sprite, it became the fastest-growing soft drink. Consequently, the Coca-Cola Company and the NBA announced a one-hundred-year marketing partnership.[17]

The Nike Company has been extremely successful in marketing a rebel image while practicing a capitalist, corporate business plan. Nike sells its logo, symbols, ideas, and values as well as shoes and clothing by portraying an independent, nonconformist image. Yet it follows an established multinational path in its operations that draws on European designs, American financing, and Asian labor. In Korea, Nike's exploited workers, including children, worked seven days per week, twelve to fourteen hours per day, for $1.50 to $2.80 an hour. When its Korean workers unionized, Nike moved elsewhere to maintain huge profits. The company enjoyed more than $9 billion in sales in 1997 and paid $200 million to have the Brazilian national soccer team, World Cup favorites in 1998, wear its shoes. The Nike logo adorned more than forty college teams, eight NFL squads, eight National Hockey League contingents, five Major League Soccer uniforms, various Tour De France bicyclists, and a rash of national teams in soccer and hockey. By 1997 Nike controlled 36 percent of the world market for sports equipment, but the decline of the Asian economy severely hurt Nike's profit margin, with a 49 percent decline, and a 50 percent drop in the company's stock. Nike's Indonesian workers stoned the local Nike factory, and the company proceeded to China, Thailand, and Vietnam, a scene reminiscent of the contested labor practices of past American employers in Asia, the Pacific, the Caribbean, and Central America.[18]

The workforce in many professional sports now consists of migratory athletes, often adorned in their Nike accoutrements or those of competitors like Adidas, Reebok, or Puma. They travel the world exchanging their nationality for lucre or a better lifestyle. The latter is more commonplace for African athletes bent on escaping poverty. Athletes from Kenya, South Africa, Namibia, and Morocco have found success on the world track tour, and other countries recruit Africans for their national teams, but no runners are among the highest-paid athletes. Black African soccer players are also sought for their skills, but they are relatively exploited when salaries are compared with white players. More than 50 percent of the players on African national teams suited up for European professional teams in 2000, but one scholar has termed their contractual arrangements a "modern form of slavery."[19]

Race remains an issue in European soccer, and it represents more than just a corporate desire to limit labor expenses. Emmanuel Ofsadebe, a Nigerian who played for Poland's national team in 2002, provided prolific scoring and revived chances for World Cup glory, something Poland had not experienced since a third-place finish in 1982. Yet in a match at Lubin, Polish fans taunted him by throwing bananas on the field. Lest that occasion be dismissed as an isolated incident by country bumpkins, seemingly more erudite fans in Warsaw repeated the affront in a match against Iceland. Tony Sanneh, an African American playing in Germany, has been subjected to ape calls. Apparently the greatness of the heroic black Brazilian star Pele failed to touch some European hearts.[20]

Sport has been, however, one of the primary catalysts in race relations over the past century. Integrated athletic competition in the colonies and the Caribbean paved the way for Joe Louis and Jackie Robinson. Muhammad Ali proved a transcendent figure who forced whites to confront their racism, and he took his messages to Africa and Asia as well. Television made Ali the most recognizable man in the world. By the late twentieth century, another African American athlete, Michael Jordan, held that distinction. Long a hero in the United States, Jordan arrived in Paris for only two games while touting the McDonald's championship and his Nike shoes. Despite the commercialism, more than twenty-seven thousand fans, including the French prime minister, watched him perform, as a thousand journalists searched for adjectives. Some claimed him to be a deity, and even American adults revered him as such. Chinese children rated him as one of the two most important people of the century, along with their own Zhou Enlai. In forty-five countries people rated him the most popular athlete. Jordan's appeal crosses cultural boundaries, and if children and fans cannot match his athleticism, they can "be like Mike" at least by purchasing the products he hawks for Nike, McDonald's, Wheaties, Coca-Cola, Gatorade, Hanes, and the NBA. His ebullient smile has ordained him "the silent messenger of global capitalism," a title that can also be assumed by Tiger Woods, the young multiracial golfer who rejects categorization. By age twenty-one, Woods had earned $24 million in endorsements. Already acclaimed as the best golfer in the world, he has a global following in an upscale sport that attracts a select clientele, a corporate promoter's dream, and he now serves as Nike's new spokesperson.[21]

The commercialization of sport is undertaken by international marketing groups or sport management firms that have reached conglomerate status. The IMG Company, founded in Cleveland by Mark McCormick, not only represents star athletes but produces their events. IMG develops young tennis hopefuls in a Florida academy, finances both the men's and women's pro tennis tours, and runs tennis and golf tournaments. It funds a developmental basketball program in China and provides television sports programming throughout the world.[22]

Sport governing bodies, such as MLB and the NFL, NBA, and NHL, have their own marketing arms, which promote the expansion of sport as they try to control it by an international draft of players or other means of limiting salaries. Such international regulatory bodies as the IOC, FIFA (Fèdèration Internationale de Football Association), and the IAAF, award their executives with a luxurious lifestyle as they set eligibility, income, and moral standards on Olympians, soccer players, and track and field athletes.

Despite such prohibitions free-spirited athletes like Dennis Rodman in basketball, Mike Tyson in boxing, and numerous soccer players refuse to accept the established WASP norms. As antiheroes, they challenge dominant groups, attracting even the discontented elements of society as fans. For others, sport builds communities in a variety of ways—in exclusive and segregated golf clubs that refuse blacks, Jews, or female members; or, conversely, in the racial solidarity of all black urban teams that confront white suburbanites in state tournaments. Cuban Communists compete for patriotism against capitalist antagonists, though defectors increasingly succumb to the promise of riches. Other Caribbean nations, Pacific islanders, and the Japanese have all found in sport a greater sense of nationalism, identity, and communal pride. At the local level sweet nostalgia of athletic feats, championships won, and honors gained mark community entry points and school hallways throughout America. Such places and times of remembrance attest to the multiple powers of sport in the production of identities: local, regional, national, ethnic, racial, gender, and religious.[23]

For some, sport has become a secular religion; for others, a surrogate form of war. As it has been for well over a century, sport is clearly part of the American imperial plan. As early as 1922 the American Olympic Association intended to "sell the United States to the rest of the world" via sport. Within a decade the federal government enacted a global marketing plan to attract foreign nationals to American sport forms and to buy American sporting goods. More recently, American soldiers carried their bats, basketballs, footballs, and golf clubs to the deserts of the Mideast. Boys in Afghanistan are learning baseball, just as Filipinos did a century ago, but both sides might be wary of lessons to be learned. Not unlike Theodore Roosevelt's schemes for American hegemony, President George W. Bush's Project for the New American Century aims to ensure American superiority. Both maintain that the United States has not only a right but a duty to bring order, justice, and civilization to despotic regions of the world, a mission beset with racial and religious overtones.[24]

In his 2004 State of the Union Address, President George W. Bush declared: "America is a nation with a mission, and that mission comes from our basic beliefs. We have no desire to dominate, no ambitions of empire."[25] While the first part of Bush's assertion rings true, the second belies American history. His pronouncements of American idealism and promotion of democracy failed to acknowledge the reality of American practices. The Spanish-American War of 1898 provided an impetus for an American empire, although Protestant missionaries from the United States had endeavored to convert foreign populations to their world-view long before that date. Similarly, the persistent, aggressive, and provocative trade policies of the U.S. capitalist economy throughout the nineteenth and twentieth centuries required the necessity of military bases on an increasingly global scale to protect American business interests. The Spanish-American War fostered the seizure of Cuba and Puerto Rico in the Caribbean, gateways to the canal then built and controlled by the United States in Panama. One hundred years before Bush's proclamation, then president Theodore Roosevelt, in his 1904 annual message to Congress, professed the need for the United States to effect an "internal police power" in the region whenever "general loosening of the ties of civilized society, may in America ultimately require intervention by some civilized nation."[26]

Yet, upon his retirement, Lieutenant General Smedley Butler, a marine hero, penned a memoir that admitted: "I spent most of my time as a high-class muscle-man for big business, for Wall Street, and the bankers. . . . Thus, I helped make Mexico and especially Tampico safe for American oil interests in 1914. I helped make Haiti and Cuba a decent place for the National City Bank boys to collect revenue in. I helped in the raping of half a dozen Central American republics for the benefit of Wall Street. . . . In China I helped to see to it that Standard Oil went its way unmolested."[27]

The War of 1898 not only gave the United States a Caribbean presence but extended its reach across the Pacific from the West Coast to the islands of Hawaii, Wake, Guam, and the Philippines. In the South Pacific the imperial domain included American Samoa. Still, the American belief in its superior form of civilization led President Woodrow Wilson to espouse a liberal idealistic foreign policy that intended to spread the virtues of democracy. Despite such egalitarian expressions he had admitted that "since trade ignores national boundaries and the manufacturer insists on having the world as a market, the law of his nation must follow him, and the doors of a nation which are closed against him must be battered down. Concessions obtained by financiers must be safeguarded by ministers of state, even if the sovereignty of unwilling nations be outraged in the process. Colonies must be obtained or planted, in order that no useful corner of the world may be overlooked or left unused." Wilson sent American troops to Nicaragua, the Dominican Republic, Haiti, and Mexico during his tenure in order to bolster U.S. interests. He explained World War I by stating: "Who does not know the seed of war in the modern world is industrial and commercial rivalry? . . . Germany was afraid her commercial rivals were going to get the better of her. . . . Some nations . . . thought Germany would get the commercial advantage of them. . . . This war, in its inception, was a commercial and industrial war. It was not a political war."[28]

Within the United States, Wilson's racial policies further humiliated African American and Japanese residents by reinforcing segregation policies. During the administration of President Calvin Coolidge, the foreign policy initiatives persisted in intervening in Latin America for the benefit of American financiers. By the 1950s the Cold War between Communism and capitalism required a global presence in the battle for economic and philosophical supremacy. President John F. Kennedy asserted that the United States would go anywhere and fight any foe to promote liberty and freedom. However, he recanted that statement well before the reverses of Vietnam exposed the limits of American impositions.[29]

Senator William Fulbright, in his 1966 book *The Arrogance of Power*, remarked on certain similarities between the United States and previous imperial powers, such as Rome and Great Britain, who overextended themselves in delusions of grandeur and self-imposed missions of cultural assimilation. Fulbright wrote: "Power tends to confuse itself with virtue and a great nation is particularly susceptible to the idea that its power is a sign of God's favor, conferring upon it a special responsibility for other nations—to remake them richer and happier and wiser, to remake them, that is, in its own shining image. . . . Once imbued with the idea of a mission, a great nation easily assumes that it has the means as well as the duty to do God's work."[30]

The administration of George W. Bush proclaimed its mission similarly, judging the United States as the "single sustainable model for national success, one that is right and true for every person in every society."[31] In so doing it identified an "arc of instability" that extends from northern South America across northern Africa and through the Mideast to Indonesia. Not coincidentally, many of the nations under scrutiny are oil-producing Muslim countries with inherent religious and economic implications. Chalmers Johnson has charged that the United States has engaged in a new form of colonization by spreading its military bases around the world. By 2003 the Pentagon admitted to having more than 6,700 military installations, more than 700 of them in about 130 foreign countries. Such figures do not include the entirety of the myriad bases in the Mideast, nor the clandestine ones operating in the United Kingdom.[32]

While such locations attest to the obvious political intentions of their purpose, the more subtle inclusions of sport and popular culture go unstudied. On such bases a strict adherence to Protestant fundamentalist beliefs prohibits abortions at military hospitals, while 234 golf courses and a ski center in Bavaria promote particular middle-class value systems. In addition to the importing of American sport forms in the Middle East, the Baghdad Airport contains the first Burger King restaurant in war-ravaged Iraq.[33] The importation of such American cultural forms as fast food, movies, music videos, and sport may produce more lasting influences than a military occupation, but history argues for a more negotiable, often slower and resistant change that produces hybrid cultures.

The Japanese transferred their samurai values to baseball, but that did not deter the nationalism that erupted into a contest for Asia and World War II. The Islamic residents of the Mideast also possess a warrior ethic (expressed in jihad or holy war) that is conducive to sport, but their religious zeal may not wilt as easily to sport's attractions. Like Canadian historian Geoffrey Smith, they may ascertain that "in most global sport—so much of it Americanized—we behold a new and insidious form of imperialism."[34]

Assimilation to American cultural values has generally failed in occupations of fewer than two generations. In almost all territories under its control, the United States proved unable to change religious values, despite ardent efforts by Protestant missionaries and the YMCA. The Americans provided an infrastructure of roads, schools, and civil services, but they could not instill democracy in Asia or the Caribbean, where dictators continued to reign. American governance too often catered to American businesses rather than promote indigenous commerce. In Panama, General Frederick Woerner admitted: "We enforced [the sanctions] quite ineffectively because we didn't want to hurt U.S. business."[35] Colonists who learn the ways of the colonizers may become a threat instead of an ally. Capitalism does not automatically breed democracy, and sport has myriad responses, ranging from acculturation to political warfare. The only given is that both the dominant and subordinate groups will be changed in the process.

Notes

1. Race, Religion, and Manifest Destiny

1. Pakenham, *The Scramble for Africa*; Said, *Culture and Imperialism*, 8; F. U. Adams, *Conquest of the Tropics*, 7.
2. Among the early historians in the heroic genre, see Dibble, *A History of the Sandwich Islands*, and F. U. Adams, *Conquest of the Tropics*. See Bogue, *Frederick Jackson Turner*, on the career of the most influential of the early historians, who posited white Americans as an exceptional people. More contemporary works in the heroic vein are those of Stephen Ambrose. Zimmerman, *First Great Triumph*, offers a recent but more balanced approach. See Hobsbawm and Ranger, *The Invention of Tradition*, on historical constructs.
3. More critical views have been asserted by Limerick, *The Legacy of Conquest*; Wei and Kamel, *Resistance in Paradise*; and Kaplan and Pease, *Cultures of United States Imperialism*.

   Several revisionists have offered new and valuable insights into the imperial process. Among them are Huntington, *The Clash of Civilizations and the Remaking of World Order*; Ferro, *Colonization*; Abernethy, *The Dynamics of Global Dominance*; Guidry, Kennedy, and Zald, *Globalizations and Social Movements*; and Heffer, *The United States and the Pacific*.
4. Blum et al., *The National Experience*, 465, 525, 526 (quote); Garraty, *The American Nation*, 419, 501; http://www.mnsu.edu/emuseum/cultural/anthropology/Morgan.html.
5. Blum et al., *The National Experience*, 525, 526 (quote); Garraty, *The American Nation*, 542; http://mail.rcas.rye.ny.us/ history/Sampson/progress_imperialism/josiah_strong.htm.
6. Gould, *The Mismeasure of Man*; Tucker, *The Science and Politics of Racial Research*; Baker, *From Savage to Negro*; Forbes, "The Manipulation of Race, Caste, and Identity"; Klineberg, *Race Differences*; Carson, *Settlement Folk*.
7. Horsman, *Race and Manifest Destiny*, 3.
8. Dibble, *A History of the Sandwich Islands*, 137; Heffer, *The United States and the*

Pacific, 32, 65, 101–15; Bartholomew, *Maui Remembers*, 11–12, 18. See Jacobson, *Whiteness of a Different Color*, 13, 22–31, on naturalization.

9. Blum et al., *The National Experience*, 334.
10. Baker, *From Savage to Negro*, 24; T. W. Allen, *The Invention of the White Race*, vol. 1, 27–28.
11. Jacobson, *Whiteness of a Different Color*, 159.
12. Lee, "Enforcing the Borders"; Franks, "Baseball and Racism's Traveling Eye."
13. Baker, *From Savage to Negro*, 27.
14. Leonard Wood to Dear Bishop Brent, March 24, 1910, Bishop Charles H. Brent Papers, Library of Congress, box 9.
15. Zimmerman, *First Great Triumph*, 471; Blum et al., *The National Experience*, 569, 584–85; Jacobson, *Barbarian Virtues*, 75–85.
16. Jacobson, *Whiteness of a Different Color*, 78; T. W. Allen, *The Invention of the White Race*; Roediger, *The Wages of Whiteness*, 133 (quote), 145–46.
17. W. W. Brown, "On Race and Change," 56–57.
18. Henry Childs Merwin, "The Irish in American Life," *Atlantic Monthly* (March 1896), 289, 294–95, 298, cited in Jacobson, *Whiteness of a Different Color*, 49.
19. Arnesen, "Whiteness and the Historians' Imagination," 18.
20. Jacobson, *Whiteness of a Different Color*, 56.
21. Jacobson, *Whiteness of a Different Color*, 56 (quote), 57.
22. Pascoe, "Miscegenation Law."
23. Brodkin, *How Jews Became White Folks*, 29.
24. Jacobson, *Whiteness of a Different Color*, 65–67; Guterl, *The Color of Race in America*, 28–44; Brodkin, *How Jews Became White Folks*, 28.
25. Henry Cabot Lodge, "The Restriction of Immigration," *North American Review* 152 (1891), cited in Jacobson, *Whiteness of a Different Color*, 42.
26. Jacobson, *Whiteness of a Different Color*, 223–43.
27. On the extensive literature on the evolution of whiteness, see Ignatiev, *How the Irish Became White*; Lott, *Love and Theft*; Roediger, *The Wages of Whiteness*; Montgomery, *Beyond Equality*; Foner, *Free Soil, Free Labor, Free Men*; Wilentz, *Chants Democratic*; Laurie, *Working People of Philadelphia*; Keil and Jentz, *German Workers in Chicago*; and Gutman, *Work, Culture, and Society in Industrializing America*.

    On the religious factor see Rosenzweig, *Eight Hours for What We Will*; Kantowicz, *Corporation Sole*; and McGreevy, *Parish Boundaries*.

    For a discussion and critique of whiteness studies, see Kolchin, "Whiteness Studies," and the special issue of *International Labor and Working Class History* 60 (Fall 2001).

28. Kasson, *Buffalo Bill's Wild West*; Slotkin, "Buffalo Bill's Wild West."
29. T. S. Hines, *Burnham of Chicago*, 74–124; Badger, *The Great American Fair*; Rydell, *All The World's a Fair*; Neufeld, "The Contribution of the World's Columbian Exposition."
30. *Columbian Exposition Album* (Chicago, 1893), 98, cited in Ziff, *The American 1890s*, 4.
31. Guttmann, *Games and Empires*, 175–77, asserts the initial religious motives of early colonizers. In Asia and Hawaii, American missionaries also turned to commercial ventures.

    See Gems, "The Construction, Negotiation, and Transformation of Racial Identity," or Gems, "The Athlete as Trickster," for alternative explanations of Native American motives.
32. D. W. Adams, *Education for Extinction*; Hoxie, *A Final Promise*; Newcombe, *The Best of the Athletic Boys*.
33. Among the broad range of studies on Progressive era sport and educational practices, see Mrozek, *Sport and American Mentality, 1880–1910*; Hardy, *How Boston Played*; Cavallo, *Muscles and Morals*; Goodman, *Choosing Sides*; and Gems, *Windy City Wars*.
34. Wei and Kamel, *Resistance in Paradise*, 6.
35. Wei and Kamel, *Resistance in Paradise*, 2–5, 33, 66; Garcia, "I Am the Other"; Zimmerman, *First Great Triumph*, 345–49; Pratt, *Expansionists of 1898*.

    On the debate over imperialism see Welch Jr., *Imperialists vs. Anti-imperialists*, 106 (Adams quote), 49–50 (Schurz).
36. Welch Jr., *Imperialists vs. Anti-imperialists*, 66 (Barrett quote), 25 (Proctor); Jacobson, *Barbarian Virtues*, 226 (Beveridge).
37. Quoted in Pratt, *Expansionists of 1898*, 5 (quote), 329.
38. Quoted in Pratt, *Expansionists of 1898*, 301.
39. Quoted in Pratt, *Expansionists of 1898*, 302–3.
40. Pratt, *Expansionists of 1898*, 304–7. Putney, *Muscular Christianity*, 164–67, offers similar responses.
41. Wei and Kamel, *Resistance in Paradise*, 66–67; Fulbright quote from Senator William Fulbright, *The Arrogance of Power* (New York: Random House, 1966), as cited by Jim Lobe at the History News Network Web site, http://hnn.us/articles/631.html.
42. W. M. Hoeger to Leonard Wood, November 7, 1904, Leonard Wood Papers, Library of Congress, Philippines box, Miscellaneous file; Leonard Wood to Dear Bishop Brent, March 24, 1910, Bishop Charles H. Brent Papers, box 9;

Pratt, *Expansionists of 1898*, 12–28; Zimmerman, *First Great Triumph*, 8–14, 88–90, 92–101, 120.

43. Karnow, *In Our Image*, 154 (quotes); Garcia, "I Am the Other," claims that 87 percent of U.S. generals in the Philippines had previously fought Native Americans.

44. P. Kramer, "Jim Crow Science and the 'Negro Problem'"; McFerson, *The Racial Dimension of American Overseas Colonial Policy*, 113; Gatewood Jr., *"Smoked Yankees" and the Struggle for Empire*, 252 (quote).

45. Annual Report, Army Navy Clubs, December 31, 1931, 11, National Archives, Reading Group 350, box 1074; Gatewood, *"Smoked Yankees" and the Struggle for Empire*, 243; McFerson, *The Racial Dimensions of American Overseas Colonial Policy*, 70–71; Dauncey, *The Philippines*, 110 (quote).

46. McFerson, *The Racial Dimensions of American Overseas Colonial Policy*; F. U. Adams, *Conquest of the Tropics*, 7; Stuart, *Isles of Empire*, 247, 260–61, 269; May, *Social Engineering in the Philippines*; Cannadine, *Ornamentalism*; P. A. Kramer, "Empires, Exceptions, and Anglo-Saxons."

For the influence of popular culture see Oriard, *Reading Football*; Hoxie, *A Final Promise*, 88–93; and Nemerov, *Frederic Remington and Turn-of-the-century America*.

On military education see Gatewood, *"Smoked Yankees" and the Struggle for Empire*, 306–9; LeRoy, *Philippine Life in Town and Country*, 214–28; Leonard Wood Papers, Library of Congress, General Orders no. 93 and 205, 1899 (vol. 1); and pp. 82–95 and 114–15 (vol. 2) of Military Orders Having Force of Law by Commanding General, Department of Porto Rico, 1898–1900, box: General Orders, Porto Rico 1898–1900; box: Cuba (1899–1902) Cuba Government folder: Circulars no. 2, 92, 127, in General Orders, Dept. of Cuba, 1901–1902. William H. Taft to Secretary of State Elihu Root, April 21, 1900, in William Howard Taft Papers, Library of Congress, Letterbooks, series 8, Philippine Commission (quote).

47. Taft, *Civil Government in the Philippines*, 49–50.

48. Charles W. Fairbanks, Dedicatory Address, 51, Manila YMCA, October 20, 1909, pamphlet, Library of Congress.

49. May, *Social Engineering in the Philippines*, 24–36, 82–83, 97–120; Constantino, "The Miseducation of the Filipino."

50. Rt. Rev. Charles H. Brent, "Religious Conditions in the Philippines," 1904 pamphlet, n.p., Library of Congress.

51. *The Greatest of Expositions*, 225–39, 272; S. W. Pope, *Patriotic Games*, 42–43; P. A. Kramer, "The Pragmatic Empire," 234–46; Hoberman, *Darwin's Athletes*, 99–109.
52. A host of works address masculinity, including Bederman, *Manliness and Civilization*; Kimmel, *Manhood in America*; Putney, *Muscular Christianity*; Townsend, *Manhood at Harvard*; Rotundo, *American Manhood*; Carnes and Griffen, *Meanings for Manhood*; Chapman, *Sandow the Magnificent*; and Ernst, *Weakness Is a Crime*.

    On feminization see Douglas, *The Feminization of American Culture*; Marks, *Bicycles, Bangs, and Bloomers*; Cahn, *Coming On Strong*; and Gordon, *Gender and Higher Education in the Progressive Era*. On bodies see Vertinsky, *The Eternally Wounded Woman*; Armstrong, *American Bodies*; and Gilman, "Damaged Men."

    On football see Gems, *For Pride, Profit, and Patriarchy*.
53. Hoganson, *Fighting for American Manhood*, 43–67; Kimmel, *Manhood in America*, 7 (quote).
54. Southgate, *History: What and Why?* 100–113; Kaplan and Pease, *Cultures of United States Imperialism*, 3–21; L. A. Perez Jr., "We Are the World." Among the numerous analyses of imperialism in the British empire, see the works of J. A. Mangan, including *The Games Ethic and Imperialism* and (as editor) *Making Imperial Mentalities*. The meager American efforts of book length consist of Guttmann, *Games and Empires*; Franks, *Hawaiian Sports in the Twentieth Century*; Franks, *Crossing Sidelines, Crossing Cultures*; and Reaves, *Taking In a Game*. See Phillips, "Deconstructing Sport History," for a critique of the field. The theoretical framework for this study is encompassed in Hoare and Smith, *Selections from the Prison Notebooks of Antonio Gramsci*.

2. China and the Rejection of Christianity

1. Ropp, *Heritage of China*; Huntington, *The Clash of Civilizations and the Remaking of World Order*, 43, 95–100; Fessler, *China*, 43–48; Eller, *History of Evangelical Missions*, 194, 232; Graham, "Gender, Culture, and Christianity," 27.
2. Graham, "Gender, Culture, and Christianity," 27, 36.
3. Jackson, *Gold Dust*, 291; Johnson, *Roaring Camp*, 240–51 (quote at 245), 306–7; Limerick, *The Legacy of Conquest*, 261–62.
4. Wallace, *California through Five Centuries*, 165, 192–94, 200–209, 308–12; Limerick, *The Legacy of Conquest*, 262–69; Roediger, *The Wages of Whiteness*, 167–70, 179–80; Jacobson, *Barbarian Virtues*, 75–82, 193–95; Lee, "Enforcing the Borders," 63–68.
5. Reaves, *Taking In a Game*, 24, 28 (quote).

6. Reaves, *Taking In a Game*, 19–27, 29–35; Latourette, *World Service*, 249; Brownell, *Training the Body for China*, 39; "A Game between Chinese Players," *Chicago Tribune*, September 1, 1888, 6 (quote).
7. *Chicago Tribune*, September 1, 1888, 6 (quote); *Chicago Tribune*, September 23, 1888, 14. See Caspar Whitney, "Non-athletic China," for an unflattering portrayal.
8. Graham, "Gender, Culture, and Christianity," 14–15, 29–75; Schoonover, *Uncle Sam's War of 1898*, 39–47.
9. Blum et al., *The National Experience*, 308–9, 525, 535–38; Putney, *Muscular Christianity*, 132; Latourette, *World Service*, 249–50; Reaves, *Taking In a Game*, xvi, 34, 36, 40; Brownell, *Training the Body for China*, 39; Graham, "Gender, Culture, and Christianity," 42–43, 79, 100–108 (quote at 108).
10. Reaves, *Taking In a Game*, 138; Brands, *Bound to Empire*, 80–81.
11. Graham, "Gender, Culture, and Christianity," 157, cites correspondence in the *Chinese Recorder*.
12. *Advance* (November 8, 1904), cited in Putney, *Muscular Christianity*, 167; *Harper's Weekly* (October 27, 1900), cited in Nemerov, *Frederic Remington and Turn-of-the-century America*, 79.
13. Reaves, *Taking In a Game*, xvi, 37; Mrs. H. C. Smith, *A History of the Young Women's Christian Association of North-Western College*, 32, 45–47, in North Central College Archives; Graham, "Gender, Culture, and Christianity," 101–4 (1908 quote at 102); Brownell, *Training the Body for China*, 40 (Ross quote).
14. Latourette, *World Service*, 266; Naismith, *Basketball*, 154–55. Naismith claims an 1898 start for basketball, while Reaves, *Taking In a Game*, 36, and Guttmann, *Games and Empires*, 101, favor earlier dates.
15. Young Men's Christian Association (YMCA) Archives, Philippines box, NP Correspondence Reports, 1911–1968, University of Minnesota; Graham, "Gender, Culture, and Christianity," 109, 141–48, 171–74.
16. Jacobson, *Barbarian Virtues*, 215–16; Reaves, *Taking In a Game*, 23, 38.
17. Reaves, *Taking In a Game*, 40; Franks, *Hawaiian Sports in the Twentieth Century*, 24–32; clipping, May 11, 1912, at the National Baseball Hall of Fame Archives, Hawaii file (quote).
18. Reaves, *Taking In a Game*, 37; Franks, *Hawaiian Sports in the Twentieth Century*, 24–34, 36 (quote); clipping, *San Jose Mercury*, April 13, 1912, National Baseball Hall of Fame Archives, Hawaii file.
19. Elwood S. Brown, *Annual Report, Oct. 1, 1911–Oct. 1, 1912*, YMCA Archives, Philip-

pines box NP, Correspondence Reports, 1911–1968 (quotes, n.p.); Davidann, "Citadels of Civilization."

20. Reaves, *Taking In a Game*, xvii; Elfers, *The Tour to End All Tours*, 125–32, 124 (quote).
21. Elfers, *The Tour to End All Tours*, 125.
22. Graham, "Gender, Culture, and Christianity," 199–201; Chengting T. Wang to My Dear Fletcher, February 19, 1915, and Report on the Chinese in Manila and the Philippines (unsigned), both in YMCA Archives, Philippines box, Int. Div. 167, local assoc., 1906–1973.
23. Jacobson, *Barbarian Virtues*, 35; Reaves, *Taking In a Game*, 40–41.
24. Eller, *History of Evangelical Missions*, 254–59; Brownell, *Training the Body for China*, 43, 48, 50, 52–53; Graham, "Gender, Culture, and Christianity," 36, 377–78, 401–8, 424–39. Hollinger, "Interchange: The Practice of History," 611, suggests the children of the missionaries proved more successful as Cold War strategists and politicians.
25. Latourette, *World Service*, 252, 275, 283; Reaves, *Taking In a Game*, 41, 58; Naismith, *Basketball*, 156; *Atlanta Highlands Journal*, May 19, 1926, and May 26, 1927, National Baseball Hall of Fame Archives, on the 1922–23 tour of the Herbert Hunter All-Stars; Graham, "Gender, Culture, and Christianity," 103, 108.
26. Olin D. Wannamaker, "Brief Description of Princeton-in-Peking," February 1923, Rockefeller Archive Center, Rockefeller University (located in folder "Princeton in Peking").
27. Franks, *Crossing Sidelines, Crossing Cultures*, xiv; Reaves, *Taking In a Game*, 41.
28. Frye and Hangen, *The Year Book of the Evangelical Church*, 35–36, at North Central College Archives.
29. Reaves, *Taking In a Game*, 42–43; Franks, "Baseball and Racism's Traveling Eye," 187–88, 191. Lee Gum Hong was also known by the Anglo appellation of Al Bowen.
30. Fan Hong, " 'Iron Bodies"; Brownell, *Training the Body for China*, 50.
31. T. W. Allen, *The Invention of the White Race*, 27; Brodkin, *How Jews Became White Folks*, 72; R. Park, "Sport and Recreation among Chinese American Communities," 462 (quote); Franks, "Baseball and Racism's Traveling Eye," 190 (on Akana).
32. Reaves, *Taking In a Game*, 7, 44–48 (quote at 47).
33. Reaves, *Taking In a Game*, 140–51.
34. http://www.gio.gov.tw/taiwan and http://www.sinica.edu.tw/tit/sports/1295-sp2.html.

3. Baseball and Bushido in Japan

1. Varley, *Japanese Culture*, 235–70; Langer, *An Encyclopedia of World History*, 920–23.
2. Varley, *Japanese Culture*, 208, 210; Davidann, *A World of Crisis and Progress*. See Mangan, *The Games Ethic and Imperialism*, and Dyreson, "Regulating the Body and the Body Politic," on the dissemination of Western ideology via sport. Various associations of sport and Japanese national character are made in Guttmann and Thompson, *Japanese Sports*, and Morris–Suzuki, "The Invention and Reinvention of 'Japanese Culture.'" The Japanese curriculum is described in A. D. Stauffacher, "Physical Education in Japan," *College Chronicle* 24, no. 10 (March 15, 1913): 159–62, available in the North Central College Archives.
3. Guthrie-Shimizu, "For Love of the Game"; Zimmerman, *First Great Triumph*, 163, 239 (quote).
4. Reaves, "A History of Baseball in China," 14–15; Latourette, *World Service*, 165–66; Roden, "Baseball and the Quest for National Dignity in Meiji Japan"; Whitney, "Non-athletic China." See Tanada, "Diffusion into the Orient," for early British initiatives.
5. McFerson, *The Racial Dimension of American Overseas Colonial Policy*, 34–39; Varley, *Japanese Culture*, 249–50.
6. Reaves, *Taking In a Game*, 49; Kusaka, "The Development of Baseball Organizations in Japan"; Roden, "Baseball and the Quest for National Dignity in Meiji Japan," 289–95 (quotes at 294).
7. Roden, "Baseball and the Quest for National Dignity in Meiji Japan," 294.
8. Roden, "Baseball and the Quest for National Dignity in Meiji Japan," 294–99; Roden, *Schooldays in Imperial Japan*, 124–25; Kusaka, "The Development of Baseball Organizations in Japan," 267.
9. Roden, "Baseball and the Quest for National Dignity in Meiji Japan," 298.
10. Roden, "Baseball and the Quest for National Dignity in Meiji Japan," 296–97; Roden, *Schooldays in Imperial Japan*, 124. On imperialism see Wei and Kamel, *Resistance in Paradise*; A. Kramer, *The Samoa Islands*; Gray, *Amerika Samoa*; Field, *Mau*; and Stuart, *Isles of Empire*.
11. Whitney, "Athletic Awakening of the Japanese," 165, 166 (quotes, respectively).
12. Leonard Wood to Dear Bishop Brent, March 24, 1910, Bishop Charles H. Brent Papers, box 9, Library of Congress. Similar and earlier concerns are expressed in M. W. Hoeger to Wood, November 7, 1904, Leonard Wood Papers, Philippines box, Library of Congress. Schoonover, *Uncle Sam's War of 1898*, 40, 51, 66.
13. Pratt, *Expansionists of 1898*, 217. A biographical sketch of Steere Gikaku Noda at

the Hawaii Sports Hall of Fame in the Bishop Museum in Honolulu states that the Asahis later won 15 championships as members of the Hawaii Baseball League. Franks, "Baseball and Racism's Traveling Eye," 184, and Sullivan, *Middle Innings*, 9, on the *L.A. Times* quotes.

14. Elfers, *The Tour to End All Tours*, 115; Kusaka, "The Development of Baseball Organizations in Japan," 268–69.
15. Stuffy (Alfred W. Place) to Amos Alonzo Stagg, November 7, 1908, Amos Alonzo Stagg Papers, box 63, folder 3, University of Chicago Special Collections.
16. Guthrie-Shimizu, "For Love of the Game," 661; A. W. Place to Stagg, November 7, 1908, Stagg Papers, box 63, folder 3; Obojski, *The Rise of Japanese Baseball Power*, 4, 7–9, 10–14; Elfers, *The Tour to End All Tours*, 111, 113; Foster, *Spalding's Official Base Ball Guide*, 1910, 303 (quote).
17. Kingman, "Japan on the Diamond"; Richter, "Collegiate 1909 Invasion of Japan," 481 (quote).
18. Stagg to R. Kurosawa, July 29, 1910, Stagg Papers, box 63, folder 3.
19. Stagg to Ralph Cleary, August 30, 1910, Stagg Papers, box 63, folder 3.
20. Stagg to Kurosawa, July 29, 1910, and A. W. Place to Alonzo Stagg, November 7, 1908, Stagg Papers, box 63, folder 3.
21. Fred Merrifield to My Dear Lon (Stagg), June 27, 1910, Stagg Papers, box 63, folder 3.
22. Pat Page, International Baseball Series, Fall 1910, correspondence; Page to Stagg, October 6, 1910, and October 14, 1910 (all in Stagg Papers, box 63, folder 3).
23. T. Takasugi, Pres. of Waseda Base Ball Assoc., to Prof. A. Alonzo Stagg, July 20, 1910; and Pat Page to Stagg, October 20, 1910 (both in Stagg Papers, box 63, folder 3).
24. Kusaka, "The Development of Baseball Organizations in Japan," 269–70; Douglas S. Knight to University of Chicago Board of Athletics, December 29, 1910, Stagg Papers, box 63, folder 3. Franks, *Crossing Sidelines, Crossing Cultures*, 58, indicates a Waseda University win over the University of Utah in Salt Lake City on its 1911 U.S. tour. Rhea Mansfield, "The Man Who Made Baseball in Japan," *Baseball Magazine*, July 1912, 26–30, National Baseball Hall of Fame Archives, Foreign: Baseball—Japan, 1880–1949 file. See Elwood S. Brown, *Annual Report, Oct. 1, 1914–Oct. 1, 1915*, n.p., Young Men's Christian Association (YMCA) Archives, Philippines box NP, Correspondence Reports, 1911–1968, University of Minnesota, on his plans for the Far East Olympics. The idea for

a regional athletic fest was inspired by a baseball game between Japan and the Philippines; see Elwood Brown, *Annual Report*, Oct. 1, 1912–Oct. 1, 1913, n.p., and *Annual Report*, Oct. 1, 1913–Oct. 1, 1914, n.p. (both in YMCA Archives).

25. Blum et al., *The National Experience*, 584–85; Jacobson, *Barbarian Virtues*, 82–85. The 1913–1914 barnstorming tour is discussed in the Barnstorming file, National Baseball Hall of Fame Archives, and Elfers, *The Tour to End All Tours*. The 1915 baseball tour is detailed in the Department of Physical Education and Athletics Papers, 1892–1974, box 27, folder 2, University of Chicago Special Collections.
26. Guthrie-Shimizu, "For Love of the Game," 651; Latourette, *World Service*, 165–66, 171–74; Davidann, *A World of Crisis and Progress*, 100–119, 128.
27. Edith Wildes, cited in Elwood S. Brown, *Annual Report*, Oct. 1, 1916–Oct. 1, 1917, n.p., YMCA Archives.
28. Brown, *Annual Report*, Oct. 1, 1916–Oct. 1, 1917.
29. Brown, *Annual Report*, Oct. 1, 1916–Oct. 1, 1917.
30. Brown, *Annual Report*, Oct. 1, 1916–Oct. 1, 1917.
31. Kusaka, "The Development of Baseball Organizations in Japan," 269; Davidann, "Citadels of Civilization," 31; Reaves, *Taking In a Game*, 52, 53 (quotes.)
32. The Okabe-Stagg correspondence is contained in box 2, folder 11, of the Stagg Papers. On the role of the organic intellectual, see Hoare and Smith, *Selections from the Prison Notebooks of Antonio Gramsci*, 3–6, 57–59.
33. Okabe to Mr. and Mrs. Stagg, February 27, 1920, and March 6, 1921, and newspaper clippings from *Japan Times*, March 2, 1921, and *Japan Advertiser*, March 2, 1921 (all in box 2, folder 11, Stagg Papers); Whitney, "Athletic Awakening of the Japanese," 165–66; Franks, *Crossing Sidelines, Crossing Boundaries*, xiv.
34. James Naismith, *Basketball*, 156. Okabe to Mr. and Mrs. Stagg, August 17, 1925; *Philippines Herald* clipping; and H. Okabe to Mr. Stagg, February 6, 1929 (quote) (all in box 2, folder 11, Stagg Papers).
35. *Philippines Herald* clipping and Okabe to Mr. and Mrs. Stagg, August 17, 1925, box 2, folder 11, Stagg Papers. Garraty, *The American Nation*, 679, indicates that while other nations received immigration quotas, Japan got none.
36. Obojski, *The Rise of Japanese Baseball Power*, 15–19; Reaves, *Taking In a Game*, 56. A 1925 baseball scorebook, box 28, folder 5, Stagg Papers, indicates that 5 games were tied. Rain and darkness ended several extra-inning contests. On Tobita Suishu see William W. Kelly, "Blood and Guts in Japanese Professional Baseball," 104–5. In addition to the Reach tour, the White Sox and Giants included Japan in their 1913 globetrotting excursion.

37. Reaves, *Taking In a Game*, 59–63; Kingman, "Japan on the Diamond."
38. Frye and Hangen, *The Year Book of the Evangelical Church*, 33–35; Eller, *History of Evangelical Missions*, 204, 228.
39. Obojski, *The Rise of Japanese Baseball Power*, 18–19; H. Okabe to Mr. Stagg, February 6, 1929, box 2, folder 11, Stagg Papers.
40. Stagg to Okabe, July 30, 1929, box 2, folder 11, Stagg Papers.
41. Stagg to Okabe, February 3, 1930; June 30, 1930; August 28, 1930; and September 23, 1930 (all in box 2, folder 11, Stagg Papers).
42. Okabe to My Dear Prof. Stagg, June 30, 1930, box 2, folder 11, Stagg Papers; A. A. Kempa, *A Survey of Physical Education in the Territory of Hawaii, 1930* (n.p)., Bishop Museum, Hawaii Sports Hall of Fame, Honolulu, 22; 1930 scorebook, box 29, folder 2, Stagg Papers (quote).
43. Abe, Kiyohara, and Nakajima, "Fascism, Sport, and Society in Japan."
44. Obojski, *The Rise of Japanese Baseball Power*, 19–20; Reaves, *Taking In a Game*, 64–67.
45. Welky, "Viking Girls, Mermaids, and Little Brown Men," 40 (quotes).
46. Obojski, *The Rise of Japanese Baseball Power*, 21–30, gives 1934 as the organizational date for the pro league, with actual play starting in 1936. See Whiting, *The Chrysanthemum and the Bat*, 221–46, for further development of pro baseball in Japan and repeated challenges to American teams. See Reaves, *Taking In a Game*, 76–78, on the 1935 Japanese tour to the United States and FDR's support. See Guthrie-Shimizu, "For Love of the Game," for a decidedly different interpretation of U.S.-Japanese relations.
47. Abe, Kiyohara, and Nakajima, "Fascism, Sport, and Society in Japan," 13.
48. Said, *Culture and Imperialism*, 209–10, details the stages of ideological and active resistance. See Davidann, *A World of Crisis and Progress*, on the inability of the YMCA to effect cultural change; and R. C. Crepeau, "Pearl Harbor," on the idealistic belief in the transformative powers of baseball.
49. Roden, "Baseball and the Quest for National Dignity in Meiji Japan," 302–3.

4. Sport and Colonialism in the Philippines

1. Mojares, "The Hills Are Still There"; P. Kramer, "Reflex Actions: Social Imperialism between the United States and the Philippines, 1898–1929" (presented at the American Historical Association 117th Annual Meeting, Chicago, January 2–5, 2003).
2. Beran, "Americans in the Philippines." Among numerous more recent works

on imperialism, see Said, *Culture and Imperialism*, and Kaplan and Pease, *Cultures of United States Imperialism*.

3. Schurz quoted in Zimmerman, *First Great Triumph*, 377.
4. *Catholic Citizen*, September 10, 1898, 4, cited in Jacobson, *Whiteness of a Different Color*, 211.
5. Welch Jr., *Imperialists vs. Anti-imperialists*.
6. Karnow, *In Our Image*, 106–30. See Guerrero, *Philippine Society and Revolution*, 26–35, for placement of the independence movement as early as 1892.
7. Wei and Kamel, *Resistance in Paradise*, 6–9; Pratt, *Expansionists of 1898*, 287–303 (quote at 301).
8. Przybyszewski, "Judicial Conservatism and Protestant Faith," 484–85 (quote).
9. Dean C. Worcester Papers, Bentley Library, University of Michigan; P. A. Kramer, "The Pragmatic Empire"; D. C. Worcester, "Field Sports among the Wild Men of Luzon"; D. C. Worcester, "The Non-Christian Peoples of the Philippine Islands." Widespread interest in such exotic "others" is also indicated in H. B. Dickson, "Personal Experiences among the Head Hunters of N.E. India," in YMCA Minutes, Missionary Committee Report, May 5–June 18, 1915, box 2, folder 6, North Central College Archives. Also see Fred Eggan Papers, University of Chicago Special Collections, on early anthropological studies in the Philippines.
10. D. C. Worcester, "The Non-Christian Peoples of the Philippines," 1180, 1182, 1189 (quotes, respectively); P. Kramer, "Jim Crow Science and the 'Negro Problem,'" 237–41, on Bean.
11. See Said, *Culture and Imperialism*, 152, on technology as power; and Nick Deocampo, "Imperialist Fictions," 225–36, on Edison. Milton W. Stahler, *College Chronicle* 36, no. 3 (October 31, 1914), 41, in North Central College Archives, describes a missionary's use of a Victrola to attract natives.
12. D. C. Worcester, *The Philippines*, vol. 2, 514 (quote).
13. D. C. Worcester, *The Philippines*, vol. 2, 515.
14. Walsh, "Baseball in the Philippines"; Reaves, *Taking In a Game*, 91–92; LeRoy, *Philippine Life in Town and Country*, 214–15.
15. Beran, "Americans in the Philippines," 71; Gleeck Jr., *American Institutions in the Philippines*, 39 (quotes).
16. Wakefield, *Playing to Win*; Steven W. Pope, "An Army of Athletes"; Nankville, *The History of the Twenty-fifth Regiment United States Infantry*, 163–69; Bell quoted in Seymour, *Baseball*, 324–25.
17. William Howard Taft to My Dear Secretary (Elihu Root), October 21, 1900,

in William Howard Taft Papers, Library of Congress, reel 463 (quote); Dery, "Prostitution in Colonial Manila"; Hoganson, *Fighting for American Manhood*, 187–91.

18. Rt. Rev. Charles H. Brent, "Religious Conditions in the Philippines," 1904 pamphlet, n.p., Library of Congress.
19. Coffman, *The Regulars*, 64.
20. Fee, *A Woman's Impression of the Philippines*, 283–86 (quote at 286). See Freer, *The Philippine Experiences of an American Teacher*, 273, 287, for another teacher's account of baseball. Also see Monroe Woolley, " 'Batter Up' in the Philippines," *Outdoor World and Recreation*, May 1913, 314–14, in National Baseball Hall of Fame Archives, Foreign: Philippines file; Walsh, "Baseball in the Philippines," 106; and Reaves, *Taking In a Game*, 94–96.
21. LeRoy, *Philippine Life in Town and Country*; clipping on cockfights, National Archives, RG 350, box 656; Gleeck Jr., *The Manila Americans*, 6; Salamanca, *The Filipino Reaction to American Rule*, 108–9, 117–20; Gates, *Schoolbooks and Krags*, 61, 63; P. A. Kramer, "The Pragmatic Empire," 167; P. Kramer, "Jim Crow Science and the 'Negro Problem,"' 231–35; May, *Social Engineering in the Philippines*, 88–92. Baseball leagues still featured integrated play. The 25th Infantry, composed of African Americans, perennially won the army championship.
22. See Parsons, "American Snobbishness in the Philippines," and Dery, "Prostitution in Colonial Manila," for indications of Americans' racial attitudes and social practices. V. Rafael, "White Women and United States Rule in the Philippines," 639–66 (quote at 658).
23. Shaw and Francia, *Vestiges of War*, 89–133 (Wood quote at 91); also see pp. 46 and 53 for accounts of massacres of five hundred to nine hundred Muslims, including women and children, under both Wood and General John J Pershing. See Coffman, *The Regulars*, 45, on Foulois quote. See Gatewood, *"Smoked Yankees,"* on African American soldiers in the islands.
24. See P. A. Kramer, "Empires, Exceptions, and Anglo-Saxons," on segregation. On Burnham see Karnow, *In Our Image*, 16–17, 211, 214–15; and T. Hines, "The Imperial Façade". Moore, *Plan of Chicago*, 29 (quote).
25. T. S. Hines, *Burnham of Chicago*, 203.
26. Burnham to William H. Taft, April 4, 1905; Burnham to J. G. White, April 10, 1905 (quote); Burnham to Forbes, August 7, 1905 (all in Daniel Burnham Papers, vol. 15, series 1, 165, 194–95, 499).
27. Karnow, *In Our Image*, 16–17.
28. T. S. Hines, *Burnham of Chicago*, 206–7.

29. T. S. Hines, *Burnham of Chicago*, 213; Boyer, *The City of Collective Memory*, 4–7, 14–15, 94, 99, 103.
30. Karnow, *In Our Image*, 214–15; Burnham Papers, 1904: 5–7, 356–57, 499, 579–80, 596–99, 629–30, 641 (quote), 675; Moore, *Plan of Chicago*, 28–29; T. S. Hines, *Burnham of Chicago*, 208–9. Burnham and Forbes were family friends who had recommended each other to President Theodore Roosevelt for the Philippine posts.
31. T. S. Hines, *Burnham of Chicago*, 209.
32. T. S. Hines, *Burnham of Chicago*, 210.
33. *Ninth Annual Report*, 1910 (Manila: Bureau of Printing, 1910), n.p., in Worcester Papers, box 3, on restructuring; Beran, "Americans in the Philippines," 72, on holidays.
34. Karnow, *In Our Image*, 139–95; Zwick, "Mark Twain's Anti-imperialist Writings in the 'American Century,"' 39; Guerrero, *Philippine Society and Revolution*, 31–35; Salamanca, *The Filipino Reaction to American Rule*, 156–57, 178–82, 185; Kaplan and Pease, *Cultures of United States Imperialism*, 189–90.
35. Karnow, *In Our Image*, 176–77 (quote); Salamanca, *The Filipino Reaction to American Rule*, 158.
36. *Manila Cablenews*, August 8, 1907, cited in Stanley, *A Nation in the Making*, 107.
37. *St. Louis Post-Dispatch*, June 19, 1904, 4, cited in P. A. Kramer, "The Pragmatic Empire," 235. For a similar reaction see Jim Zwick, "How the Filipinos Feel about the Exhibition of the Igorottes in the United States" (editorial), *The Public* 8 (March 3, 1906), available at http://www.boondocksnet.com/expos/wfe_publico60303.html; *The Greatest of Expositions*, 230–39; Annette Hofmann, "The German and German-American Contribution to the 1904 Olympic Games in St. Louis" (presented at the North American Society for Sport History Conference, May 28–31, 2004, Pacific Grove CA). Rosaldo, *Ilongot Headhunting*, 2, 260–63, asserts that the American-trained Philippines Constabulary retaliated for the death of an American anthropologist by headhunting in 1909.
38. Sixto Lopez and Thomas T. Patterson, "The Filipinos Will Not 'Take Up the White Man's Burden,"' *The Public* 7 (May 21, 1904), cited in Jim Zwick, "Anti-imperialism in the United States, 1898–1935," http://www.boondocksnet.com/./kipling/lopez_wmb.html.
39. Salamanca, *The Filipino Reaction to American Rule*, 87, 160–63; V. L. Rafael, "White Love"; Gleeck Jr., *The Manila Americans*, 57.
40. May, *Social Engineering in the Philippines*, 93, 96; Coffman, *The Regulars*, 73; Salamanca, *The Filipino Reaction to American Rule*, 77–80; Pratt, *Expansionists of*

1898, 312; Gleeck Jr., *The Manila Americans*, 48–49. Homer C. Stuntz to Arthur J. Brown, September 30, 1910, Bishop Charles H. Brent Papers, Library of Congress, box 9, addresses concerns in the religious debate.

41. Bocobo-Olivar, *History of Physical Education in the Philippines*, 24–33.
42. Karnow, *In Our Image*, 216; May, *Social Engineering in the Philippines*, 20–21; W. Cameron Forbes, *Football Notebook*, 1901, HUD 10897.29, Harvard Archives; W. Cameron Forbes, clipping of 1898 season, in HUD 10898, Harvard Archives. Remson B. Ogilby to George Wharton Pepper, December 19, 1912, Brent Papers, indicates a family contribution toward the building of a gym at Brent's private school in Baguio as well. See Pier, *American Apostles to the Philippines*, ix, and P. A. Kramer, "The Pragmatic Empire," for divergent views on Forbes's influence in the Philippines. Licuanen, *Filipinos and Americans*, 38–44, 68–92, is a more measured response. Alcantara, "Baguio between Two Wars"; Stanley, *A Nation in the Making*, 138, on the *Manila Times*.
43. Gleeck Jr., *The Manila Americans*, 25, 64–72; Licuanen, *Filipinos and Americans*, 41–42, 56–67; T. Hines, "The Imperial Façade"; Alcantara, "Baguio between the Wars," 221. YMCA Archives, Philippines box, NP Correspondence, 1911–1968, Admin. Reports, 1912–1917, indicates that the city moat was filled to create football and baseball fields as well as courts for volleyball and tennis. Annual Report, Army and Navy Club, December 31, 1931, National Archives, RG 350, box 1074, on segregation; Brent Papers, box 47, Philippines Islands folder, Baguio School pamphlet (quote).
44. Frederic S. Marquardt Papers, Bentley Library, University of Michigan.
45. Marquadt Papers; Woolley, " 'Batter Up"'; Calo, *Organization and Management of Athletic Meets*, 2–3.
46. Marquardt Papers; National Baseball Hall of Fame Archives, Foreign: Philippines file; Woolley, " 'Batter Up,"' 313–14 (quotes). Reaves, *Taking In a Game*, 94–97, describes Cebu as a "hotbed" of baseball with top American coaches.
47. Reaves, *Taking In a Game*, 95, 102; Walsh, "Baseball in the Philippines," 106; A. J. Puhl to Pat Page, September 9. 1910, and A. J. Puhl to Frank McIntyre, September 9, 1910 (both in box 63, folder 1, Amos Alonzo Stagg Papers, University of Chicago Special Collections); Pat Page, "International Baseball Series, Fall 1910," Stagg Papers, box 63, folder 3.
48. Stanley Weston, "Pancho Villa, the Gigantic Runt," clipping, 64; Hal Hennesey, "Pancho Villa: The Tiniest Giant," clipping, 40; Bill Miller, "Boxing's Mosquito Fleet," 6–6 (all in Villa [Francisco Guilledo] file, International Boxing Hall of Fame). Remson B. Ogilby to My Dear Bishop, September 5, 1910, in Brent

Papers (quote). Private Carmi L. Williams Co. G, 13th Infantry, to Rt. Rev. Charles H. Brent, November 19, 1914, indicates that the YMCA experienced similar difficulties.

49. D. L. Andrews, "Desperately Seeking Michel"; Okihiro, *Margins and Mainstreams*, 28, 56–57, 111; Coffman, *The Regulars*, 62 (quote).
50. George A. Dorsey, "Lazy Streak in Philippines," *Chicago Tribune*, July 7, 1912, 8.
51. R. F. Barton to Dear professor [sic] Starr, July 16, 1914, Frederick Starr Papers, University of Chicago Special Collections.
52. Goldberg, *Racist Culture*, 41–47; Coffman, *The Regulars*, 67 (quote), 80.
53. Bulosan, *America Is in the Heart*, 66–67 (quote); Coffman, *The Regulars*, 66; San Juan Jr., *On Becoming Filipino*, 62.
54. Coffman, *The Regulars*, 66.
55. Ontal, "Fagen and Other Ghosts"; Nankville, *The History of the Twenty-fifth Regiment United States Infantry*, 163, 166, 169; Coffman, *The Regulars*, 111, 127.
56. Marquardt Papers; Bocobo-Olivar, *History of Physical Education in the Philippines*, 46–48; Witi Ross, "Education in the Philippines," 17, box 142, folder 13, Fred Eggan Papers, University of Chicago.
57. Beran, "Americans in the Philippines," 74; Sabas Tordesillas, "How Our Team Surprised the People of Patnongon," *Teachers' Assembly Herald* 6, no. 19 (May 3, 1913): 112–13, and Luis Santiago, "The Organization of the San Mateo Baseball Team," *Teachers' Assembly Herald* 5, no. 26 (1912): 142–43, both in Pecson and Racelis, *Tales of the American Teachers in the Philippines*, 192 and 195–99, respectively.
58. Starr Papers, box 11, notebook 7, describes Forbes's attempts to entice the Moros via baseball in 1908, while Governor Wood used technology to awe natives in Mindanao, in "Report of the First Annual Moro Agricultural and Industrial Fair, Aug. 1–4, 1906," in Wood Papers, Philippines box.
59. Bocobo-Olivar, *History of Physical Education in the Philippines*, 47; W. W. Marquardt, Dir. of Education, Manila, October 25, 1916, in National Archives, RG 350, box 931, on playgrounds.
60. Latourette, *World Service*, 317. Gleeck Jr., *American Institutions in the Philippines*, 72–77, dates the building from 1908, while Latourette indicates 1909. YMCA Archives, Philippines box, Manila file, indicates building plans as early as 1901, and the request for tax-exempt status.
61. Beran, "Americans in the Philippines," 78–79; Gleeck Jr., *American Institutions in the Philippines*, 75; Bocobo-Olivar, *History of Physical Education in the Philippines*,

55–56; Elwood S. Brown, *Annual Report, Oct. 1, 1911–Oct. 1, 1912*, Philippines Correspondence Reports, 1911–1968, YMCA Archives, n.p. (quote).

62. Governor-General Harrison, Executive Order 79, September 16, 1914, National Archives, R 350, box 931, on Brown's appointment; Gleeck Jr., *American Institutions in the Philippines*, 74–74; Philippines Correspondence Reports, 1911–1968, YMCA Archives, Administrative Reports file, n.p.,
63. Elwood S. Brown, *Annual Report, Oct. 1, 1912–Oct. 1, 1913*, YMCA Archives, n.p. (quote).
64. Elwood S. Brown, *Annual Report, Oct. 1, 1914–Oct. 1, 1915*, YMCA Archives, n.p.
65. On YMCA segregation policies, see Philippines, International Division 167, local associations, 1906–1973, YMCA Archives, Philippines box, Manila file, 1906–1907; William H. Taft to James F. Smith, Gov.-Gen. of the Philippines, December 31, 1906; Chengting T. Wang to My Dear Fletcher, February 19, 1915; and H. W. Lowe to George I. Babcock, March 21, 1921 (latter three from YMCA Archives, Philippines correspondence file, 1906–1908).

    On volleyball results see Brown, *Annual Report, Oct. 1, 1914–Oct. 1, 1915*, n.p.; and Clymer, *Protestant Missionaries in the Philippines*, 66, 92.
66. Damon Runyon, "Briton Outclassed by Filipino Demon in Bloody Fight," clipping, and Weston, "Pancho Villa," 64 (quote), both in Villa (Francisco Guilledo) file, International Boxing Hall of Fame. On boxing legislation see National Archives, RG 350, box 691.
67. Weston, "Pancho Villa," 66; T. S. Andrews, *Ring Battles of Centuries and Sporting Almanac*, 29.
68. Espana-Maram, "Negotiating Identity," 118–26; Roger Mooney, "Going Home a Hero: How Ceferino Garcia Finally Realized His Dreams," *Ring*, April 1994, 26–28, 60, in Garcia file, International Boxing Hall of Fame; *School News Review*, October 1, 1935, 8, National Archives, RG 350, box 1187.
69. Bocobo-Olivar, *History of Physical Education in the Philippines*, 49.
70. Bocobo-Olivar, *History of Physical Education in the Philippines*, 50.
71. Coffman, *The Regulars*, 338; Bocobo-Olivar, *History of Physical Education in the Philippines*, 50 (quote).
72. Bocobo-Olivar, *History of Physical Education in the Philippines*, 48.
73. Karnow, *In Our Image*, 20–22, 228; Guerrero, *Philippine Society and Revolution*, 184.
74. V. L. Rafael, "White Love," 186–87.
75. Salamanca, *The Filipino Reaction to American Rule*, 139; Karnow, *In Our Image*, 13; Guerrero, *Philippine Society and Revolution*, 47, 52, 134–35, 167, 169.

76. Salamanca, *The Filipino Reaction to American Rule*, 109–10, 117–20; Gleeck Jr., *American Institutions in the Philippines*, 78.
77. J. Truitt Maxwell to Elwood S. Brown, April 18, 1922, YMCA Archives, Philippines correspondence file, 1920–1923.
78. *School News Review*, July 15, 1934, 8, in National Archives, RG 350, box 1187; Earl Carroll, Sec. of Luzon, *Annual Administrative Report*, 1932, and E. S. Turner to Frank V. Slack, August 7, 1935 (both in YMCA Archives, Correspondence and Reports file, 1930–1936).
79. Salamanca, *The Filipino Reaction to American Rule*, 87; Gleeck Jr., *American Institutions in the Philippines*, 45, 301–2; Stanley, *A Nation in the Making*, 315, n. 2.

    On the incorporation of Spanish and tribal languages into the local vernacular, see William D. MacClintock, "The Philippine Teachers' Vacation Assembly," *The World Today* 16 (January 1909), http://www.boondocksnet.com/centennial/sctexts/teachers.html; and Maurice P. Dunlap, "What Americans Talk in the Philippines," *American Review of Reviews* 48 (August 1913), http://www.boondocksnet.com/centennial/sctexts/talk.html. Wood, *Report of the Special Mission to the Philippine Islands*, 29–30, details English woes. Coffman, *The Regulars*, 339.
80. Bocobo-Olivar, *History of Physical Education in the Philippines*, 61;*Annual Report*, Philippine Amateur Athletic Federation, 1926, n.p., YMCA Archives, Philippines box, Miscellaneous Reports file.
81. *Annual Report*, Philippine Amateur Athletic Federation, 1926, n.p; Gleeck Jr., *The Manila Americans*, 119.
82. "What Basketball Is Doing for the Girls in Zambales," *Teachers' Assembly Herald* 6, no. 19 (May 3, 1913): 112; in Pecson and Racelis, *Tales of the American Teachers in the Philippines*, 191; Bocobo-Olivar, *History of Physical Education in the Philippines*, 44. On basketball see Paras, "A Nation Hooked on Hoops."
83. *Annual Report*, Philippine Amateur Athletic Federation, 1926, n.p.; *Philippines Herald*, September 30, 1933, clipping, National Archives, RG 350, box 656, on cockfights; Gleeck Jr., *American Institutions in the Philippines*, 97.
84. Lardizabal, "Pioneer American Teachers and Philippine Education," 106–7; Gleeck Jr., *American Institutions in the Philippines*, 279.
85. Madison, "American Military Bases in the Philippines," 135.
86. Bocobo-Olivar, *History of Physical Education in the Philippines*, 153–60.

5. Hawaii as a Cultural Crossroads of Sport

1. On globalization and imperialism, see Guidry, Kennedy, and Zald, "Global-

ization and Social Movements," and Kaplan and Pease, *Cultures of United States Imperialism*.

2. Bartholomew, *Maui Remembers*, 35.
3. Sheldon Dibble, one of the early ministers, provided the accounts of Hawaiian life in *A History of the Sandwich Islands*. Bowling consisted of rolling stones for distance or accuracy between stakes. Schmitt, *Firsts and Almost Firsts in Hawaii*, 185, indicated Anglos bowling at ten pins in a tavern as early as the 1820s.
4. Cited in "Expansion in the Pacific," http://www.smplanet.com/imperialism/hawaii.html.
5. Dibble, *A History of the Sandwich Islands*, 151 (quote), 320–56, describes the religious quarrels.
6. Dibble, *A History of the Sandwich Islands*, 276.
7. Dibble, *A History of the Sandwich Islands*, 320–408; Bartholomew, *Maui Remembers*, 16, 18, 22, 26, 28, 104, 106; Takaki, *Pau Hana*, 17–18; Buck, *Paradise Remade*, 68–71, 152; Dudley and Agard, "A History of Dispossession." The 1840 constitution officially declared Hawaii as a "Christian" nation and required school attendance for children ages four to fourteen.
8. Takaki, *Pau Hana*, 3–9, 10 (quote).
9. Cisco, *Hawaii Sports*, 1–2, credits Cartwright with the first baseball diamond in Hawaii, while Schmitt, "Some Firsts in Island Leisure," and Ardolino, "Missionaries, Cartwright, and Spalding," specify earlier play. On language see Buck, *Paradise Remade*, 132.
10. Schmitt, "Some Firsts in Island Leisure," 113; *The Islander*, vol. 1, no. 23 (August 6, 1875): 145, and vol. 1, no. 25 (August 20, 1875): 160, both in National Baseball Hall of Fame Archives, Hawaii file; Cisco, *Hawaii Sports*, 221, 328; Ardolino, "Missionaries, Cartwright, and Spalding," 36–38.
11. Cisco, *Hawaii Sports*, 46, 130, 328, 346, 371; Takaki, *Pau Hana*, 44; Bishop Museum Photo Collection, Hawaii Sports Hall of Fame, Honolulu.
12. Cisco, *Hawaiian Sports*, 107; Buck, *Paradise Remade*, 75–77, 87, 118–20, 133, 155–56; Jacobson, *Barbarian Virtues*, 234; Pratt, *Expansionists of 1898*.
13. Love, *Race over Empire*, 126.
14. Love, *Race over Empire*, 124.
15. Cited in Pratt, *Expansionists of 1898*, 217.
16. Wei and Kamel, *Resistance in Paradise*, 133–43; Jacobson, *Barbarian Virtues*, 236; G. E. Allen, *The Y.M.C.A. in Hawaii*, 30; Zimmerman, *First Great Triumph*, 291.
17. Bartholomew, *Maui Remembers*, 28.

18. Takaki, *Pau Hana*, 127–32; Bartholomew, *Maui Remembers*, 96; Franks, *Hawaiian Sports in the Twentieth Century*, 8–9.
19. Love, *Race over Empire*, 95, indicates that Japanese workers made up 60 percent of the Hawaiian labor force by 1896. Guthrie-Shimizu, "For Love of the Game," 646–47; Steere Gikaku Noda biography, Bishop Museum, Hawaii Sports Hall of Fame; Franks, *Hawaiian Sports in the Twentieth Century*, 20–27.
20. Franks, *Crossing Sidelines, Crossing Cultures*, 58–61; Franks, "Baseball and Racism's Traveling Eye"; Franks, *Hawaiian Sports in the Twentieth Century*, 24–32; newspaper clippings, National Baseball Hall of Fame, Hawaii file.
21. Ben R. Finney, "The Development and Diffusion of Modern Hawaiian Surfing"; Booth, "Ambiguities in Pleasure and Discipline"; Yost, *The Outrigger Canoe Club of Honolulu, Hawaii*; Franks, *Crossing Sidelines, Crossing Cultures*, 140.
22. Finney, "The Development and Diffusion of Modern Hawaiian Surfing," 324; Franks, *Crossing Sidelines, Crossing Cultures*, 63–64, 140–41. See *Chicago Tribune*, July 10, 1912, 4, and July 19, 1924, 7, on inclusion and "bronze skinned." Jim Nendel, "New Hawaiian Monarchy: The Media Representations of Duke Kahanamoku 1911–1912," unpublished manuscript, 20–21; Yost, *The Outrigger Canoe Club*, 65. Franks reports the rescinding of Lang Akana's 1914 contract in the Pacific Coast League due to skin color, and Frank Blukoi's service with the All-Nations team and the Kansas City Monarchs; Franks, *Hawaiian Sports in the Twentieth Century*, 61, indicates four Hawaiian swimmers and a Hawaiian coach on the 1920 Olympic team. G. E. Allen, *The Y.M.C.A. in Hawaii*, 98, also lists Ludy Langer and W. H. Harris as Olympians. Bishop Museum, Hawaii Sports Hall of Fame, biographies.
23. Hall and Ambrose, *Memories of Duke*; G. E. Allen, *The Y.M.C.A. in Hawaii*, 98.
24. T. Takasugi, Pres. of Waseda Base Ball Assoc., to Prof. A. Alonzo Stagg, July 20, 1910, Amos Alonzo Stagg Papers, box 63, folder 3, University of Chicago Special Collections; Franks, *Hawaiian Sports in the Twentieth Century*, 21, 54, 57, 60; Takaki, *Pau Hana*, 104 (quote).
25. Okihiro, *Margins and Mainstreams*, 135, 157; Salyer, "Baptism by Fire."
26. Nankville, *The History of the Twenty-fifth Regiment United States Infantry*, 163–65, 171–73; Beaven biographical sketch, Bishop Museum, Hawaii Sports Hall of Fame.
27. Franks, *Hawaiian Sports in the Twentieth Century*, 9.
28. Lauren S. Morimoto, "An Oral (Hi)story of Barefoot Football: Sport, Plantation Culture and Community on Kaua'i" (presented at the North American Society for Sport History Conference, Pacific Grove, California, May 31, 2004), 7;

Lauren S. Morimoto, " 'Locals Only': Barefoot Football and the Construction of 'Local' Culture on Kaua'i" (presented at the North American Society for Sport History Conference, Green Bay, Wisconsin, May 30, 2005).

29. Morimoto, "An Oral (Hi)story of Barefoot Football," 3, 6, 10; Franks, *Hawaiian Sports in the Twentieth Century*, 57–59, 66–68; Diaz, "Fight Boys 'til the Last," 187; Otto "Proc" Krum biography, Bishop Museum, Hawaii Sports Hall of Fame; Bartholomew, *Maui Remembers*, 96; Franks, *Crossing Sidelines, Crossing Cultures*, 85–87; Kempa, *A Survey of Physical Education in the Territory of Hawaii*, 26; Recreation Commission, *A History of Recreation in Hawaii*, 27, 47, 65, 100.
30. Franks, *Hawaiian Sports in the Twentieth Century*, 52; Yost, *The Outrigger Canoe Club*, 68; Bartholomew, *Maui Remembers*, 96.
31. Yost, *The Outrigger Canoe Club*, 54.
32. Yost, *The Outrigger Canoe Club*, 55; Wei and Kamel, *Resistance in Paradise*, 135; Bartholomew, *Maui Remembers*, 84–97; Recreation Commission, *A History of Recreation in Hawaii*, 106–7.
33. Villa (Francisco Guilledo) file, International Boxing Hall of Fame; Franks, *Crossing Sidelines, Crossing Boundaries*, 16, 32–37, 44. Dado was state champion during the 1930s, while Marino gained his title in 1950. Kempa, *A Survey of Physical Education in the Territory of Hawaii*, 26, indicates three hundred professional boxers by that time. They earned $50 to $250 per fight. Cisco, *Hawaii Sports*, 98; Franks, *Hawaiian Sports in the Twentieth Century*, 63–66, 190.
34. On swimming see G. E. Allen, *The Y.M.C.A. in Hawaii, 1869–1969*, 120, and Bartholomew, *Maui Remembers*, 35, 96–97. The 1930 win was a YMCA national championship, while Hawaiians won individual and team national AAU titles from 1939 to 1941. Franks, *Hawaiian Sports in the Twentieth Century*, 167–68, indicates national AAU titles in 1946, 1949, and 1950 as well.
35. Kempa, *A Survey of Physical Education in the Territory of Hawaii*, 22; Franks, *Hawaiian Sports in the Twentieth Century*, 68–71.
36. Bailey and Farber, *The First Strange Place*, 5–6, 110–11; Franks, *Hawaiian Sports in the Twentieth Century*, 66–68, 119–20. The Asahis retrieved their original name in 1947.
37. Steere Gikaku Noda, Henry Tadashi "Bozo" Wakabayashi, and Wally Yonamine biographies, Bishop Museum, Hawaii Sports Hall of Fame; Morimoto, "An Oral (Hi)story of Barefoot Football," 2; Reaves, *Taking In a Game*, 139; Franks, *Hawaiian Sports in the Twentieth Century*, 77–97.
38. Morimoto, "An Oral (Hi)story of Barefoot Football," 9–17.
39. Blackford, *Fragile Paradise*; Franks, *Hawaiian Sports in the Twentieth Century*, 175;

Noda biography, Hawaii Sports Hall of Fame; Buck, *Paradise Remade*, 171–88 (quote at 177).

40. Buck, *Paradise Remade*, 180–82; Blackford, *Fragile Paradise*, 66–73 (quote at 69); Kamana and Wilson, "The Tip of the Spear."
41. Blackford, *Fragile Paradise*, 58–74, 95–110, 202–30; Buck, *Paradise Remade*, 186–88; Kane, "Arrested Development"; Bartholomew, *Maui Remembers*, 157–59.
42. Buck, *Paradise Remade*, 164; "More Than Just a Tiny Timbre"; O'Neill, "96795"; Sodetani, "The Lazarus Language," 28, 30; Ryan, "Lessons with Love."
43. Linnekin and Poyer, *Cultural Identity and Ethnicity in the Pacific*; Franks, *Hawaii Sports in the Twentieth Century*, 171, 177–79; Blackford, *Fragile Paradise*, 224–30.

6. Cuba and the Rehabilitative Qualities of Sport

1. Wei and Kamel, *Resistance in Paradise*, 30; Pettavino and Pye, *Sport in Cuba*, 17; L. A. Perez Jr., *Cuba and the United States*, xv, 18–25, 43, 54; L. A. Perez Jr., *On Becoming Cuban*, 18–23.
2. Pettavino and Pye, *Sport in Cuba*, 17, 26–27; L. A. Perez Jr., *On Becoming Cuban*, 75–76; Echevarría, *The Pride of Havana*, 90–93, 100. Pettavino and Echevarría agree on Nemesio Guillo as the student who introduced the game to Cuba, but they disagree on the location of his schooling. Pettavino claims Fordham, while Echevarría asserts Springhill College in Mobile, Alabama.
3. L. A. Perez Jr., *On Becoming Cuban*, 80.
4. L. A. Perez Jr., *On Becoming Cuban*, 57–58, 72–75, 78; Echevarría, *The Pride of Havana*, 89, 103; Pettavino and Pye, *Sport in Cuba*, 40–41; L. A. Perez Jr., *Cuba and the United States*, 25 (quote).
5. Echevarría, *The Pride of Havana*, 97, 99, 105, 109, 114; L. A. Perez Jr., *On Becoming Cuban*, 75–77, 90.
6. L. A. Perez Jr., *On Becoming Cuban*, 75; Echevarría, *The Pride of Havana*, 115.
7. L. A. Perez Jr., *On Becoming Cuban*, 81, 76 (quote, April 9, 1893, 3).
8. L. A. Perez Jr., *On Becoming Cuban*, 81–83, 257; Pettavino and Pye, *Sport in Cuba*, 27, 60; L. A. Perez Jr., *Cuba and the United States*, 71–72; Bjarkman, *Baseball with a Latin Beat*, 239–40.
9. T. B. Allen, "Remember the Maine?" 92–109. The most recent investigations of the sinking determined internal causes for the blast and a faulty design that placed fueling coal next to a powder magazine, resulting in a spontaneous combustion.
10. L. A. Perez Jr., *Cuba and the United States*, 97–100. See Millis, *The Martial Spirit*,

for a narrative account of the war, and Jeffers, *Colonel Roosevelt*, for one of the war's biggest promoters and beneficiaries.

11. Blum et al., *The National Experience*, 537; L. A. Perez Jr., *Cuba and the United States*, 109–16; L. A. Perez Jr., *On Becoming Cuban*, 322, 323 (quotes).
12. L. A. Perez Jr., *On Becoming Cuban*, 396; Echevarría, *The Pride of Havana*, 87; Pettavino and Pye, *Sport in Cuba*, 48–51.
13. Leonard Wood Papers, Library of Congress, Cuba box [1899–1902], General Orders, Special Orders—Dept. of Cuba 1901–1902, Circulars No. 2, 92, 127; Millett, *The Politics of Intervention*, 34, 38; L. A. Perez Jr., *On Becoming Cuban*, 161, 405–6; Magoon, *Republic of Cuba*, 349–50; L. A. Perez Jr., *Cuba and the United States*, 128 (quote), 133–34.
14. Wilson L. Gill to William H. Taft, July 1, 1905, William Howard Taft Papers, Library of Congress reel 624; L. A. Perez Jr., *Cuba and the United States*, 128 (quote).
15. L. A. Perez Jr., *Cuba and the United States*, 130–32; Pettavino and Pye, *Sport in Cuba*, 53; L. A. Perez Jr., *On Becoming Cuban*, 255 (quote).
16. Musicant, *The Banana Wars*, 118 (quote).
17. Echevarría, *The Pride of Havana*, 120–36 (quote at 129).
18. L. A. Perez Jr., *On Becoming Cuban*, 256–57.
19. J. E. Hubbard to Assoc. friends, July 5, 1904, Young Men's Christian Association (YMCA) Archives, Cuba box, Correspondence, 1904–1919, University of Minnesota.
20. Undated, unsigned letter, YMCA Archives, Cuba box, Correspondence, 1904–1919, file 1; J. E. Hubbard to Mr. Anderson, February 9, 1905; J. E. Hubbard to Dear friends, October 28, 1905; J. E. Hubbard to John R. Mott, April 9, 1908 (quote).
21. J. E. Hubbard to J. R. Mott, October 17, 1906, YMCA Archives, Cuba box, file 1.
22. Magoon, *Republic of Cuba*, 326–28; L. A. Perez Jr., *On Becoming Cuban*, 109; Healy, *Drive to Hegemony*, 127–32; Musicant, *The Banana Wars*, 53–67 (quote at 60).
23. Memorandum for Chief of Staff, February 17, 1908, National Archives, Cuba, RG 395.
24. Memorandum for the Chief of Staff, September 23, 1908, National Archives, Cuba, RG 395.
25. Healy, *Drive to Hegemony*, 210–13.
26. Pettavino and Pye, *Sport in Cuba*, 54; Royce, "The Blond Terror"; J. E. Hubbard to John R. Mott, April 9, 1908, YMCA Archives, Cuba box, file 1 (quote).

27. J. E. Hubbard to J. R. Mott, November 9, 1908, YMCA Archives, Cuba box, file 1.
28. J. E. Hubbard to W. T. Diack, March 22, 1909, YMCA Archives, Cuba box, file 1. See *Chicago Tribune*, October 24, 1998, pt. 3: 1, 6, for a history of Cuban football into the 1950s.
29. L. A. Perez Jr., *On Becoming Cuban*, 260; *Chicago Tribune*, January 2, 1910, pt. 3: 1.
30. Musicant, *The Banana Wars*, 67–71; Healy, *Drive to Hegemony*, 210–16.
31. L. A. Perez Jr., *Cuba and the United States*, 137–46; L. A. Perez Jr., *On Becoming Cuban*, 177–98, 220–55; Echevarría, *The Pride of Havana*, 190–96; F. U. Adams, *Conquest of the Tropics*, 247, 260, 294.
32. Joseph E. Hubbard, *1911 Annual Report*, September 30, 1911, YMCA Archives, Cuba box, file 2; Pettavino and Pye, *Sport in Cuba*, 29–33; Echevarría, *The Pride of Havana*, 162, 173–74; Regalado, *Viva Baseball!*, 19–21, 28.
33. Pettavino and Pye, *Sport in Cuba*, 42.
34. Roberts, *Papa Jack*.
35. L. A. Perez Jr., *On Becoming Cuban*, 397.
36. George F. Tibbetts, Sec. for West Indies, to John R. Mott, September 8, 1911, YMCA Archives, Cuba box, file 2; J. E. Hubbard, report for quarter ending June 30, 1916, YMCA Archives, Cuba box, file 3; G. W. Garniss, *Annual Report of the Physical Dept., Oct. 2, 1916–Sept. 29, 1917*, YMCA Archives, Cuba box, file 3 (quote).
37. Guttmann, *Games and Empires*, 82; Musicant, *The Banana Wars*, 71–78; Healy, *Drive to Hegemony*, 203–8.
38. Healy, *Drive to Hegemony*, 203, 208; L. A. Perez Jr., *On Becoming Cuban*, 168–69, 90 (quote).
39. L. A. Perez Jr., *On Becoming Cuban*, 261.
40. Echevarría, *The Pride of Havana*, 169–70, 206, 215, 225–26; L. A. Perez Jr., *On Becoming Cuban*, 260, 267–70.
41. E. J. Simonds, report, October 25, 1921, and E. J. Simonds, 1924 report, both in YMCA Archives, Cuba box, file 4; Pettavino and Pye, *Sport in Cuba*, 61–65.
42. Sugden, *Boxing and Society*, 134; L. A. Perez Jr., *On Becoming Cuban*, 175–76; Kid Chocolate file, International Boxing Hall of Fame.
43. L. A. Perez Jr., *On Becoming Cuban*, 263–64; L. A. Perez Jr., *Cuba and the United States*, 170–201; Hugo Hartenstein to Frank W. Slack, March 7, 1933; G. I. Babcock to E. R. Liebert, February 4, 1934, YMCA Archives, Cuba box, file 6, Correspondence 1930–1939. See Diane Van Weele, History 3961 papers, June 10, 1992, on reasons for the YMCA failure, in YMCA Archives, Cuba box, file 6.

44. Echevarría, *The Pride of Havana*, 48, 71, 225–51, 407n7; L. A. Perez Jr., *On Becoming Cuban*, 274; Pettavino and Pye, *Sport in Cuba*, 36–37; L. A. Perez Jr., *Cuba and the United States*, 209–14; Wagner, "Sport in Revolutionary Societies."
45. Echevarría, *The Pride of Havana*, 339 (quote).
46. L. A. Perez Jr., *On Becoming Cuban*, 274.
47. Kid Gavilan file, International Boxing Hall of Fame.
48. Regalado, *Viva Baseball!*; L. A. Perez Jr., *On Becoming Cuban*, 258–66 (quote at 259), 465–505.
49. Pettavino, "Novel Revolutionary Forms"; Sugden, *Boxing and Society*, 149–66; Chappell, "The Soviet Protégé," 193 (quote).
50. Chappell, "The Soviet Protégé," 199–201; Carter, "Baseball Arguments"; "Orioles' Cuba Trip More than Fun and Games," *Chicago Sun-Times*, March 28, 1999; Carlos Rodriguez Acosta, Commissioner of Cuban Baseball, "Baseball and Society," http://www.pbs.org/stealinghome/debate/bands.html.

7. Sport and Restoration of Pride

1. Wei and Kamel, *Resistance in Paradise*, 64–65; *Chicago Sun-Times*, July 17, 2001, 26A.
2. Garcia, "I Am the Other"; Stuart, *Isles of Empire*, 353n12 (quote).
3. Garcia, "I Am the Other," 39, 63.
4. Duany, *The Puerto Rican Nation on the Move*, 65–121 (quote at 70). See Leonard Wood Papers, box: General Orders, Porto Rico, 1898–1900, vol. 1, on dueling and gambling.
5. Military Orders Having Force of Law by Commanding General, Government of Porto Rico, 1898–1900, National Archives, RG 395, vol. 2, 76–115 (quote at 82).
6. Military Orders Having Force of Law by Commanding General, vol. 2, 82–84; Stuart, *Isles of Empire*, 361–62.
7. Garcia, "I Am the Other," 61; Stuart, *Isles of Empire*, 28, 59n16, contends that four U.S. corporations owned the twelve largest sugar plantations and that 1.2 percent of the population owned 36 percent of the cultivated land within twenty years; also see p. 445 on Union de Puerto Rico.

   National Geographic published nine articles on Puerto Rico between 1898 and 1900. See LaGorce, "Porto Rico," for continued coverage.
8. Van Hyning, *Puerto Rico's Winter League*, 1; A. C. Sharpe, Report to Adjutant General, July 25, 1900, in National Archives, RG 395.
9. YMCA Archives, Puerto Rico, Correspondence files, 1920–1929: John R. Mott

to George F. Tibbetts, June 18, 1908; Manuel Bueno, General Secretary Report to the Board of Directors, January 25, 1938; W. G. Coxhead, Report for Quarter Ending June 30, 1915. R. J. Park, " 'Forget about That Pile of Papers"'; Report of the Physical Director of the YMCA, Oct. 1, 1915–Sept. 30, 1916, YMCA Archives, Puerto Rico, Correspondence files, 1920–1929, p. 9 (quote).

10. Report of the Physical Director of the YMCA, 6; W. G. Coxhead, Report Ending Sept. 30, 1914, n.p. (quotes).
11. Dr. P. S. Spence to Sir, September 23, 1915, National Archives, RG 350, box 931; Coxhead, Report of the Physical Director, 1915–1916, 13; R. J. Park, " 'Forget about That Pile of Papers,"' 52; Cannon cited in Stuart, *Isles of Empire*, 333.
12. Report of Physical Director of the YMCA, San Juan, P.R., Oct. 1, 1817–Sept. 30, 1918, YMCA Archives, Puerto Rico box.
13. Stuart, *Isles of Empire*, 405; *Porto Rican Interests*, 9–10; Healy, *Drive to Hegemony*, 267; R. J. Park, " 'Forget about That Pile of Papers,"' 53.
14. National Archives, RG 350, box 1074; Stuart, *Isles of Empire*, 99. Healy, *Drive to Hegemony*, 267, claims an average daily wage of 70 cents in 1928; LaGorce, "Porto Rico," 615, 622 (quotes).
15. Duany, *The Puerto Rican Nation on the Move*, 187–90; Briggs, *Reproducing Empire*, 162–74, 180–82; Mac Aloon, "La Pitada Olimpica," claims that several political groups fractured along commonwealth, statehood, and independence desires.
16. Van Hyning, *Puerto Rico's Winter League*, 1; *San Juan Times*, clipping, May 16, 1928, and Orval P. Townshend to Walter F. O'Brien, January 13, 1925, both in box 1074, National Archives, RG 350. The government finally relented, legalizing cockfights in 1933.
17. W. G. Coxhead to George I. Babcock, November 7, 1924, YMCA Archives, correspondence file, 1920–1929.
18. Everett J. Symonds, 1927 *Annual Report*, n.p., YMCA Archives, file 4, Correspondence 1920–1925.
19. Symonds, 1927 *Annual Report*, n.p.; George I. Babcock to Frank Slack, May 27, 1931, YMCA Archives, Correspondence file; R. J. Park, " 'Forget about That Pile of Papers,"' 52.
20. Mac Aloon, "La Pitada Olimpica," 326; Sixto Escobar file, International Boxing Hall of Fame.
21. Briggs, *Reproducing Empire*, 75, 220; Stuart, *Isles of Empire*, 446, 457n37; Van Hyning, *Puerto Rico's Winter League*, 81–83.
22. Van Hyning, *Puerto Rico's Winter League*, 2–9, 36–37; Mayo-Santana, "Puerto Ricans," 377.

23. Roosevelt cited in Stuart, *Isles of Empire*, 362–63.
24. Stuart, *Isles of Empire*, 25, 83; Wakefield, *Playing to Win*, 77.
25. R. J. Park, "'Forget about That Pile of Papers,"' 54–59; "Engendering Colonialism: The Effects of U.S. Colonialism on Women from Puerto Rico, Cuba, Hawaii, and the Philippines" (panel discussion at a De Paul University seminar, October 17, 1998).
26. Mac Aloon, "La Pitada Olimpica," 348; Duany, *The Puerto Rican Nation on the Move*, 122–23.
27. Cockburn, "True Colors"; Wei and Kamel, *Resistance in Paradise*, 67–70; Stuart, *Isles of Empire*, 38. "Engendering Colonialism" claimed a sterilization rate of more than 45 percent by 1996 in a campaign that began in the 1930s. Briggs, *Reproducing Empire*, 107–11, 125 (quote), 143, cites a lower figure of 33 percent through the 1980s.
28. Stuart, *Isles of Empire*, 442–43; Mac Aloon, "La Pitada Olimpica," 328; Echevarría, *The Pride of Havana*, 318; Duany, *The Puerto Rican Nation on the Move*, 192–235 (quote at 197).
29. Kirsch, Harris, and Nolte, *Encyclopedia of Ethnicity and Sports in the United States*, 375, 462; Duany, *The Puerto Rican Nation on the Move*, 238; Regalado, *Viva Baseball!*, 72 (quote).
30. Bjarkman, *Baseball with a Latin Beat*, 95; Regalado, *Viva Baseball!*, 65–66, 84–85, 134–35; Cepeda, "From Hardball to Hard Times and Back,"; Orlando Cepeda file, Baseball Hall of Fame.
31. Kirsch, Harris, and Nolte, *Encyclopedia of Ethnicity and Sports in the United States*, 104–5; Roberto Clemente file, National Baseball Hall of Fame; Mac Aloon, "La Pitada Olimpica," 323; Rob Ruck, "Remembering Roberto Clemente," *Pittsburgh*, December 1992, 36, 42, in Clemente file (quote).
32. Richard Lapchick, "Recalling Roberto," *Sporting News*, October 27, 1997, 7, Roberto Clemente file, National Baseball Hall of Fame; R. J. Park, "'Forget about That Pile of Papers," 51.
33. Mac Aloon, "La Pitada Olimpica"; Kirsch, Harris, and Nolte, *Encyclopedia of Ethnicity and Sport in the United States*, 62.
34. Kirsch, Harris, and Nolte, *Encyclopedia of Ethnicity and Sport in the United States*, 111, 154, 375, 391.
35. Van Hyning, *Puerto Rico's Winter League*, 46.
36. Stuart, *Isles of Empire*, 56, 74, 98, 126; Cockburn, "True Colors," 46 (quote).
37. Mac Aloon, "La Pitada Olimpica," 330 and 318 (quotes), 326.
38. Murray Polner, "Sports: My or No Way," http://hnn.us/articles/12438.html;

Ron Briley, "Baseball Player Carlos Delgado's Summer of Discontent: Dissent and the National Pastime," http://hnn.us/articles/6485.html; "Puerto Rico Stuns Dream Team, 92–73," http://www.rednova.com/news/general/79232/puerto_rico_stuns_dream_team_9273.

39. Mac Aloon, "La Pitada Olimpica," 327–29; Stuart, *Isles of Empire*, 48–54, 216–18, 240; Cockburn, "True Colors"; Duany, *The Puerto Rican Nation on the Move*, 10–35; Zimmerman, *First Great Triumph*, 489.

8. Sport and Economic Retaliation

1. Atkins and Wilson, *The Dominican Republic and the United States*, 5–32.
2. A. M. Klein, *Sugarball*, 16; Bjarkman, *Baseball with a Latin Beat*, 252–53; Ruck, "Three Kings Day in Consuelo."
3. Healy, *Drive to Hegemony*, 71–76, 98–99, 111–23; Musicant, *The Banana Wars*, 239–40 (quote).
4. Healy, *Drive to Hegemony*, 160–63, 197; Atkins and Wilson, *The Dominican Republic and the United States*, 39–45; Musicant, *The Banana Wars*, 235–84.
5. A. M. Klein, *Sugarball*, 110.
6. A. M. Klein, *Sugarball*, 17; Guttmann, *Games and Empires*, 87; Healy, *Drive to Hegemony*, 244–45; Musicant, *The Banana Wars*, 269–79 (quote at 274).
7. Musicant, *The Banana Wars*, 276–79 (quote at 277).
8. Healy, *Drive to Hegemony*, 197.
9. Atkins and Wilson, *The Dominican Republic and the United States*, 54–55, 59; Schoenrich, *Santo Domingo*, 169, 199–200.
10. Musicant, *The Banana Wars*, 280.
11. Musicant, *The Banana Wars*, 281; A. M. Klein, *Sugarball*, 19–20, 115–28.
12. Howard, *Coloring the Nation*, 118; Ruck, "Three Kings Day in Consuelos," 80 (quote).
13. Healy, *Drive to Hegemony*, 226; Musicant, *Banana Wars*, 274; A. Klein, "American Hegemony, Dominican Resistance, and Baseball"; A. M. Klein, *Sugarball*, 20.
14. A. M. Klein, "Culture, Politics, and Baseball in the Dominican Republic." A. M. Klein, *Sugarball*, 29, places the advent of *béisbol romantico* in the 1950s but admits the chronology is debated.
15. Ribowsky, *A Complete History of the Negro Leagues*, 208–9; A. M. Klein, *Sugarball*, 21–23.
16. A. M. Klein, *Sugarball*, 23–27 (quote at 26).
17. A. M. Klein, *Sugarball*, 27–29.
18. A. M. Klein, *Sugarball*, 30–35.

19. Regalado, *Viva Baseball!*, 127–28; Juan Marichal file, National Baseball Hall of Fame.
20. Regalado, *Viva Baseball!*, 126–27, 134–35, 144–45.
21. A. M. Klein, *Sugarball*, 13, 35; Krich, *El Béisbol*, 106; Musicant, *The Banana Wars*, 362–69; Blum et al., *The National Experience*, 825–26.
22. A. M. Klein, "Culture, Politics, and Baseball in the Dominican Republic"; A. M. Klein, *Sugarball*, 42, 47, 51.
23. Atkins and Wilson, *The Dominican Republic and the United States*, 169–70.
24. Bjarkman, *Baseball with a Latin Beat*, 347–84; Baldassaro and Johnson, *The American Game*, xiv; Stuart, *Isles of Empire*, 69n77; A. Klein, "American Hegemony, Dominican Resistance, and Baseball," 302; A. M. Klein, *Sugarball*, 58 (quote).
25. Knisely, "Everybody Has the Dream," states that 71 of the 750 MLB players in 2000 came from the Dominican Republic. See Le Batard, "Next Detour," 105–11, on the Dominican dream.
26. Le Batard, "Next Detour," 105–11.
27. Le Batard, "Next Detour," 105–11.
28. Le Batard, "Next Detour," 105–11; A. M. Klein, "Culture, Politics, and Baseball in the Dominican Republic," 127.
29. Howard, *Coloring the Nation*, 118; Yerxa, *Admirals and Empire*; A. M. Klein, *Sugarball*, 1.

9. The Outposts of Empire

1. Gray, *Amerika Samoa*, 20–46; Lay, Murrow, and Meleisa, *Samoa*, 1–15; Stuart, *Isles of Empire*, 24, 57n3, 57n4, 242; "Cultural History of American Samoa," http://www.ashpo.org/history.htm.
2. Lay, Murrow, and Meleisa, *Samoa*, 18; Wei and Kamel, *Resistance in Paradise*, 92, 101–2; A. Kramer, *The Samoa Islands*, vol. 1: 135, 137, 545, 546, 660; vol. 2: 68, 305–8, 381–94 (quote at 381).
3. Stuart, *Isles of Empire*, 73, 332–33; Gray, *Amerika Samoa*, 60–64; Welch, *Imperialists vs. Anti-imperialists*, 32–33; Heffer, *The United States and the Pacific*, 192–95.
4. Gray, *Amerika Samoa*, 99–102, 107; Stuart, *Isles of Empire*, 363–65, 408.
5. Stuart, *Isles of Empire*, 83, 98, 265, 283n22; Gray, *Amerika Samoa*, 154, 173–75.
6. Stuart, *Isles of Empire*, 27, 183, 408; Field, *Mau*, 27–28.
7. Field, *Mau*, 73–111, 126, 147–59, 166; Stuart, *Isles of Empire*, 172; Wei and Kamel, *Resistance in Paradise*, 91, 107.
8. Stuart, *Isles of Empire*, 26, 159, 174n7.
9. "American Samoa National Olympic Committee," http://www.oceania-olym

pic.org/members/am_samoa.html; Reaves, *Taking In a Game*, xxi; Stuart, *Isles of Empire*, 48–49, 52–54, 56, 126, 133, 157, 260–61, 269. Stuart states a per capita income of $9,440 for the Virgin Islands, $7,747 for Guam, and $4,177 for Puerto Rico.

10. Stuart, *Isles of Empire*, 265, 336; Wei and Kamel, *Resistance in Paradise*, 97; Lay, Murrow, and Meleisa, *Samoa*, 70, 73.
11. http://basketball.sportingpulse.com/oceania/background.shtml, 1–5; http://www.oceania-olympic.org/members/amsamoa.html, 1–10.
12. Ibid.; "Trevor the Tortoise Trails in Last," http://news.bbc.co.uk/sport1/hi/in_depth/2001/world_athletics/1474290.stm.
13. M. P. Perez, "Interethnic Antagonism in the Wake of Colonialism"; Stuart, *Isles of Empire*, 241, 243, 266, 331. The ban on friars and religious processions proved temporary. Wei and Kamel, *Resistance in Paradise*, 111–12, 114, 117.
14. Stuart, *Isles of Empire*, 268, 276; "English in the Schools of Guam," *Guam Recorder*, September 1925, quoted in Wei and Kamel, *Resistance in Paradise*, 123.
15. Diaz, " 'Fight Boys 'til the Last . . ."
16. McFerson, *The Racial Dimension of American Overseas Colonial Policy*, 112; Stuart, *Isles of Empire*, 46–54, 105–6, 116–17; M. A. Perez, "Interethnic Antagonism in the Wake of Colonialism"; Wei and Kamel, *Resistance in Paradise*, 110.
17. Stuart, *Isles of Empire*, 161, 172, 174n11.
18. See Diaz, "Pappy's House," on the pluralistic nature of culture in Guam; Diaz, "Fight Boys 'til the Last . . ."
19. Musicant, *The Banana Wars*, 158–59; Renda, *Taking Haiti*, 30, 39, 52, 98–100; G. W. Brown, "Haiti and the United States."
20. Renda, *Taking Haiti*, 40–46, 97–100; Logan, "Education in Haiti," gives a 92 percent illiteracy rate in 1915 compared to a slightly larger U.S. claim of 98 percent. "Wards of the United States," 152, 162–63 (quotes.)
21. Renda, *Taking Haiti*, 10, 51–53; Brown, "Haiti and the United States," 137–38; Simmons, *The United States Marines*, 80; Musicant, *The Banana Wars*, 158–60 (quote at 160).
22. Musicant, *The Banana Wars*, 158, 163–64, 179; Renda, *Taking Haiti*, 10, 30–31, 96, 117; Brown, "Haiti and the United States," 148–49; "Wards of the United States," 177 (quote).
23. Renda, *Taking Haiti*, 80–88; Musicant, *The Banana Wars*, 166–71, 180, 188 (quote).
24. Renda, *Taking Haiti*, 85.
25. Musicant, *The Banana Wars*, 164.

26. Musicant, *The Banana Wars*, 188–201.
27. Musicant, *The Banana Wars*, 213; "Wards of the United States," 153, 159 (quotes.)
28. Renda, *Taking Haiti*, 232–33, 241 (quote at 233).
29. "Wards of the United States," 149, 173, 177; Musicant, *The Banana Wars*, 207.
30. Musicant, *The Banana Wars*, 202–3; Simmons, *The United States Marines*, 79–82; Renda, *Taking Haiti*, 10, 30–31, 61, 100–108 (quote at 100).
31. Logan, "Education in Haiti"; Renda, *Taking Haiti*, 32, 84, 148–50.
32. Musicant, *The Banana Wars*, 212–19; Renda, *Taking Haiti*, 11, 33, 156–62, 171–73, 186–202 (quotes at 156 and 158).
33. Renda, *Taking Haiti*, 126, 130 (quote), 212.
34. Renda, *Taking Haiti*, 11, 130–36, 167–71, 212, 232–36.
35. Renda, *Taking Haiti*, 136, 143, 146, 155–56 (quote); Musicant, *The Banana Wars*, 223–30.
36. Musicant, *The Banana Wars*, 230–33; Renda, *Taking Haiti*, 34; Logan, "Education in Haiti," 460.
37. Renda, *Taking Haiti*, 36, 265, 301, 306.
38. Langley and Schoonover, *The Banana Men*, 6–37.
39. Richard McGehee, "The King and His Court: Early Baseball and Other Sports in Nicaragua" (presented at the North American Society for Sport History Conference, Auburn University, May 24–27, 1996); Healy, *Drive to Hegemony*, 263; Bjarkman, *Baseball with a Latin Beat*, 238; Wagner, "Sport in Revolutionary Societies," 119, claims "well organized baseball leagues by 1890."
40. Langley and Schoonover, *The Banana Men*, 41–160 (quote at 85).
41. Langley and Schoonover, *The Banana Men*, 190n4.
42. Healy, *Drive to Hegemony*, 153–60, 234–37; Langley and Schoonover, *The Banana Men*, 92–110 (quote at 92).
43. Langley and Schoonover, *The Banana Men*, 111–12; Musicant, *The Banana Wars*, 140–43.
44. Musicant, *The Banana Wars*, 143. At the same time, American mercenaries backed by an American banana baron overthrew the Honduran government, further damaging any vestiges of American popularity in the area. The United States had previously engineered a Panamanian revolt from Colombia to gain the Canal Zone.
45. Musicant, *The Banana Wars*, 286; McGehee, "Sport in Nicaragua," 184 (quote).
46. McGehee, "Sport in Nicaragua."
47. McGehee, "Sport in Nicaragua," 193–94.

48. Musicant, *The Banana Wars*, 286–333 (quotes at 333); Sandino to U.S. Navy Admiral David F. Sellers in 1928.
49. Musicant, *The Banana Wars*, 347–61 (quote at 351–52).
50. Zoss and Bowman, *Diamonds in the Rough*, 405–6.
51. Alexis Arguello file, International Boxing Hall of Fame; Randy Wayne White, "Far from Home Plate," *Outside*, October 2001, 51.

IN 52. Healy, *Drive to Hegemony*, 27–28; Musicant, *The Banana Wars*, 79–113 (quote at 113).

53. Musicant, *The Banana Wars*, 113–36; Heffer, *The United States and the Pacific*, 142–47; Healy, *Drive to Hegemony*, 77–98 (quotes at 90).
54. F. U. Adams, *Conquest of the Tropics*, 161.
55. F. U. Adams, *Conquest of the Tropics*, 163–64.
56. Julie Greene, "Spaniards on the Silver Roll: The U.S. Government, Liminality, and Labor Troubles in the Panama Canal Zone" (presented at the Newberry Library Labor History Seminar, Chicago, September 21, 2001) stated that more than 60 percent of the labor force were black Caribbeans.
57. F. U. Adams, *Conquest of the Tropics*, 149.
58. Greene, "Spaniards on the Silver Roll"; Putney, *Muscular Christianity*, 186–87; Bjarkman, *Baseball with a Latin Beat*, 237.
59. Greene, "Spaniards on the Silver Roll."
60. Healy, *Drive to Hegemony*, 227; Panama Al Brown file and Kid Chocolate file, International Boxing Hall of Fame.
61. Ray Arcel, "Remembering Roberto Duran," *KO Magazine* (1984), 20–29, Roberto Duran file, International Boxing Hall of Fame.
62. Jeremy Greenwood, "Roberto Duran . . . Latin Ambassador of Macho," *World Wide Boxing Digest*, clipping, 4–5, Roberto Duran file, International Boxing Hall of Fame.
63. "Beyond the Glory," Fox Sports Network, February 4, 2001; William Nack, "Back, but Still a Long Way to Go," *Sports Illustrated*, clipping, 16–17, Roberto Duran file, International Boxing Hall of Fame.
64. Musicant, *The Banana Wars*, 390–417; Bjarkman, *Baseball with a Latin Beat*, 347–84.

10. The Globalization of Sport

1. Wallerstein, *The Modern World System II*; Joseph Maguire, *Global Sport*; Miller et al., *Globalization and Sport*; Mangan and DaCosta, *Sport in Latin American Society*; Mangan, *The Cultural Bond*.

2. Hardt and Negri, *Empire*, 347; Mangan, *Europe, Sport, World*, 2–3; Guidry, Kennedy, and Zald, *Globalizations and Social Movements*, 11–30; Joseph Maguire, *Global Sport*, 150 (quote).
3. Dunand, "Worldwide It's a Hit"; Ferguson, "America."
4. Beth Harris, "Matsui Homer off Nomo Powers Yankees Past L.A.," *Chicago Sun-Times*, June 20, 2004, 94, states that the game featuring the two Japanese stars drew a record crowd of 55,207 to Dodger Stadium.
5. David Maraniss, *When Pride Still Mattered: A Life of Vince Lombardi* (New York: Simon and Schuster, 1999), 118–20, states that the United States sent West Point coaches to Japan, Okinawa, and the Philippines to introduce football in 1951.
6. Miller et al., *Globalization and Sport*, 3, 9–10; Mangan, *The Cultural Bond*; Mangan, *The Games Ethic and Imperialism*.
7. Bale, *Sports Geography*, 56–57.
8. Freeman, ESPN; R. Crepeau and Nathan, "Two Views of ESPN"; Miller et al., *Globalization and Sport*, 65; LaFeber, *Michael Jordan and the New Global Capitalism*, 110 (quote).
9. "Not Just a Game."
10. Joseph Maguire, *Global Sport*, 150–54.
11. Joseph Maguire, *Global Sport*, 158–69, 178; Miller et al., *Globalization and Sport*, 14–19.
12. Gems, *For Pride, Profit, and Patriarchy*; Joe Maguire, "The Media-sport Production Complex"; NFL International, http://nfl.com/international/2000countries.html; Jarrett Bell, "American Bowl May Go to China," *USA Today*, May 27, 2004, 6C; NFLChina.com Web site, http://www.NFLChina.com; Tagliabue quoted in Rick Telander, "Tag's Day a Regal Show of Force," *Chicago Sun-Times*, February 1, 2004, 111A.

    Joliet (IL) Evening Herald News, December 7, 1921, cited in "An 1896 Xmas Vacation," indicates U.S. college teams playing football in Monterey, Mexico, and Mexico City as early as 1896. See the *Los Angeles Times*, October 6, 1929, for an account of another game in Mexico City (courtesy of Ray Schmidt, College Football Historical Society). See Kuchar, "Northern Exposure," on college football scholarships for non-U.S. players.
13. Spalding Company, official history of sports, at http://www.spalding.com; "Albert Goodwill Spalding," *Spalding Store News*, September 9, 1915, 3–20; Levine, *A. G. Spalding and the Rise of Baseball*, 97–122; Miller et al., *Globalization and Sport*, 14–17, 64; Gustafson, "Next Country"; Hirdt, "Foreign Legions"; Baldassaro

and Johnson, *The American Game*, 2; "Matsui Fever Taking Hold," *Chicago Sun-Times*, April 13, 2003, 128A; Toni Ginnetti, "Cubs Tapping Asian Pipeline," *Chicago Sun-Times*, May 5, 2002, 117A.

14. Zoss and Bowman, *Diamonds in the Rough*, 416.
15. A. A. Stagg to Pauline Stagg, March 10, 1892, Amos Alonzo Stagg Papers, University of Chicago Special Collections; Josephine Wilkin to her mother, March 6, 1892, Smith College Archives, on the original games.

    Grundman, "A.A.U.-N.C.A.A. Politics"; Joseph Maguire, *Global Sport*, 126–27, 180; *Chicago Sun-Times*, October 28, 2001, 118A; "International House of Hoops"; Bucher, "Uber Star"; Bucher, "Euro Trail"; M. Adams, "Export . . . in Spain"; Fussman, "Next Athlete"; Joe Maguire, "The Commercialization of English Elite Basketball."
16. Avrahmi, "Isolation Play"; LaFeber, *Michael Jordan and the New Global Capitalism*, 131, 138; Miller et al., *Globalization and Sport*, 64; Van Bottenburg, *Global Games*, 10, claims another American YMCA invention, volleyball, as most popular, with participants in 217 countries.
17. Miller et al., *Globalization and Sport*, 6, 14–19.
18. Miller et al., *Globalization and Sport*, 56–59; Joseph Maguire, *Global Sport*, 14, 130; LaFeber, *Michael Jordan and the New Global Capitalism*, 104, 144–57; Reilly, "The Swooshification of the World."
19. Joseph Maguire, *Global Sport*, 97–127; "Playing for Profit"; Darby, "The New Scramble for Africa," 227 (quote).
20. Jere Longman, "Poland's Top Scorer Gets a Cold Welcome," New York Times.com, May 28, 2002.
21. Rushin, "World Domination"; Miller et al., *Globalization and Sport*, 8, 17; Andrews et al., "Jordanscapes," 452 (quote); "Not Just a Game," *The Economist*, 9, 14, 16.
22. "Not Just a Game," *The Economist*, 16–18.
23. "Not Just a Game," *The Economist*, 7.
24. Paino, "Hoosiers in a Different Light"; Bale, *Sports Geography*, 15–16, 20–26; Dyreson, "Globalizing American Sporting Culture," 145–51 (quote at 146).
25. Bush cited in Robert Schmuhl, "World Views America as Empire in Denial," *Chicago Sun-Times*, February 8, 2004, 38A.
26. Anderson and Cayton, *The Dominion of War*, details the centrality of imperialism in American culture. Roosevelt quoted in "Echoes from the Past," History News Network, http://hnn.us/articles/631.html.
27. Butler quoted in Stanley Kutler, "Review of Chalmers Johnson's *The Sorrows of*

Empire," History News Network, January 14, 2004, http://hnn.us/articles/3015.html.

28. Kutler, "Review of Chalmers Johnson's *The Sorrows of Empire*"; Blum et al., *The National Experience*, 584–87; Garraty, *The American Nation*, 594–97. Wilson quotes from William Loren Katz, "George 'Woodrow Wilson' Bush," History News Network, http://hnn.us/articles/6188.html.
29. Blum et al., *The National Experience*, 641–43.
30. Fulbright quoted in "Echoes from the Past," History News Network, http://hnn.us/articles/631.html.
31. Bush cited by Kutler, "Review of Chalmers Johnson's *The Sorrows of Empire*," 2.
32. Chalmers Johnson, "The Arithmetic of America's Military Bases Abroad: What Does It All Add Up To?" January 21, 2004, History News Network, http://hnn.us/articles/3097.html.
33. Johnson, "The Arithmetic of America's Military Bases Abroad."
34. Joseph Maguire, *Global Sport*, 63–64; LaFeber, *Michael Jordan and the New Global Capitalism*, 141 (quote).
35. Musicant, *The Banana Wars*, 392.

Bibliography

Archives

Bishop Museum, Hawaii Sports Hall of Fame, Honolulu, Hawaii
Chicago Art Institute
    Daniel Burnham Papers
Chicago Historical Society
Harvard University: W. Cameron Forbes Papers
International Boxing Hall of Fame
Library of Congress
    Stephen Bonsal Papers
    Bishop Charles H. Brent Papers
    William Howard Taft Papers
    Leonard Wood Papers
National Archives
National Baseball Hall of Fame
North Central College
Philippines National Library
Rockefeller University: Rockefeller Archive Center
Smith College Archives
University of Chicago
    Department of Physical Education and Athletic Papers
    Fred Eggan Papers
    Presidents' Papers
    Amos Alonzo Stagg Papers
    Frederick Starr Papers
University of Michigan, Bentley Library
    Frederic S. Marquardt Papers
    Dean C. Worcester Papers
University of Minnesota: Young Men's Christian Association (YMCA)
    Archives

Books, Articles, and Dissertations

"1896 Xmas Vacation, An." *College Football Historical Society* 10, no. 2 (February 1997): 11–12.

Abe, Ikuo, Yasuhara Kiyohara, and Ken Nakajima. "Fascism, Sport, and Society in Japan." *International Journal of the History of Sport* 9, no. 1 (April 1992): 1–28.

Abernethy, David B. *The Dynamics of Global Dominance: European Overseas Empires, 1415–1980*. New Haven CT: Yale University Press, 2000.

Adams, David Wallace. *Education for Extinction: American Indians and the Boarding School Experience, 1875–1928*. Lawrence: University Press of Kansas, 1995.

Adams, Frederick Upham. *Conquest of the Tropics*. Garden City NY: Doubleday, Page, 1914.

Adams, Mark. "Export . . . in Spain." *ESPN Magazine*, October 28, 2002, 78–82.

Alcantara, Erlyn Ruth E. "Baguio between Two Wars: The Creation and Destruction of a Summer Capital." In *Vestiges of War: The Philippine-American War and the Aftermath of an Imperial Dream, 1899–1999*, ed. Angel Velasco Shaw and Luis H. Francia, 207–23. New York: New York University Press, 2002.

Allen, Gwenfreade E. *The Y.M.C.A. in Hawaii, 1869–1969*. Honolulu: Young Men's Christian Association (YMCA), 1969.

Allen, Theodore W. *The Invention of the White Race: Racial Oppression and Social Control*. London: Verso, 1998.

Allen, Thomas B. "Remember the Maine?" *National Geographic*, February 1998, 92–109.

Anderson, Fred, and Andrew Cayton. *The Dominion of War: Empire and Liberty in North America, 1500–2000*. New York: Viking, 2005.

Andrews, David L. "Desperately Seeking Michel: Foucault's Genealogy, the Body, and Critical Sport Sociology." *Sociology of Sport Journal* 10, no. 2 (June 1993): 148–67.

Andrews, David L., Ben Carrington, Steven J. Jackson, and Zbigniew Mazur. "Jordanscapes: A Preliminary Analysis of the Global Popular." *Sociology of Sport Journal* 13 (1996): 428–57.

Andrews, T. S., ed. *Ring Battles of Centuries and Sporting Almanac*. N.p.: Tom Andrews Record Book Company, 1924.

Arbena, Joseph L., ed. *Sport and Society in Latin America: Diffusion, Dependency, and the Rise of Mass Culture*. New York: Greenwood, 1988.

Arbena, Joseph L., and David G. LaFrance, eds. *Sport in Latin America and the Caribbean*. Wilmington DE: Scholarly Resources, 2002.

Ardolino, Frank. "Missionaries, Cartwright, and Spalding: The Development of Baseball in Nineteenth-century Hawaii." *Nine: A Journal of Baseball History and Culture* 10, no. 2 (2002): 27–45.

Armstrong, Tim, ed. *American Bodies: Cultural Histories of the Physique*. New York: New York University Press, 1996.

Arnesen, Eric. "Whiteness and the Historians' Imagination." *International Labor and Working Class History* 60 (Fall 2001): 3–32.

Atkins, G. Pope, and Larman C. Wilson. *The Dominican Republic and the United States: From Imperialism to Transnationalism*. Athens: University of Georgia Press, 1998.

Avrahmi, Ze'ev, with Chad Millman. "Isolation Play." *ESPN Magazine*, April 28, 2003, 45–51.

Badger, Reid. *The Great American Fair*. Chicago: Nelson Hall, 1979.

Baker, Lee D. *From Savage to Negro: Anthropology and the Construction of Race, 1896–1954*. Berkeley: University of California Press, 1998.

Bailey, Beth, and David Farber. *The First Strange Place: Race and Sex in World War II Hawaii*. Baltimore: Johns Hopkins University Press, 1992.

Baldassaro, Lawrence, and Richard A. Johnson, eds. *The American Game: Baseball and Ethnicity*. Carbondale: Southern Illinois University Press, 2002.

Bale, John. *Sports Geography*. 1989. Reprint, London: Routledge, 2003.

Bartholomew, Gail. *Maui Remembers: A Local History*. Honolulu: Mutual Publishing, 1994.

Bederman, Gail. *Manliness and Civilization: A Cultural History of Gender and Race in the United States, 1880–1917*. Chicago: University of Chicago Press, 1995.

Bennett, Mrs. H. *Her Story: A History of the Woman's Missionary Society*. Cleveland OH: Mattill and Lamb, n.d.

Beran, Janice A. "Americans in the Philippines: Imperialism or Progress through Sports?" *International Journal of the History of Sport* 6 (May 1989): 62–87.

Berger, Maurice, Brian Wallis, and Simon Watson, eds. *Constructing Masculinity*. New York: Routledge, 1995.

Bjarkman, Peter C. *Baseball with a Latin Beat: A History of the Latin American Game*. Jefferson NC: McFarland, 1994.

Blackford, Mansel G. *Fragile Paradise: The Impact of Tourism on Maui, 1959–2000.* Lawrence: University Press of Kansas, 2001.

Blum, John M., Edmund S. Morgan, Willie Lee Rose, Arthur M. Schlesinger Jr., Kenneth M. Stampp, and C. Vann Woodward. *The National Experience: A History of the United States.* New York: Harcourt, Brace, Jovanovich, 1981.

Bocobo-Olivar, Celia. *History of Physical Education in the Philippines.* Quezon City: University of the Philippines Press, 1972.

Bogue, Allan G. *Frederick Jackson Turner: Strange Roads Going Down.* Norman: University of Oklahoma Press, 1998.

Booth, Douglas. "Ambiguities in Pleasure and Discipline: The Development of Competitive Surfing." *Journal of Sport History* 22, no. 3 (Fall 1995): 189–206.

Boyer, Christine M. *The City of Collective Memory: Its Historical Imagery and Architectural Entertainments.* 1994. Reprint, Cambridge MA: MIT Press, 1996.

Brands, H. W. *Bound to Empire: The United States and the Philippines.* New York: Oxford University Press, 1992.

Briggs, Laura. *Reproducing Empire: Race, Sex, Science, and U.S. Imperialism in Puerto Rico.* Berkeley: University of California Press, 2002.

Brodkin, Karen. *How Jews Became White Folks and What That Says about Race in America.* New Brunswick NJ: Rutgers University Press, 1998.

Brown, Bill. "Waging Baseball, Playing War: Games of American Imperialism." *Cultural Critique* 17 (Winter 1990–91): 51–78.

Brown, George W. "Haiti and the United States." *Journal of Negro History* 2 (April 1923): 134–52.

Brown, William Wells. "On Race and Change." In *Black on White: Black Writers on What It Means to Be White*, ed. David R. Roediger, 56–57. New York: Schocken Books, 1998.

Brownell, Susan. *Training the Body for China: Sports in the Moral Order of the People's Republic.* Chicago: University of Chicago Press, 1995.

Bucher, Ric. "Euro Trail." *ESPN Magazine*, November 12, 2001, 91–99.

———. "Uber Star." *ESPN Magazine*, November 12, 2001, 83–88.

Buck, Elizabeth. *Paradise Remade: The Politics of Culture and History in Hawaii.* Philadelphia: Temple University Press, 1993.

Bukosan, Carlos. *America Is in the Heart: A Personal History.* New York: Harcourt, Brace, 1946.

Cahn, Susan. *Coming On Strong: Gender and Sexuality in Twentieth-century Women's Sport*. New York: Free Press, 1994.

Calo, Lucrezia T. *Organization and Management of Athletic Meets*. Manila: Rex Book Store, 1984.

Cannadine, David. *Ornamentalism: How the British Saw Their Empire*. Oxford: Oxford University Press, 2001.

Carnes, Mark C., and Clyde Griffen, eds. *Meanings for Manhood: Constructions of Masculinity in Victorian America*. Chicago: University of Chicago Press, 1990.

Carr, Kevin Gray. "Making War: War, Philosophy, and Sport in Japanese Judo." *Journal of Sport History* 20, no. 2 (Summer 1993): 167–88.

Carson, Mina. *Settlement Folk: Social Thought and the American Settlement Movement, 1885–1930*. Chicago: University of Chicago Press, 1990.

Carter, Thomas. "Baseball Arguments: Aficionismo and Masculinity at the Core of Cubanidad." In *Sport in Latin American Society: Past and Present*, ed. J. A. Mangan and Lamartine P. DaCosta, 117–38. London: Frank Cass, 2002.

Cavallo, Dominick. *Muscles and Morals: Organized Playgrounds and Urban Reform, 1880–1920*. Philadelphia: University of Pennsylvania Press, 1981.

Cepeda, Orlando, with Herb Fagen. "From Hardball to Hard Times and Back." In *Baseball and the American Dream: Race, Class, Gender and the National Pastime*, ed. Robert Elias, 76–89. Armonk NY: M. E. Sharpe, 2001.

Chadwick, Henry, ed. *Spalding's Base Ball Guide and Official League Book for 1901*. New York: American Sports Publishing, 1901.

Chapman, David L. *Sandow the Magnificent: Eugen Sandow and the Beginnings of Body Building*. Urbana: University of Illinois Press, 1994.

Chappell, Robert. "The Soviet Protégé: Cuba, Modern Sport and Communist Comrade." In *Europe, Sport, World: Shaping Global Societies*, ed. J. A. Mangan, 181–204. London: Frank Cass, 2001.

Cisco, Dan. *Hawaii Sports: History, Facts, and Statistics*. Honolulu: University of Hawaii Press, 1999.

Clymer, Kenton J. *Protestant Missionaries in the Philippines, 1898–1916: An Inquiry into the American Colonial Mentality*. Urbana: University of Illinois Press, 1986.

Cockburn, Andrew. "True Colors: Divided Loyalties in Puerto Rico." *National Geographic*, March 2003, 34–55.

Coffman, Edward M. *The Regulars: The American Army, 1898–1941*. Cambridge MA: Belknap, 2004.

Constantino, Renato. "The Miseducation of the Filipino." In *Vestiges of War: The Philippine-American War and the Aftermath of an Imperial Dream, 1899–1999*, ed. Angel Velasco Shaw and Luis H. Francia, 177–92. New York: New York University Press, 2002.

Crepeau, Richard, and Daniel A. Nathan. "Two Visions of ESPN." *Journal of Sport History* 27, no. 3 (Fall 2000): 525–31.

Crepeau, Richard C. "Pearl Harbor: A Failure of Baseball." *Journal of Popular Culture* 15, no. 4 (Spring 1982): 67–74.

Darby, Paul. "The New Scramble for Africa: The African Football Labour Migration to Europe." In *Europe, Sport, World: Shaping Global Societies*, ed. J. A. Mangan, 217–44. London: Frank Cass, 2001.

Dauncey, Mrs. Campbell. *The Philippines: An Account of Their People, Progress, and Condition*. Boston: J. B. Millet, 1910.

Davidann, Jon. "Citadels of Civilization: U.S. and Japanese Visions of World Order in the Interwar Period." In *Trans-Pacific Relations: America, Europe, and Asia in the Twentieth Century*, ed. Richard Jensen, Jon Davidann, and Yoneyuki Sugita, 21–43. Westport CT: Praeger, 2003.

Davidann, Jon Thares. *A World of Crisis and Progress: The American YMCA in Japan, 1890–1930*. Bethlehem PA: Lehigh University Press, 1998.

Deocampo, Nick. "Imperialist Fictions: The Filipino in the Imperialist Imaginary." In *Vestiges of War: The Philippine-American War and the Aftermath of an Imperial Dream, 1899–1999*, ed. Angel Velasco Shaw and Luis H. Francia, 225–36. New York: New York University Press, 2002.

Dery, Luis. "Prostitution in Colonial Manila." *Philippine Studies* 39, no. 4 (1991): 475–89.

Diaz, Vicente M. "Fight Boys 'til the Last . . . : Island Style Football and the Remasculinization of Indigeneity in the Militarized American Pacific Islands." In *Pacific Diaspora: Island Peoples in the United States and across the Pacific*, ed. Paul Spickard, Joanne L. Rondilla, and Debbie Hippolyte Wright, 169–94. Honolulu: University of Hawaii Press, 2002.

———. "Pappy's House: History, Pop Culture and the Reevaluation of a Filipino-American 'Sixty Cents' in Guam." In *Vestiges of War: The Philippine-American War and the Aftermath of an Imperial Dream, 1899–*

1999, ed. Angel Velasco Shaw and Luis H. Francia, 318–28. New York: New York University Press, 2002.

Dibble, Sheldon. *A History of the Sandwich Islands*. 1843. Reprint, Honolulu: Thos. G. Thrum, 1909.

Dolan, Ronald E., ed. *Philippines: A Country Study*. Washington DC: Library of Congress, 1993.

Douglas, Ann. *The Feminization of American Culture*. New York: Anchor, 1977.

Dreifort, John E., ed. *Baseball History from Outside the Lines: A Reader*. Lincoln: University of Nebraska Press, 2001.

Duany, Jorge. *The Puerto Rican Nation on the Move: Identities on the Island and in the United States*. Chapel Hill: University of North Carolina Press, 2002.

Dudley, Michael Kioni, and Keoni Kealoha Agard. "A History of Dispossession." In *Pacific Diaspora: Island Peoples in the United States and across the Pacific*, ed. Paul Spickard, Joanne L. Rondilla, and Debbie Hippolyte Wright, 309–21. Honolulu: University of Hawaii Press, 2002.

Dunand, Emmanuel. "Worldwide It's a Hit." *National Geographic*, April 2004.

Dyreson, Mark. "Globalizing American Sporting Culture: The U.S. Government Plan to Conquer the World Sports Market in the 1930s." *Sportwissenschaft* 34, no. 2 (2004): 145–51.

———. *Making the American Team: Sport, Culture, and the Olympic Experience*. Urbana: University of Illinois Press, 1998.

———. "Regulating the Body and the Body Politic: American Sport, Bourgeois Culture, and the Language of Progress, 1880–1920." In *The New American Sport History: Recent Approaches and Perspectives*, ed. S. W. Pope, 121–44. Urbana: University of Illinois Press, 1997.

Echevarría, Roberto González. *The Pride of Havana: A History of Cuban Baseball*. New York: Oxford University Press, 1999.

Elfers, James E. *The Tour to End All Tours: The Story of Major League Baseball's 1913–1914 World Tour*. Lincoln: University of Nebraska Press, 2003.

Elias, Robert, ed. *Baseball and the American Dream: Race, Class, Gender, and the National Pastime*. Armond NY: M. E. Sharpe, 2001.

Eller, Paul Himmel. *History of Evangelical Missions*. Harrisburg PA: Evangelical Press, 1942.

Ernst, Robert. *Weakness Is a Crime: The Life of Bernarr MacFadden*. Syracuse NY: Syracuse University Press, 1991.

Espana-Maram, Linda N. "Negotiating Identity: Youth, Gender, and Popular Culture in Los Angeles's Little Manila, 1920s–1940s." PhD diss., University of California, Los Angeles, 1996.

Fauriol, Georges, and Eva Loser, eds. *Cuba: The International Dimension*. New Brunswick NJ: Transaction, 1990.

Fee, Mary H. *A Woman's Impression of the Philippines*. Chicago: McClurg, 1910.

Feldman, Bruce. "Rock Star." ESPN *Magazine*, November 26, 2001, 50–54.

Ferguson, Niall. "America: An Empire in Denial." *Chronicle of Higher Education*, March 28, 2003, B7–B10.

Ferro, Marc. *Colonization: A Global History*. London: Routledge, 1997.

Fessler, Loren. *China*. New York: Time Inc., 1963.

Field, Michael J. *Mau: Samoa's Struggle for Freedom*. 1984. Reprint, Auckland, New Zealand: Polynesian Press, 1991.

Finney, Ben R. "The Development and Diffusion of Modern Hawaiian Surfing." *Journal of the Polynesian Society* 69 (1960): 315–31.

Foner, Eric. *Free Soil, Free Labor, Free Men: The Ideology of the Republican Party before the Civil War*. New York: Oxford University Press, 1970.

Forbes, Jack D. "The Manipulation of Race, Caste, and Identity: Classifying Afroamericans, Native Americans, and Red-Black People." *Journal of Ethnic Studies* 17, no. 4 (Winter 1990): 1–51.

Fossett, Judith Jackson, and Jeffrey A. Tucker, eds. *Race Consciousness: African-American Studies for the New Century*. New York: New York University Press, 1997.

Foster, John B., ed. *Spalding's Official Base Ball Guide, 1910*. New York: American Sports Publishing, 1910.

———, ed. *Spalding's Official Base Ball Record, 1909*. New York: American Sports Publishing, 1908.

Franks, Joel S. "Baseball and Racism's Traveling Eye: The Asian Pacific Experience." In *The American Game: Baseball and Ethnicity*, ed. Lawrence Baldassaro and Richard A. Johnson, 177–96. Carbondale: Southern Illinois University Press, 2002.

———. *Crossing Sidelines, Crossing Cultures: Sport and Asian Pacific American Cultural Citizenship*. Lanham MD: University Press of America, 2000.

———. *Hawaiian Sports in the Twentieth Century*. Lewiston NY: Edward Mellen Press, 2002.

Freeman, Michael. ESPN: *The Uncensored History*. Dallas: Taylor, 2000.

Freer, William B. *The Philippine Experiences of an American Teacher: A Narrative of*

Work and Travel in the Philippine Islands. New York: Charles Scribner's Sons, 1906.

Frye, Edwin G., and A. E. Hangen, eds. *The Year Book of the Evangelical Church, 1927*. Cleveland OH: Evangelical Publishing House, 1927.

Fussman, Cal. "Next Athlete." *ESPN Magazine*, December 25, 2000, 78–87.

Garcia, Gervasio Luis. "I Am the Other: Puerto Rico in the Eyes of North Americans, 1898." *Journal of American History* 87, no. 1 (June 2000): 39–64.

Garraty, John A. *The American Nation: A History of the United States*. New York: Harper and Row, 1983.

Gates, John M. *Schoolbooks and Krags: The United States Army in the Philippines, 1898–1902*. Westport CT: Greenwood, 1973.

Gatewood, Willard B., Jr. *"Smoked Yankees" and the Struggle for Empire: Letters from Negro Soldiers, 1898–1902*. Fayetteville: University of Arkansas Press, 1987.

Gems, Gerald R. "The Athlete as Trickster." *Ethnic Studies Review* 24, no. 1–3 (Winter 2001): 48–57.

———. "The Construction, Negotiation, and Transformation of Racial Identity in American Football." *American Indian Culture and Research Journal* 22, no. 2 (July 1998): 131–50.

———. *For Pride, Profit, and Patriarchy: Football and the Incorporation of American Cultural Values*. Lanham MD: Scarecrow, 2000.

———. *Windy City Wars: Labor, Leisure, and Sport in the Making of Chicago*. Lanham MD: Scarecrow, 1997.

Gillette, Howard. "The Military Occupation of Cuba, 1899–1902: Workshop for American Progressivism." *American Quarterly* 25 (1973): 410–25.

Gilman, Sander L. "Damaged Men: Thoughts on Kafka's Body." In *Constructing Masculinity*, ed. Maurice Berger, Brian Wallis, and Simon Watson, 176–89. New York: Routledge, 1995.

Gleeck, Lewis E., Jr. *American Institutions in the Philippines (1898–1941)*. Manila: Historical Conservation Society, 1976.

———. *The Manila Americans (1901–1964)*. Manila: Carmelo and Bauermann, 1977.

Goldberg, David Theo. *Racist Culture: Philosophy and the Poetics of Meaning*. Cambridge MA: Blackwell, 1993.

Goodman, Cary. *Choosing Sides: Playgrounds and Street Life on the Lower East Side*. New York: Schocken Books, 1979.

Gordon, Lynn D. *Gender and Higher Education in the Progressive Era*. New Haven CT: Yale University Press, 1990.

Gould, Stephen Jay. *The Mismeasure of Man*. 1981. Reprint, New York: Norton, 1996.

Graham, Gael. "Gender, Culture, and Christianity: American Protestant Mission Schools in China, 1880–1930." PhD diss., University of Michigan, 1990.

Gray, J.A.C. *Amerika Samoa: A History of American Samoa and Its United States Naval Administration*. Annapolis MD: U.S. Naval Institute, 1960.

Greatest of Expositions, The. St. Louis: Louisiana Purchase Exposition Company, 1904.

Grundman, Adolph H. "A.A.U.-N.C.A.A. Politics: Forest C. 'Phog' Allen and America's First Olympic Basketball Team." *Olympika* 5 (1996): 111–26.

Guerrero, Amado. *Philippine Society and Revolution*. Hong Kong: Ta Kung Pao, 1971.

Guidry, John A., Michael D. Kennedy, and Mayer N. Zald. "Globalization and Social Movements." In *Globalizations and Social Movements: Culture, Power, and the Transnational Public Sphere*, 1–32. Ann Arbor: University of Michigan Press, 2000.

———. *Globalizations and Social Movements: Culture, Power, and the Transnational Public Sphere*. Ann Arbor: University of Michigan Press, 2000.

Gulick, Sidney L. *Mixing the Races in Hawaii: A Study of the Coming Neo-Hawaiian American Race*. Honolulu: Porter Printing, 1937.

Gustafson, John. "Next Country." ESPN *Magazine*, December 27, 1999, 91.

Guterl, Matthew Pratt. *The Color of Race in America, 1900–1940*. Cambridge MA: Harvard University Press, 2001.

Guthrie-Shimizu, Sayuri. "For Love of the Game: Baseball in Early U.S.-Japanese Encounters and the Rise of a Transnational Sporting Fraternity." *Diplomatic History* 28, no. 5 (November 2004): 637–62.

Gutman, Herbert. *Work, Culture, and Society in Industrializing America*. New York: Vintage Books, 1976.

Guttmann, Allen. *Games and Empires: Modern Sports and Cultural Imperialism*. New York: Columbia University Press, 1994.

Guttmann, Allen, and Lee Thompson. *Japanese Sports: A History*. Honolulu: University of Hawaii Press, 2001.

Hall, Sandra Kimberley, and Greg Ambrose. *Memories of Duke: The Legend Comes to Life*. Honolulu: Bess Press, 1995.

Hardt, Michael, and Antonio Negri. *Empire*. Cambridge MA: Harvard University Press, 2000.

Hardy, Stephen. *How Boston Played: Sport, Recreation, and Community, 1865–1915*. Boston: Northeastern University Press, 1982.

Hawaiian Promotion Committee. *Hawaii: A Primer*. Honolulu: Mercantile Printing, 1908.

Healy, David. *Drive to Hegemony: The United States in the Caribbean, 1898–1917*. Madison: University of Wisconsin Press, 1988.

Heffer, Jean. *The United States and the Pacific: History of a Frontier*. Notre Dame IN: Notre Dame University Press, 2002.

Higgs, Robert J. *God in the Stadium: Sports and Religion in America*. Lexington: University Press of Kentucky, 1995.

Hines, Thomas. "The Imperial Façade: Daniel Burnham and American Architecture in the Philippines." *Pacific Historical Review* 41, no. 1 (1972): 33–53.

Hines, Thomas S. *Burnham of Chicago: Architect and Planner*. Chicago: University of Chicago Press, 1979.

Hirdt, Steve. "Foreign Legions." *ESPN Magazine*, February 17, 2003, 16.

Hoare, Quintin, and Geoffrey N. Smith, eds. *Selections from the Prison Notebooks of Antonio Gramsci*. New York: International Publishers, 1972.

Hoberman, John. *Darwin's Athletes: How Sport Has Damaged Black America and Preserved the Myth of Race*. Boston: Houghton Mifflin, 1997.

Hobsbawm, Eric, and Terence Ranger, eds. *The Invention of Tradition*. Cambridge: Cambridge University Press, 1983.

Hoganson, Kristin L. *Fighting for American Manhood: How Gender Politics Provoked the Spanish-American and Philippine-American Wars*. New Haven CT: Yale University Press, 1998.

Hollinger, David. "Interchange: The Practice of History." *Journal of American History* 90, no. 2 (September 2003).

Hong, Fan. "'Iron Bodies': Women, War, and Sport in the Early Communist Movement in Modern China." *Journal of Sport History* 24, no. 1 (Spring 1997): 1–23.

Horsman, Reginald. *Race and Manifest Destiny: The Origins of American Racial Anglo-Saxonism*. Cambridge MA: Harvard University Press, 1981.

Howard, David. *Coloring the Nation: Race and Ethnicity in the Dominican Republic.* Boulder CO: L. Rienner, 2001.

Hoxie, Frederick E. *A Final Promise: The Campaign to Assimilate the Indians, 1880–1920.* New York: Cambridge University Press, 1989.

Huntington, Samuel P. *The Clash of Civilizations and the Remaking of World Order.* New York: Simon and Schuster, 1996.

Ignatiev, Noel. *How the Irish Became White.* New York: Routledge, 1995.

"International House of Hoops." *ESPN Magazine*, August 5, 2002, 74.

Jackson, Donald Dale. *Gold Dust.* New York: Knopf, 1980.

Jacobson, Matthew Frye. *Barbarian Virtues: The United States Encounters Foreign Peoples at Home and Abroad, 1876–1917.* New York: Hill and Wang, 2000.

———. *Whiteness of a Different Color: European Immigrants and the Alchemy of Race.* Cambridge MA: Harvard University Press, 1998.

Jeffers, H. Paul. *Colonel Roosevelt: Theodore Roosevelt Goes to War, 1897–1898.* New York: Wiley, 1996.

Johnson, Susan Lee. *Roaring Camp: The Social World of the California Gold Rush.* New York: Norton, 2000.

Kamana, Kauanoe, and William H. Wilson. "The Tip of the Spear: Hawaiian Language Educators Reclaim a Cultural Legacy." *Teaching Tolerance* (Spring 2002): 20–24.

Kane, Joe. "Arrested Development." *Outside*, May 2001, 68–78.

Kantowicz, Edward R. *Corporation Sole: Cardinal Mundelein and Chicago Catholicism.* Notre Dame IN: Notre Dame University Press, 1983.

Kaplan, Amy, and Donald E. Pease, eds. *Cultures of United States Imperialism.* Durham NC: Duke University Press, 1993.

Karnes, Thomas L. *Tropical Enterprise: Standard Fruit and Steamship Company in Latin America.* Baton Rouge: Louisiana State University Press, 1978.

Karnow, Stanley. *In Our Image: America's Empire in the Philippines.* New York: Random House, 1989.

Kasson, Joy S. *Buffalo Bill's Wild West: Celebrity, Memory, and Popular History.* New York: Hill and Wang, 2000.

Keil, Hartmut, and John B. Jentz, eds. *German Workers in Chicago: A Documentary History of Working-class Culture from 1850 to World War I.* Urbana: University of Illinois Press, 1988.

Kelley, Robin D. G. "'But a Local Phase of a World Problem': Black History's

Global Vision, 1883–1950." *Journal of American History* 86, no. 3 (December 1999): 1045–77.

Kelly, William W. "Blood and Guts in Japanese Professional Baseball." In *The Culture of Japan as Seen through Its Leisure*, ed. Sepp Linhart and Sabine Fruhstuck. Albany: State University of New York Press, 1998.

Kempa, A. A. *A Survey of Physical Education in the Territory of Hawaii*. N.p., 1930.

Keown, Tim. "Special Team." *ESPN Magazine*, April 14, 2003, 23–30.

Kijokawa, Masaji. "Swimming into History." *Journal of Olympic History* 5, no. 3 (Fall 1997): 10–14.

Kimmel, Michael. *Manhood in America: A Cultural History*. New York: Free Press, 1996.

Kingman, Harry. "Japan on the Diamond." *Asia*, February 1928, 163.

Kirsch, George B., Othello Harris, and Claire E. Nolte, eds. *Encyclopedia of Ethnicity and Sports in the United States*. Westport CT: Greenwood, 2000.

Klein, Alan. "American Hegemony, Dominican Resistance, and Baseball." *Dialectical Anthropology* 13 (1988): 301–12.

Klein, Alan M. "Culture, Politics, and Baseball in the Dominican Republic." *Latin American Perspectives* 22, no. 3 (Summer 1995): 111–30.

———. *Sugarball: The American Game, the Dominican Dream*. New Haven CT: Yale University Press, 1991.

Klineberg, Otto. *Race Differences*. New York: Harper and Bros., 1935.

Knisely, Michael. "Everybody Has the Dream: Baseball Scouting and Players' Hopes of Success in Dominican Republic." *Sporting News*, February 19, 2001.

Kolchin, Peter. "Whiteness Studies: The New History of Race in America." *Journal of American History* 89, no. 1 (June 2002): 154–73.

Kramer, Augustin. *The Samoa Islands: An Outline of a Monograph with Particular Consideration of German Samoa*. 1901. Reprint, Honolulu: University of Hawaii Press, 1994.

Kramer, Paul. "Jim Crow Science and the 'Negro Problem' in the Occupied Philippines, 1898–1914." In *Race Consciousness: African-American Studies for the New Century*, ed. Judith Jackson Fossett and Jeffrey A. Tucker, 227–46. New York: New York University Press, 1997.

Kramer, Paul A. "Empires, Exceptions, and Anglo-Saxons: Race and Rule between the British and the United States Empires, 1880–1910." *Journal of American History* 88, no. 4 (March 2002): 1315–53.

———. "The Pragmatic Empire: U.S. Anthropology and Colonial Politics in the Occupied Philippines, 1898–1916." PhD diss., Princeton University, 1998.

Krich, John. *El Béisbol: Travels through the Pan-American Pastime*. New York: Atlantic Monthly Press, 1989.

Kuchar, Mike. "Northern Exposure." ESPN *Magazine*, February 18, 2002, 98.

Kusaka, Yuko. "The Development of Baseball Organizations in Japan." *International Review for the Sociology of Sport* 22, no. 4 (1987): 266–77.

LaFeber, Walter. *Michael Jordan and the New Global Capitalism*. New York: Norton, 1999.

LaGorce, John O. "Porto Rico: The Gate of Riches." *National Geographic*, December 1924, 599–651.

Langer, William L., ed. *An Encyclopedia of World History*. Boston: Houghton Mifflin, 1972.

Langley, Lester D., and Thomas Schoonover. *The Banana Men: American Mercenaries and Entrepreneurs in Central America, 1880–1930*. Lexington: University Press of Kentucky, 1995.

Lardizabal, Amparo Santamaria. "Pioneer American Teachers and Philippine Education." In *Tales of the American Teachers in the Philippines*, ed. Geronima T. Pecson and Maria Racelis, 85–118. Manila: Carmelo and Bauermann, 1959.

Latourette, Kenneth S. *World Service: A History of Foreign Work and World Service of the Young Men's Christian Association of the United States and Canada*. New York: Association Press, 1957.

Laurie, Bruce. *Working People of Philadelphia, 1800–1850*. Philadelphia: Temple University Press, 1980.

Lay, Graeme, Tony Murrow, and Malama Meleisa. *Samoa: Pacific Pride*. Auckland, New Zealand: Pasifika Press, 2000.

Le Batard, Dan. "Next Detour." ESPN *Magazine*, December 24, 2001, 105–11.

Lee, Erika. "Enforcing the Borders: Chinese Exclusion along the U.S. Borders with Canada and Mexico, 1882–1924." *Journal of American History* 89, no. 1 (June 2002): 54–86.

LeRoy, James A. *Philippine Life in Town and Country*. New York: G. P. Putnam's Sons, 1905.

Lester, Larry, and Sammy J. Miller. *Black Baseball in Kansas City*. Chicago: Arcadia, 2001.

Levine, Peter. *A. G. Spalding and the Rise of Baseball: The Promise of American Sport.* New York: Oxford University Press, 1985.

Licuanen, Virginia Benitez. *Filipinos and Americans: A Love-Hate Relationship.* Manila: Baguio Country Club, 1982.

Limerick, Patricia Nelson. *The Legacy of Conquest: The Unbroken Past of the American West.* New York: Norton, 1987.

Linhart, Sepp, and Sabine Fruhstruck, eds. *The Culture of Japan as Seen through Its Leisure.* Albany: State University of New York Press, 1998.

Linnekin, Jocelyn, and Lin Poyer, eds. *Cultural Identity and Ethnicity in the Pacific.* Honolulu: University of Hawaii Press, 1990.

Logan, Rayford. "Education in Haiti." *Journal of Negro History* 15 (October 1930): 401–60.

Lott, Eric. *Love and Theft: Blackface Minstrelsy and the American Working Class.* New York: Oxford University Press, 1993.

Love, Eric T. *Race over Empire: Racism and U.S. Imperialism, 1865–1900.* Chapel Hill: University of North Carolina Press, 2004.

Mac Aloon, John J. "La Pitada Olimpica: Puerto Rico, International Sport, and the Constitution of Politics." In *Text, Play, and Story: The Construction and Reconstruction of Self and Society*, ed. Edward Bruner, 315–55. Washington DC: American Ethnological Society, 1984.

Madison, Julian. "American Military Bases in the Philippines, 1945–1965: Neo-Colonialism and Its Demise." In *Trans-Pacific Relations: America, Europe, and Asia in the Twentieth Century*, ed. Richard Jensen, Jon Davidann, and Yoneyuki Sugita, 125–45. Westport CT: Praeger, 2003.

Magoon, Charles E. *Republic of Cuba: Report of Provisional Administration.* Havana: Rambla and Bouza, 1908.

Maguire, Joe. "The Commercialization of English Elite Basketball, 1972–1988." *International Review of the Sociology of Sport* 23 (1988): 305–24.

———. "The Media-sport Production Complex: The Case of American Football in Western European Societies." *European Journal of Communications* 6 (1991): 315–35.

Maguire, Joseph. *Global Sport: Identities, Societies, Civilizations.* Cambridge UK: Polity Press, 1999.

Mangan, J. A., ed. *The Cultural Bond: Sport, Empire, Society.* London: Frank Cass, 1992.

———, ed. *Europe, Sport, World: Shaping Global Societies*. London: Frank Cass, 2001.

———. *The Games Ethic and Imperialism: Aspects of the Diffusion of an Ideal*. London: Frank Cass, 1998.

———, ed. *The Imperial Curriculum: Racial Images and Education in the British Colonial Experience*. London: Routledge, 1993.

———, ed. *Making Imperial Mentalities: Socialisation and British Imperialism*. Manchester UK: Manchester University Press, 1990.

Mangan, J. A., and Lamartine P. DaCosta, eds. *Sport in Latin American Society: Past and Present*. London: Frank Cass, 2002.

Mansfield, Rhea. "The Man Who Made Baseball in Japan." *Baseball Magazine*, July 1912, 26–30.

Maraniss, David. *When Pride Still Mattered: A Life of Vince Lombardi*. New York: Simon and Schuster, 1999.

Marks, Patricia. *Bicycles, Bangs, and Bloomers: The New Woman in the Popular Press*. Lexington: University Press of Kentucky, 1990.

Matz, Eddie. "Good Morning, Iraq." *ESPN Magazine*, April 14, 2003, 34.

May, Glenn. *Social Engineering in the Philippines: The Aims, Execution, and Impact of American Colonial Policy, 1900–1913*. Westport CT: Greenwood, 1980.

Mayo-Santana, Raul. "Puerto Ricans." In *Encyclopedia of Ethnicity and Sports in the United States*, ed. George Kirsch, Othello Harris, and Claire E. Nolte, 373–78. Westport CT: Greenwood, 2000.

McFerson, Hazel M. *The Racial Dimension of American Overseas Colonial Policy*. Westport CT: Greenwood, 1997.

McGehee, Richard V. "Sport in Nicaragua, 1889–1926." In *Sport in Latin America and the Caribbean*, ed. Joseph L. Arbena and David G. LaFrance, 175–205. Wilmington DE: Scholarly Resources, 2002.

McGreevy, John T. *Parish Boundaries: The Catholic Encounter with Race in the Twentieth-Century Urban North*. Chicago: University of Chicago Press, 1996.

Merrifield, Fred. "University Athletics in Japan." *University of Chicago Magazine* 2, no. 3 (1910): 102–6.

Miller, Toby, Geoffrey Lawrence, Jim McKay, and David Rowe. *Globalization and Sport: Playing the World*. London: Sage, 2001.

Millett, Allan R. *The Politics of Intervention: The Military Occupation of Cuba, 1906–1909*. Columbus: Ohio State University Press, 1968.

Millis, Walter. *The Martial Spirit*. Chicago: Ivan R. Dee, 1989.

Mojares, Resil. "The Hills Are Still There." In *Vestiges of War: The Philippine-American War and the Aftermath of an Imperial Dream, 1899–1999*, ed. Angel Velasco Shaw and Luis H. Francia, 81–86. New York: New York University Press, 2002.

Montgomery, David. *Beyond Equality: Labor and the Radical Republicans, 1862–1872*. New York: Knopf, 1967.

Moore, Charles, ed. *Plan of Chicago*. Chicago: Commercial Club, 1909.

"More Than Just a Tiny Timbre." *National Geographic*, February 2001, xvi.

Morris-Suzuki, Tessa. "The Invention and Reinvention of 'Japanese Culture.'" *Journal of Asian Studies* 54, no. 3 (August 1995): 759–80.

Mrozek, Donald J. *Sport and American Mentality, 1880–1910*. Knoxville: University of Tennessee Press, 1983.

Musicant, Ivan. *The Banana Wars: A History of the United States Military Intervention in Latin America from the Spanish-American War to the Invasion of Panama*. New York: Macmillan, 1990.

Naismith, James. *Basketball: Its Origin and Development*. New York: Association Press, 1941.

Nankville, John H., ed. *The History of the Twenty-fifth Regiment United States Infantry, 1869–1926*. 1927. Reprint, Fort Collins CO: Old Army Press, 1972.

Nemerov, Alexander. *Frederic Remington and Turn-of-the-century America*. New Haven CT: Yale University Press, 1995.

Neufeld, Maurice F. "The Contribution of the World's Columbian Exposition to the Idea of a Planned Society in the United States." PhD diss., University of Wisconsin, 1935.

Newcombe, Jack. *The Best of the Athletic Boys: The White Man's Impact on Jim Thorpe*. Garden City NJ: Doubleday, 1975.

"Not Just a Game." *The Economist*, June 6, 1998, 68.

Obojski, Robert. *The Rise of Japanese Baseball Power*. Radnor PA: Chilton Books, 1975.

Okihiro, Gary Y. *Margins and Mainstreams: Asians in American History and Culture*. Seattle: University of Washington Press, 1994.

O'Neill, Tom. "96795: The Hawaiians' Hawaii." *National Geographic*, February 2001, 126–30.

Ontal, Rene G. "Fagen and Other Ghosts: African-Americans and the Philippine-American War." In *Vestiges of War: The Philippine-American War and the Aftermath of an Imperial Dream, 1899–1999*, ed. Angel Velasco

Shaw and Luis H. Francia, 118–33. New York: New York University Press, 2002.

Oriard, Michael. *Reading Football: How the Popular Press Created an American Spectacle*. Chapel Hill: University of North Carolina Press, 1993.

Paino, Troy. "Hoosiers in a Different Light: Forces of Change v. the Power of Nostalgia." *Journal of Sport History* 28, no. 1 (Spring 2001): 63–80.

Pakenham, Thomas. *The Scramble for Africa*. New York: Random House, 1991.

Paras, Wilhelmina. "A Nation Hooked on Hoops." *Asiaweek*, October 24, 1997, 47.

Park, Roberta. "Sport and Recreation among Chinese American Communities of the Pacific Coast from Time of Arrival to the 'Quiet Decade' of the 1950s." *Journal of Sport History* 27, no. 3 (Fall 2000): 445–80.

Park, Roberta J. " 'Forget about That Pile of Papers': Second World War Sport, Recreation and the Military on the Island of Puerto Rico." *International Journal of the History of Sport* 20, no. 1 (March 2003): 50–64.

Parsons, Elsie. "American Snobbishness in the Philippines." *Independent* 60, no. 8 (February 1906): 332–33.

Pascoe, Peggy. "Miscegenation Law, Court Cases and Ideologies of 'Race' in Twentieth-century America." *Journal of American History* 83, no. 1 (June 1996): 44–69.

Pecson, Geronima T., and Maria Racelis, eds. *Tales of the American Teachers in the Philippines*. Manila: Carmelo and Bauermann, 1959.

Perez, Louis A., Jr. *Cuba and the United States: Ties of Singular Intimacy*. Athens: University of Georgia Press, 1997.

———. *On Becoming Cuban: Identity, Nationality, and Culture*. Chapel Hill: University of North Carolina Press, 1999.

———. "We Are the World: Internationalizing the National, Nationalizing the International." *Journal of American History* 89, no. 2 (September 2002): 558–66.

Perez, Michael P. "Interethnic Antagonism in the Wake of Colonialism: U.S. Territorial Racial and Ethnic Relations at the Margins." *Ethnic Studies Review* 23, no. 1–3 (2000): 1–32.

Pettavino, Paula, and Geralyn Pye. *Sport in Cuba: The Diamond in the Rough*. Pittsburgh: University of Pittsburgh Press, 1994.

Pettavino, Paula J. "Novel Revolutionary Forms: The Use of Unconventional Diplomacy in Cuba." In *Cuba: The International Dimension*, ed.

Georges Fauriol and Eva Loser, 373–403. New Brunswick NJ: Transaction, 1990.

Phillips, Murray G. "Deconstructing Sport History: The Postmodern Challenge." *Journal of Sport History* 28, no. 3 (Fall 2001): 327–43.

Pier, Arthur S. *American Apostles to the Philippines*. Boston: Beacon, 1950.

"Playing for Profit." *Economist*, June 6, 1998, 8.

Pope, S. W., ed. *The New American Sport History: Recent Approaches and Perspectives*. Urbana: University of Illinois Press, 1997.

———. *Patriotic Games: Sporting Traditions in the American Imagination, 1876–1926*. New York: Oxford University Press, 1997.

Pope, Steven W. "An Army of Athletes: Playing Fields, Battlefields, and the American Military Experience, 1890–1920." *Journal of Military History* 59 (July 1995): 435–56.

Porto Rican Interests: Hearings before the Committee on Insular Affairs, House of Representatives. Washington DC: Government Printing Office, 1919.

Pratt, Julius W. *Expansionists of 1898: The Acquisition of Hawaii and the Spanish Islands*. Gloucester MA: Peter Smith, 1959.

Przybyszewski, Linda. "Judicial Conservatism and Protestant Faith: The Case of Justice David J. Brewer." *Journal of American History* 91, no. 2 (September 2004): 471–96.

Putney, Clifford. *Muscular Christianity: Manhood and Sports in Protestant America, 1880–1920*. Cambridge MA: Harvard University Press, 2001.

Rafael, Vicente. "White Women and United States Rule in the Philippines." *American Literature* 67, no. 4 (December 1995): 639–66.

Rafael, Vicente L. "White Love: Surveillance and Nationalist Resistance in the U.S. Colonization of the Philippines." In *Cultures of United States Imperialism*, ed. Amy Kaplan and Donald E. Pease, 185–218. Durham NC: Duke University Press, 1993.

Reaves, Joseph A. "A History of Baseball in China: How America's Game Helped End Educational Exchanges in the Late Qing Dynasty, Taught Sun Yat-sen's Revolutionaries to Throw Hand Grenades, and Endured the Cultural Revolution." *North American Society for Sport History Proceedings* (1998).

———. *Taking In a Game: A History of Baseball in Asia*. Lincoln: University of Nebraska Press, 2002.

Recreation Commission. *A History of Recreation in Hawaii*. Honolulu: Recreation Commission, 1936.

Regalado, Samuel O. *Viva Baseball!: Latin Major Leaguers and Their Special Hunger.* Urbana: University of Illinois Press, 1998.

Reilly, Rick. "The Swooshification of the World." *Sports Illustrated*, February 24, 1997, 78.

Renda, Mary A. *Taking Haiti: Military Occupation and the Culture of U.S. Imperialism 1915–1940*. Chapel Hill: University of North Carolina Press, 2001.

Ribowsky, Mark. *A Complete History of the Negro Leagues, 1884–1955*. Secaucus NJ: Citadel, 1995.

Richter, Francis C. "Collegiate 1909 Invasion of Japan." In *The Reach Official American League Base Ball Guide for 1910*, ed. Francis C. Richter. Philadelphia: A. J. Reach, 1910.

———, ed. *The Reach Official American League Base Ball Guide for 1910*. Philadelphia: A. J. Reach, 1910.

Roberts, Randy. *Papa Jack: Jack Johnson and the Era of White Hopes*. New York: Free Press, 1983.

Roden, Donald. "Baseball and the Quest for National Dignity in Meiji Japan." In *Baseball History from Outside the Lines: A Reader*, ed. John E. Dreifort, 280–303. Lincoln: University of Nebraska Press, 2001.

———. *Schooldays in Imperial Japan: A Study in the Culture of a Student Elite.* Berkeley: University of California Press, 1980.

Roediger, David R., ed. *Black on White: Black Writers on What It Means to Be White*. New York: Schocken Books, 1998.

———. *The Wages of Whiteness: Race and the Making of the American Working Class.* London: Verso, 1999.

Ropp, Paul S., ed. *Heritage of China: Contemporary Perspectives on Chinese Civilization*. Berkeley: University of California Press, 1990.

Rosaldo, Renato. *Ilongot Headhunting, 1883–1974: A Study in Society and History.* Stanford CA: Stanford University Press, 1980.

Rosenzweig, Roy. *Eight Hours for What We Will: Workers and Leisure in an Industrial City, 1870–1920*. Cambridge: Cambridge University Press, 1983.

Rotundo, E. Anthony. *American Manhood: Transformations in Masculinity from the Revolution to the Modern Era*. New York: Basic Books, 1993.

Royce, Bob. "The Blond Terror." *College Football Historical Society* 9, no. 3 (May 1996): 2–3.

Ruck, Rob. "Three Kings Day in Consuelo: Cricket, Baseball, and the Co-

colos in San Pedro de Macoris." In *Sport in Latin America and the Caribbean*, ed. Joseph L. Arbena and David G. LaFrance, 75–88. Wilmington DE: Scholarly Resources, 2002.

Rushin, Steve. "World Domination." *Sports Illustrated*, October 7, 1997, 68–71.

Ryan, Tim. "Lessons with Love." *Islands*, July–August 2001, 44–49.

Rydell, Robert. *All the World's a Fair: Visions of Empire at American International Expositions, 1876–1916*. Chicago: University of Chicago Press, 1984.

Said, Edward. *Culture and Imperialism*. New York: Knopf, 1994.

Salamanca, Bonifacio S. *The Filipino Reaction to American Rule, 1901–1913*. Norwich CT: Shoe String Press, 1968.

Salyer, Lucy E. "Baptism by Fire: Race, Military Service, and U.S. Citizenship Policy, 1918–1935." *Journal of American History* 91, no. 3 (December 2004): 847–76.

San Juan Jr., E., ed. *On Becoming Filipino: Selected Writings of Carlos Bukosan*. Philadelphia: Temple University Press, 1995.

Schmitt, Robert C. *Firsts and Almost Firsts in Hawaii*. Honolulu: University of Hawaii Press, 1995.

———. "Some Firsts in Island Leisure." *Hawaiian Journal of History* 12 (1978): 99–119.

Schoenrich, Otto. *Santo Domingo: A Country with a Future*. New York: Macmillan, 1918.

Schoonover, Thomas. *Uncle Sam's War of 1898 and the Origins of Globalization*. Lexington: University Press of Kentucky, 2003.

Sexton, William T. *Soldiers in the Sun: An Adventure in Imperialism*. Freeport NY: Books from Libraries Press, 1939.

Seymour, Harold. *Baseball: The People's Game*. New York: Oxford University Press, 1990.

Shaw, Angel Velasco, and Luis H. Francia, eds. *Vestiges of War: The Philippine-American War and the Aftermath of an Imperial Dream, 1899–1999*. New York: New York University Press, 2002.

Simmons, Edward H. *The United States Marines, 1775–1975*. New York: Viking, 1976.

Slotkin, Richard. "Buffalo Bill's Wild West and the Mythologization of the American Empire." In *Cultures of United States Imperialism*, ed. Amy Kaplan and Donald E. Pease, 164–81. Durham NC: Duke University Press, 1993.

Smith, Mrs. H. C. *A History of the Young Women's Christian Association of North-Western College*. Naperville IL: n.p., 1908.

Soberano, Rawlein G. *The Politics of Independence: The American Colonial Experiment in the Philippines*. New Orleans: Alive Associates, 1983.

Sodetani, Naomi. "The Lazarus of Language." *Islands*, April 2001, 28, 30.

Southgate, Beverley. *History: What and Why? Ancient, Modern, and Postmodern Perspectives*. London: Routledge, 1996.

Spickard, Paul, Joanne L. Rondilla, and Debbie Hippolite Wright, eds. *Pacific Diaspora: Island Peoples in the United States and across the Pacific*. Honolulu: University of Hawaii Press, 2002.

Stanley, Peter W. *A Nation in the Making: The Philippines and the United States, 1899–1921*. Cambridge MA: Harvard University Press, 1974.

Stuart, Peter C. *Isles of Empire: The United States and Its Overseas Possessions*. Lanham MD: University Press of America, 1999.

Sugden, John. *Boxing and Society: An International Analysis*. Manchester UK: Manchester University Press, 1996.

Sullivan, Dean A., ed. *Middle Innings: A Documentary History of Baseball, 1900–1948*. Lincoln: University of Nebraska Press, 1998.

Taft, William H. *Civil Government in the Philippines*. New York: Outlook Company, 1902.

Takaki, Ronald. *Pau Hana: Plantation Life and Labor in Hawaii*. Honolulu: University of Hawaii Press, 1983.

Tanada, Shinsuke. "Diffusion into the Orient: The Introduction of Western Sports in Kobe, Japan." *International Journal of the History of Sport* 5, no. 3 (December 1988): 372–76.

Theroux, Paul. "The Hawai'ians." *National Geographic*, December 2002, 2–41.

Townsend, Kim. *Manhood at Harvard: William James and Others*. New York: Norton, 1996.

Tucker, William H. *The Science and Politics of Racial Research*. Urbana: University of Illinois Press, 1994.

Van Bottenburg, Maarten. *Global Games*. Urbana: University of Illinois Press, 2001.

Van Hyning, Thomas E. *Puerto Rico's Winter League: A History of Major League Baseball's Launching Pad*. Jefferson NC: McFarland, 1995.

Varley, Paul. *Japanese Culture*. Honolulu: University of Hawaii Press, 2000.

Vertinsky, Patricia. *The Eternally Wounded Woman: Women, Exercise, and Doctors in the Late Nineteenth Century*. Manchester UK: Manchester University Press, 1990.

Wagner, Eric A. "Sport in Revolutionary Societies: Cuba and Nicaragua." In *Sport and Society in Latin America: Diffusion, Dependency, and the Rise of Mass Culture*, ed. Joseph L. Arbena, 113–36. New York: Greenwood, 1988.

Wakefield, Wanda Ellen. *Playing to Win: Sports and the American Military, 1898–1945*. Albany: State University of New York Press, 1997.

Wallace, Katherine. *California through Five Centuries*. New York: AMSCO School Publications, 1974.

Wallerstein, Imanuel. *The Modern World System II: Mercantilism and the Consolidation of the European World Economy, 1600–1750*. New York: Academic Press, 1980.

Walsh, Tom. "Baseball in the Philippines: A Capsule History." *Bulletin of the American Historical Collection* 23, no. 3 (July–September 1995): 106–9.

"Wards of the United States: Notes on What Our Country Is Doing for Santo Domingo, Nicaragua, and Haiti." *National Geographic*, August 1916, 143–77.

Wei, Deborah, and Rachael Kamel, eds. *Resistance in Paradise: Rethinking 100 Years of U.S. Involvement in the Caribbean and the Pacific*. Philadelphia: American Friends Service Committee, 1998.

Welch, Richard E., Jr. *Imperialists vs. Anti-imperialists: The Debate over Expansionism in the 1890s*. Itasca IL: F. E. Peacock, 1972.

Welky, David B. "Viking Girls, Mermaids, and Little Brown Men: U.S. Journalism and the 1932 Olympics." *Journal of Sport History* 24, no. 1 (Spring 1997): 24–49.

Wells, Lawrence, ed. *Football Powers of the South*. Oxford MS: Sports Yearbook, 1983.

White, Randy Wayne. "Far from Home Late." *Outside*, October 2001, 51.

Whiting, Robert. *The Chrysanthemum and the Bat: Baseball Samurai Style*. New York: Dodd, Mead, 1977.

Whitney, Caspar. "Athletic Awakening of the Japanese." *Harper's Weekly*, February 12, 1898, 165–66.

———. "Non-athletic China." *Harper's Weekly*, February 12, 1898, 189–90.

Wilentz, Sean. *Chants Democratic: New York City and the Rise of the American Working Class, 1780–1850*. New York: Oxford University Press, 1984.

Wilson, William H., and Kauanoe Kamana. "The Tip of the Spear: Hawaiian Language Educators Reclaim a Cultural Legacy." *Teaching Tolerance*, Spring 2002, 20–24.

Wood, Leonard. *Report of the Special Mission to the Philippine Islands to the Secretary of War*. Washington DC: Government Printing Office, 1922.

Woolley, Monroe. " 'Batter Up' in the Philippines." *Outdoor World and Recreation*, May 1913, 313–14.

Worcester, Dean. "Field Sports among the Wild Men of Luzon." *National Geographic*, March 1911, 215–67.

———. "The Non-Christian Peoples of the Philippine Islands." *National Geographic*, November 1913, 1157–1256.

Worcester, Dean C. *The Philippines: Past and Present*. New York: Macmillan, 1914.

Yerxa, Donald A. *Admirals and Empire: The United States Navy and the Caribbean, 1898–1945*. Columbia: University of South Carolina Press, 1991.

Yim, Susan. "For the Love of the Game." *Islands*, December 2000, 38–43.

Yost, Howard H. *The Outrigger Canoe Club of Honolulu, Hawaii*. Honolulu: Outrigger Canoe Club, 1971.

Zabriskie, Alexander C. *Bishop Brent: Crusader for Christian Unity*. Philadelphia: Westminster, 1948.

Ziff, Larzer. *The American 1890s*. New York: Viking, 1973.

Zimmerman, Warren. *First Great Triumph: How Five Americans Made Their Country a World Power*. New York: Farrar, Straus, and Giroux, 2002.

Zoss, Joel, and John Bowman. *Diamonds in the Rough: The Untold History of Baseball*. Chicago: Contemporary Books, 1996.

Zwick, Jim. "Mark Twain's Anti-imperialist Writings in the 'American Century.'" In *Vestiges of War: The Philippine-American War and the Aftermath of an Imperial Dream, 1899–1999*, ed. Angel Velasco Shaw and Luis H. Francia, 38–56. New York: New York University Press, 2002.

Index

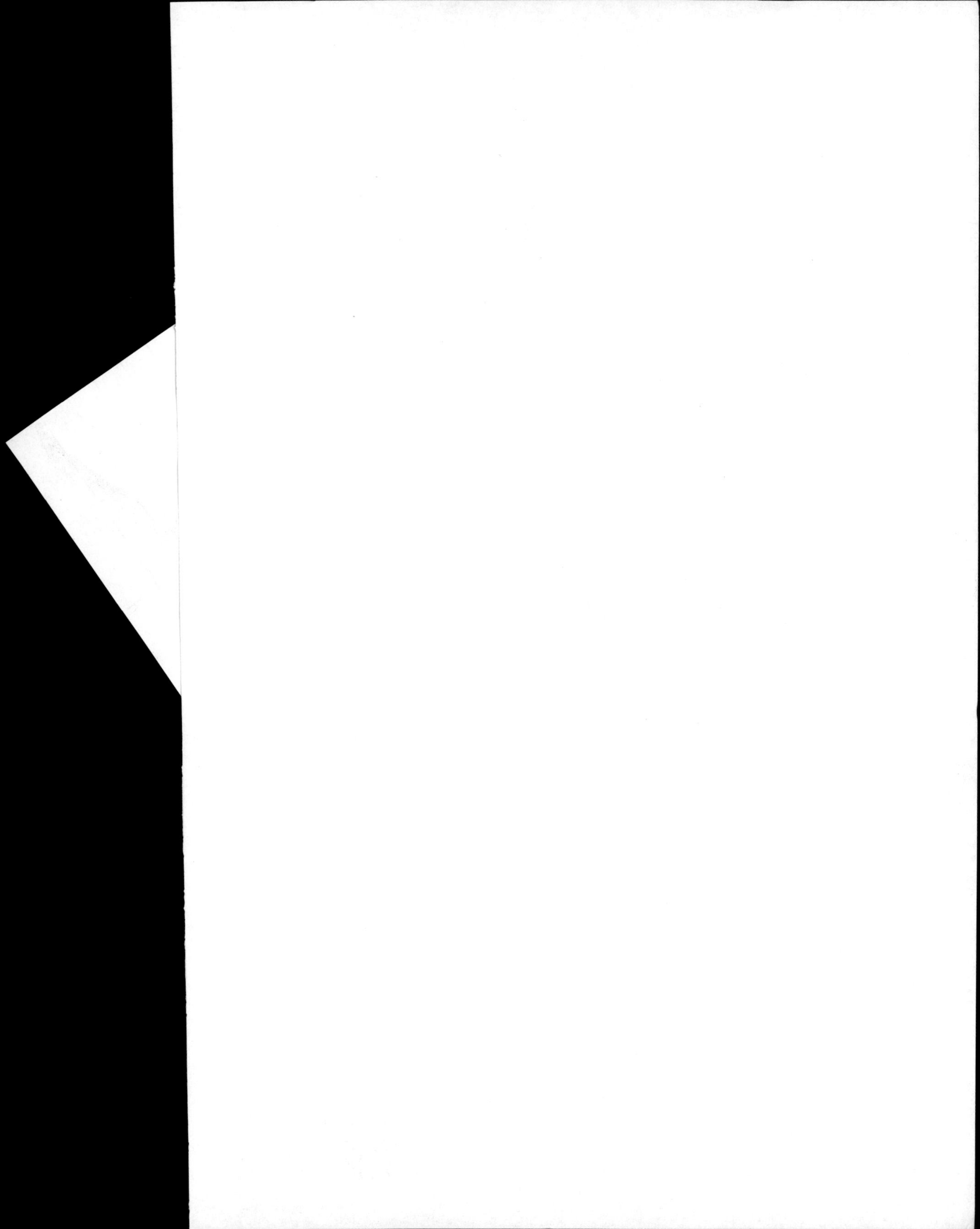

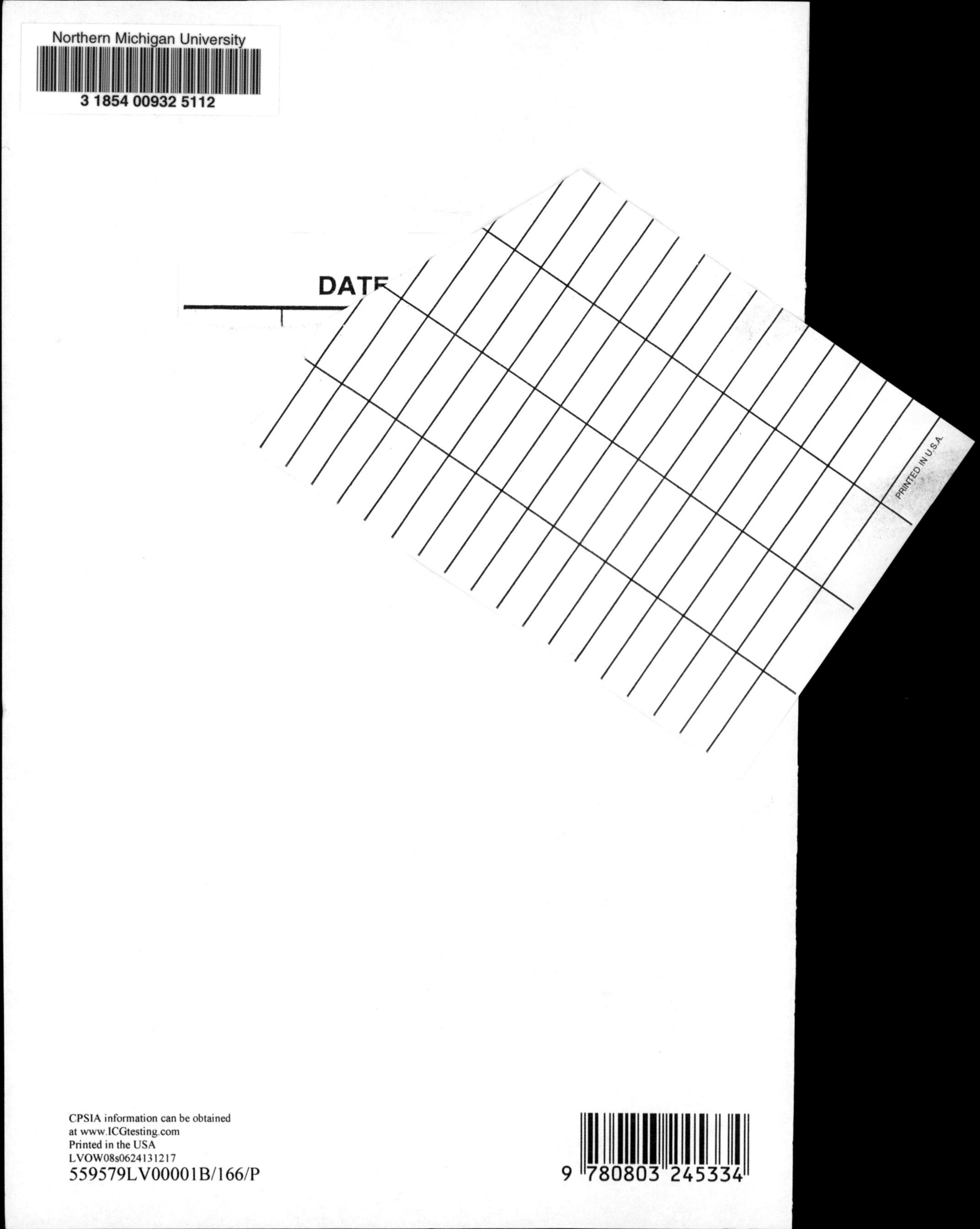

Northern Michigan University
3 1854 00932 5112

CPSIA information can be obtained
at www.ICGtesting.com
Printed in the USA
LVOW08s0624131217
559579LV00001B/166/P

9 780803 245334